Quarto is the authority on a wide range of topics.

Quarto educates, entertains and enriches the lives of our readers—enthusiasts and lovers of hands-on living.

www.quartoknows.com

© 2017 Quarto Publishing Group USA Inc.
Text © 2005, 2010, 2012 Philip Varney
Text © 2010 Jim Hinckley

First published in 2017 by Voyageur Press, an imprint of Quarto Publishing Group USA Inc., 400 First Avenue North, Suite 400, Minneapolis, MN 55401 USA.
Telephone: (612) 344-8100 Fax: (612) 344-8692

quartoknows.com
Visit our blogs at quartoknows.com

Voyageur Press titles are also available at discounts in bulk quantity for industrial or sales-promotional use. For details contact the Special Sales Manager at Quarto Publishing Group USA Inc., 400 First Avenue North, Suite 400, Minneapolis, MN 55401 USA.

10 9 8 7 6 5 4 3 2 1

ISBN: 978-0-7603-5041-6

Library of Congress Cataloging-in-Publication Data

Names: Varney, Philip, author. | Hinckley, Jim, 1958- co-author. | James, Kerrick, photographer.
Title: Ghost towns of the West / by Philip Varney and Jim Hinckley ; photography by Philip Varney and Kerrick James.
Description: Minneapolis, MN : Voyageur Press, 2017.
Identifiers: LCCN 2016044995 | ISBN 9780760350416 (paperback)
Subjects: LCSH: Ghost towns--West (U.S.)--Guidebooks. | West (U.S.)--Guidebooks. | West (U.S.)--History, Local. | BISAC: TRAVEL / United States / West / General. | TRAVEL / United States / West / Mountain (AZ, CO, ID, MT, NM, UT, WY). | TRAVEL / United States / West / Pacific (AK, CA, HI, NV, OR, WA).
Classification: LCC F590.7 .V377 2017 | DDC 978--dc23
LC record available at https://lccn.loc.gov/2016044995

Acquiring Editor: Todd R. Berger
Project Managers: Caitlin Fultz and Alyssa Bluhm
Art Direction and Cover Design: Cindy Samargia Laun
Page Design and Layout: Bradford Foltz
Maps: Patti Isaacs

On the cover: © UTBP/Shutterstock
On the frontis: © Zack Frank/Shutterstock

Printed in China

GHOST TOWNS
OF THE WEST

PHILIP VARNEY AND JIM HINCKLEY
PHOTOGRAPHY BY PHILIP VARNEY AND KERRICK JAMES

VOYAGEUR
PRESS

CONTENTS

INTRODUCTION
PAGE 6

ABOUT THE AUTHORS AND PHOTOGRAPHERS
PAGE 336

☞ INTRODUCTION ☜

Ghost Towns of the West is intended for people who seek the unusual, enjoy history, and savor solitude. Chasing down the ghost towns and mining camps in this book will take you from sea level to elevations exceeding 11,000 feet. You will view some of the West's loveliest rivers, driest deserts, and grandest mountaintops. In the process, I hope you will see the West as you have never seen it before.

The book you have in your hands takes the best ghost towns from four separate books, three by this writer, Philip Varney, and one by Jim Hinckley. My three books are Ghost Towns of California, Ghost Towns of the Pacific Northwest, and Ghost Towns of the Mountain West. Hinckley's book is Ghost Towns of the Southwest. Voyageur Press published all four titles between 2010 and 2013. Photographer Kerrick James took all the images for the Arizona and New Mexico ghost towns, while I photographed all the other sites.

Each state's chapter features a map of the area, a history of each town, specific directions to each site, and recommendations when necessary for vehicle requirements. For example, some towns are on paved roads near major highways, while others are on dirt roads and may require a high-clearance vehicle and even, rarely, four-wheel drive.

But each ghost town included in this volume is, in some way, very special. I have visited more than six hundred ghost towns in more than forty years of searching, and these eighty-four entries are my personal favorites.

A person new to ghost town hunting might tour the second entry in this book, Volcano, California, and wonder just what I consider a ghost town to be, because Volcano has shops, a hotel, and a few residents. By my definition, a ghost town has two characteristics: the population has decreased markedly and the initial reason for its settlement (such as mining) no longer keeps people there. At the peak of its mining frenzy, Volcano had an estimated population of well over 5,000 citizens; as of the 2010 census, 115 people lived there, and virtually no one makes a living in a mine. A ghost town, then, can be completely deserted, like Carson, Colorado, and Miner's Delight, Wyoming; it can have a few residents, like White Oaks, New Mexico, and Goldfield, Nevada; it can be protected for posterity as a state park, like Bannack, Montana, and incomparable Bodie, California; or it can have genuine signs of vitality, like Jerome, Arizona, and Idaho City, Idaho. But in each case, the town is a shadow of its former self.

Why are we called to these places where so many lives have toiled and so many have been forgotten? My late friend, mystery writer Tony Hillerman, in a foreword to my book *New Mexico's Best Ghost Towns*, captured the answer: "To me, to many of my friends, to scores of thousands of Americans, these ghost towns offer a sort of touching-place with the past. We stand in their dust and try to project our imagination backward into what they were long ago. Now and then, if the mood and the light and the weather are exactly right, we almost succeed."

Our "touching-places with the past," however, are in immediate and long-term danger. Vandals tear up floorboards hoping for a nonexistent coin. Looters remove an old door with the vague notion of using it, only to discard it later. Thieves dislodge a child's headstone, heartlessly assuming no one will miss it.

Remember: These old towns are to be explored and photographed, but also protected and treasured. You must be a part of the preservation, not the destruction. As you visit the places in this book, please remember that ghost towns are extremely fragile. Leave a site as you found it. I have seen many items on the back roads that tempted me, but I have no collection of artifacts. If you must pick up something, how about a fast food wrapper or a soft-drink can?

When I was doing fieldwork for my book *Ghost Towns of Colorado*, I found the following notice posted in a lovely but deteriorating house. It eloquently conveys what our deportment should be at ghost towns and historic spots:

Attention:

We hope that you are enjoying looking at our heritage. The structure may last many more years for others to see and enjoy if everyone like you treads lightly and takes only memories and pictures.

BEDS
WITH
SPRINGS

The City Hotel in Columbia offers only the finest amenities. *Philip Varney*

CALIFORNIA

CHAPTER 1

The California gold rush changed the course of human history, not just in the United States, but also across the globe. People worldwide, hoping for a markedly better life, headed for California. The population of California exploded from about 26,000 to more than 380,000 in only twelve years.

The original gold strikes were in an area that became known as the Mother Lode, an immense body of gold that extended down the western foothills of the Sierra Nevadas (Spanish for "snow-covered range") for an unbelievable distance of 100 miles. The first six historic towns in this chapter are in the Mother Lode and vary from two state parks, Coloma and Columbia, to the charming, picturesque communities of Volcano and Murphys. Even with all the gift shops, wineries, bed-and-breakfast inns, and historic hotels, there is still room in the Mother Lode for two real ghost towns: Campo Seco and Chinese Camp.

The second group of towns, Nevada City, Bloomfield, and Downieville, were referred to by the miners as the "Northern Mines." The richest of those mines, located in Nevada County, were not the small-time workings of hardy prospectors but rather the province of investors with deep pockets and owners with enormous capital at stake. These mines were among the longest-lasting and best-producing: Nevada County, with $440 million, produced more than twice as much gold between 1848 and 1965 as any other California county.

The third group of ghosts is in a most unlikely place: in or near San Francisco Bay. The premier attraction is Alcatraz, originally a military stronghold and later a famous prison—but also a ghost town. Angel Island offers two ghostly forts in a stunningly beautiful, peaceful setting. China Camp, now a state park, is a ghost fishing village and a reminder that injustices done to the Chinese were not confined to the Mother Lode. And, finally, the tiny river delta town of Locke is a unique former agricultural community also settled by the Chinese.

The fourth and final group of ghost towns is in a far more rural setting than any of the other California ghosts and features two of the best ghost towns in the American West: Bodie and Cerro Gordo (and Cerro Gordo's tiny shipping port, Keeler). It also displays some of the West's most spectacular scenery, because you'll be looking at some of the highest peaks in the contiguous states of our nation, including the highest, Mount Whitney, at an elevation of 14,505 feet. Furthermore, you are likely to find something fairly rare in California—relative solitude, because you will be in some of the least populated of the fifty-eight counties in California. The eastern slopes of the Sierra Nevada are far more rugged than its western slopes (where the gold rush began), and the high desert below the mountains has a desolate beauty. And south of those two great ghosts is one site worth exploring in the vast Mojave Desert: Randsburg, a gold-bearing bonanza.

Your California ghost town adventure begins here.

oloma is the logical place to begin California's gold rush history, since it was in Coloma, on January 24, 1848, that James Marshall peered into the American River. He later recalled, "My eye was caught by something shining in the bottom of the ditch. . . . It made my heart thump, for I was certain it was gold. . . . Then I saw another."

John Augustus Sutter, German-born in 1803 of Swiss parents, came to California (then a part of Mexico) in 1839 and became a Mexican citizen. He received a fifty-thousand-acre land grant and was appointed the *alcalde* (a title embracing the duties of judge, lawyer, marshal, and mayor) for the entire Sacramento Valley.

His empire, which he called New Helvetia, featured a large adobe fort (still standing in Sacramento) that offered protection, food, and retail goods to nearby settlers. He also laid out a town called Sutterville, constructed a flour mill, and, providentially for California, sent James Marshall to the Coloma Valley, along the south fork of the American River. There Marshall was to supervise the building of a sawmill, with Sutter and Marshall sharing the profits.

As sawmill construction neared completion, Marshall was inspecting the millrace, the channel through which the

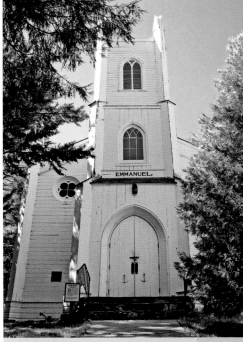

Coloma's Emmanuel Church was the site of gold discoverer James Marshall's funeral in 1885. *Philip Varney*

river would run to turn a wheel to power the sawmill. That is where he saw the glitter in the river, changing the course of California and utterly ruining Sutter's vision of a frontier agricultural dynasty.

As word of the gold discovery spread, Sutter's workers abandoned the unfinished sawmill, and his fieldworkers and other tradesmen quit to find their fortunes. The New Helvetia that Sutter had envisioned was doomed, and Coloma became not a quiet sawmill town but a camp of frenzied argonauts.

Because there was no law enforcement, neither Sutter nor Marshall could

St. John's Catholic Church, built in 1856, features an unusual bell tower that is separate from the church itself. *Philip Varney*

Sutter's sawmill was reconstructed in 1968 using the methods of the 1840s, with wooden pegs and hand-adzed timbers. *Philip Varney*

keep squatters out, and the banks of the American River became alive with prospectors as the gold fever spread. Although Sutter tried to profit from the fabulous find, he never did. He lamented, "What a great misfortune was this sudden gold discovery for me!" He attempted to get compensation for his lost lands, but the American courts ruled that his Mexican land grants were invalid. He eventually left New Helvetia for Pennsylvania, where he was buried in 1880.

Coloma was the first gold rush town, but it was hardly the richest. The river's placer deposits were depleted quickly, and the town, with a population of five thousand in 1849, was in decline by 1851, although many of the buildings you will visit were erected after that year.

Most of Coloma today is within Marshall Gold Discovery State Park. Begin at the visitors' center—the Gold Discovery Museum—where, in addition to paying a modest fee (for admission to the museum and park, a guide booklet, and brochures), you can see exhibits of artifacts, descriptions of gold processes, and presentations of videos. Since you will have a guide booklet, I'll mention only a few highlights.

East of the visitors' center is a reconstruction of Sutter's Mill. The mill is not on the original site, but a nearby trail takes you there. Adjacent to the mill is the Mormon Cabin, a 1948 replica that features a short history of the Mormons who were in Coloma in 1848.

The Coloma Schoolhouse is a 1995 reconstruction of the building brought from Slatington in 1920, restored in 1987, but destroyed that same year by a runaway logging truck. *Philip Varney*

South of the sawmill on California Highway 49 are several historic buildings, including Robert Bell's Brick Store, a general merchandise and feed store that also housed the post office. Across the street but partially hidden from view is the 1854 Independent Order of Odd Fellows (I.O.O.F.) Hall.

Beyond Bell's store stands the one-room Coloma Schoolhouse. The 1890 building was brought in pieces from Slatington to Coloma in 1920. The school was completely restored in July of 1987, but, because of its location at a bend in the highway, a runaway logging truck destroyed it a mere three months later. A coalition of organizations combined their efforts to reconstruct it, completing the task in 1995.

Southwest of the visitors' center are several buildings worth seeing, including two attractive churches. The first is the 1856 St. John's Catholic Church, where services were held until 1925. Behind the church is its cemetery. Across the road from that cemetery is a reconstruction of the cabin James Marshall built in 1856.

Down Church Street from St. John's is the 1856 Emmanuel Church, built jointly by Methodist and Episcopal congregations. James Marshall's funeral was held there in 1885.

At the end of Church Street is Cold Springs Road, where you will find Coloma's Pioneer Cemetery just beyond the turnoff to the James Marshall Monument. A brochure at the cemetery suggests a walking tour.

Monument Road goes to the James Marshall Monument, a bronze statue erected in 1890 that shows Marshall dramatically pointing down to the spot where he found gold. Marshall, like John Sutter, never prospered from his discovery. He spent much of his life vainly searching hills and streams for another strike. He died a bitter recluse in nearby Kelsey and is buried at the monument.

WHEN YOU GO

Coloma is 18 miles southeast of Auburn and 9 miles northwest of Placerville on California Highway 49.

VOLCANO

olcano is one of my favorite Mother Lode mining camps, because it has eschewed touristy touches and remains a peaceful, lovely town with friendly citizens and many excellent buildings.

Discharged New York volunteers of the then-recently completed Mexican-American War discovered gold here in 1848. They called their young mining camp Volcano because they believed, erroneously, that the craterlike cup in which the town stood was volcanic. The soldiers-turned-miners even called the area's light gray-, yellow-, and reddish-colored stone "lava."

Where there was no lava, there certainly was gold. Working the placers of Soldier's Gulch, one miner netted $8,000 in a few days. Another extracted twenty-eight pounds of gold from a single pocket.

Volcano became a booming town of five thousand citizens and could boast of such refinements as a thespian society, a debating society, a Miners' Library Association, a private law school, and an astronomical observatory, reportedly all "firsts" in California.

When placer deposits were exhausted in 1855, hydraulicking was used to uncover more gold, but the boom was over by 1865. (For more on the hydraulicking process, see either page 325 of the glossary or the North Bloomfield entry on page 32 later in this chapter.)

As you enter Volcano from the southwest, you will immediately face the town's most splendid building, the St. George Hotel, a three-story brick structure with wooden porches on all floors, built sometime between 1862 and 1867.

Walk around Volcano to take in its wonderful buildings, many of which have

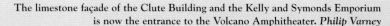

The limestone façade of the Clute Building and the Kelly and Symonds Emporium is now the entrance to the Volcano Amphitheater. *Philip Varney*

Volcano's St. George Hotel, a three-story brick structure with wooden porches, was built sometime between 1862 and 1867. *Philip Varney*

historic markers. Highlights include the two large brick and limestone façades—the remains of the Clute Building and the Kelly and Symonds Emporium—and, across the street, the General Store, in continuous use since 1852, which is the hub of the goings-on in town.

Volcano's schoolhouse, in use from 1855 until 1956, stands east of the General Store and is now a private residence.

North on Plug Street at Emigrant Road is St. Bernard's Catholic Church, which dates from 1854 (rebuilt in 1931). On a hill northeast of the church are the town's graveyards, the Volcano Pioneer Methodist Cemetery and the Catholic cemetery.

Your walk should also include the wooden, two-story 1880 Union Hotel, now the Volcano Union Inn, which once went by the weighty title of the Union Hotel Billiards, Saloon, and Boarding House.

Beyond the hotel is the 1912 Armory Hall, followed by Old Abe, a bronze cannon cast in 1837 that was smuggled into Volcano in a hearse in 1862 by Union sympathizers. As a plaque succinctly puts it, Old Abe was meant to "discourage the rebel element." During the Civil War, Volcano gold went to support the Union cause. Old Abe never fired a shot, which was just as well, since the Unionists reportedly had no cannonballs, only river rocks.

Next door to Old Abe is the Sing Kee Store, built in 1854 or 1855 as both a general merchandise and the Adams Express Agency office, the predecessor of Wells Fargo.

Volcano's Masonic Hall, built in 1860, originally housed the offices of the *Volcano Weekly Ledger*. *Philip Varney*

Attached to the back of the Sing Kee Store, but facing west, is the 1854 Masonic Hall. It originally housed the *Volcano Weekly Ledger*, with office upstairs and printing press downstairs. By 1860 the building was used by both the Masons and the Odd Fellows.

Directly across the street from the Masonic Hall is the 1871 jailhouse. It looks rather insubstantial, with its outer walls of two-by-twelve timbers. Another identical wall is on the inside, but between the two is a layer of boilerplate. The incommodious jail features two small windows made of iron plate with small holes drilled in them.

WHEN YOU GO

From Jackson, head northeast on California Highway 88 to Pine Grove, a distance of 8.8 miles. Turn left on the Pine Grove–Volcano Road and follow it for 3.2 miles to Volcano.

CAMPO SECO

Mexicans settled Campo Seco ("dry camp") in 1849. The site was located in Oregon Gulch, named for an early group of prospectors from that territory who worked the area. But "seco" was the operant word: a thriving town in 1850, it had lost half of its population by the end of that year because scarce water sent prospectors elsewhere. In 1853, however, two Mexicans extracted $5,700 in gold in one morning from Sullivan's Gulch, and, one year later, a ninety-three-ounce nugget was found, further fueling the gold frenzy. By that time the community featured two churches, the usual saloons, a brewery, two hotels, a blacksmith's shop, assorted stores, and a post office. A fire in that same year virtually destroyed the town, so many of the citizens rebuilt using stone. It is those stone buildings that offer the most interesting remnants you will see today.

Although the town was settled because of placer gold, it was the copper and zinc deposits at the Penn Mine, which opened in the 1860s and lasted until the 1940s, that provided the greatest prosperity.

There is still much to see in one of the true ghost towns of the Mother Lode. The Adams Express Agency Building, on the east side of Campo Seco Road as you enter town, provides the town's most photogenic remnants. West of those ruins on Penn Mine Road stand two mortared stone ruins that were part of the Chinese community. Surrounding these ruins are *Ailanthus altissima*, the "Tree-of-Heaven," which Chinese often brought from their native land.

The stone ruins of Campo Seco's Adams Express Agency Building are among the Mother Lode's most ghostly remnants. *Philip Varney*

Farther south of town on the east side of the road stands an attractive Victorian home with an offset triple-bay window. Across the street, heading west, is College Street, which leads to Campo Seco's old schoolhouse. One wonders if the town's founding fathers named the street to inspire their youth.

Adjacent to the school is the Protestant cemetery, where there are more than fifty graves.

South on Campo Seco Road 0.2 of a mile from College Street is the Catholic cemetery, where natives of Spain, Ireland, France, and Chile are buried.

WHEN YOU GO

From Jackson, drive 6.6 miles south on California Highway 49 to the turnoff to Mokelumne Hill, a charming gold rush town worth exploring. Campo Seco is 11.7 miles southwest of Mokelumne Hill. From Main Street, proceed southwest to California Highway 49. Turn left and then take an immediate right onto California Highway 26, the road to Valley Springs. In 3.8 miles, turn right on Paloma Road. In 5.5 miles, you will come to Campo Seco Road. Turn right. In 1.1 miles turn right again, which actually keeps you on Campo Seco Road, and proceed to Campo Seco, which is 1 mile away.

MURPHYS

Murphys is another of my favorite gold rush mining camps. With streets lined with locust trees, its central business district invites a stroll. In fact, staying the night and walking Murphys's streets in the evening is a requirement for each of my Mother Lode visits.

Murphys is named for John M. Murphy, who came to California from Canada in 1844. Four years later, John and his brother Daniel camped along Angels Creek at a place later known as Murphys New Diggings—but shortened to Murphys when it received a post office in 1851. By that time, the Murphy brothers were long gone. They opened a trading post to sell to the hordes of hopeful miners, made their fortune, and left town in 1849.

Early claims were restricted to a tiny eight-foot square; nevertheless, one claim is said to have yielded thirty-seven pounds of gold in a single afternoon and another sixty-three pounds the following morning.

Murphys's peak year was 1855, but, like dozens of other camps, the town began declining in the 1860s despite attempts at hard-rock and hydraulic mining.

Main Street in Murphys today features a number of excellent buildings, with the most obvious the rough-quarried limestone Murphys Hotel, at the southwest corner of Main and Algiers Streets. It opened in 1856 as the Sperry and Perry Hotel and was later known as Mitchler's Hotel. It became the Murphys Hotel in 1945. The hotel has a

The former Murphys Grammar School, built in 1860, was in use until 1973. It was called Pine Grove College by its students. *Philip Varney*

register containing the names of some of America's most famous figures: Mark Twain, Horatio Alger Jr., J. Pierpont Morgan, and Ulysses S. Grant. It also features one of California's most infamous: Charles E. Bolton, the highwayman known as Black Bart.

Diagonally across from the hotel is the former Jones Apothecary. Constructed after an 1859 fire, it was rebuilt never to burn: in addition to its limestone and brick walls and iron doors, it has windows only on its one street-facing wall. It later became the I.O.O.F. Hall and in 1886 became Ben and James Stephens's store. An old painted sign on the building's west side announces that business: "Stephens Bros. Cheap Cash Store."

The presidential suite in the Murphys Hotel honors its most famous occupant, President Ulysses S. Grant. *Philip Varney*

West on Main and across from a modern section of the Murphys Hotel is the 1856 Peter L. Traver Building, which features a gold rush–era museum open Friday through Sunday. Attached to the Traver Building on the west is the Thompson Building, built around 1856.

St. Patrick's Catholic Church is located 0.2 of a mile north of the business district at 619 Sheep Ranch Road. The attractive church was begun in 1858 and dedicated in 1861. A well-kept cemetery is within the church grounds.

The 1856 Murphys Hotel features a still-popular saloon, a dining room featuring excellent meals, and an upstairs of restored rooms. Think twice before choosing a room above the saloon on weekends. *Philip Varney*

St. Patrick's Catholic Church in Murphys, dedicated in 1861, features precise brickwork and lancet windows. *Philip Varney*

To visit another cemetery, head east from downtown Murphys on Main. Jones Street veers off to the right behind a large monument. Follow Jones for 0.2 of a mile to the turnoff to the Buena Vista Cemetery, which has hundreds of graves in a pleasant, tree-lined setting.

Immediately east of the cemetery entrance is the former Murphys Grammar School. Built in 1860, it was continuously in use until 1973. It was called Pine Grove College by its pupils, one of whom, physicist Albert Michelson, was the first American to win a Nobel Prize.

WHEN YOU GO

From Campo Seco, return the way you came, but only for 1 mile. Then turn south on Watertown Road, which will lead you 2.7 miles to the community of Valley Springs and California Highway 12. From there, take that road east to California Highway 49, a distance of 8.2 miles. Then drive south on Highway 49 for 12.2 miles to a left turn onto Murphys Grade Road. That turnoff is 1 mile north of Angels Camp, so if you enter Angels Camp, you have missed the turn. Murphys is 6.5 miles northeast from the left turn onto Murphys Grade Road off of Highway 49.

During the gold rush, the town of Columbia was hailed as the "Gem of the Southern Mines." More than 150 years later, the "gem" remains unflawed. Now a state park, Columbia features attractions such as restaurants, shops, stagecoach rides, a hotel, a theater, and even a saloon. But despite all this activity, Columbia retains a dignity that makes it a most enjoyable place.

The Mother Lode consisted of one incredible place to find gold after another, but fortuitous Columbia is geologically unique: it sits on a limestone bed pock-marked with potholes that for thousands of years conveniently collected placer gold, seemingly waiting for someone to retrieve it.

That someone was Dr. Thaddeus Hildreth, who in 1850 camped in the area with a group of prospectors. The gold was so plentiful that others swarmed to the new camp, first called Hildreth's Diggings, later American Camp, and finally Columbia.

Despite an acute shortage of water (eventually solved with an elaborate series of flumes and ditches), Columbia prospered wildly, becoming a town of six thousand—the biggest camp in the Mother Lode. Although Columbia now has the permanence of brick, it began, like other mining camps, as a mere tent city with

Columbia's Wells Fargo office, built in 1858 by William Daegner, was in service until 1917. *Philip Varney*

an occasional rough-sawn wood structure. After fires in 1854 and 1857, it was rebuilt with locally made brick and fireproof iron doors shipped from eastern states.

As placer gold gave out in the 1860s, Columbia declined. By the 1880s its population had dropped to about five hundred, but not before an estimated $87

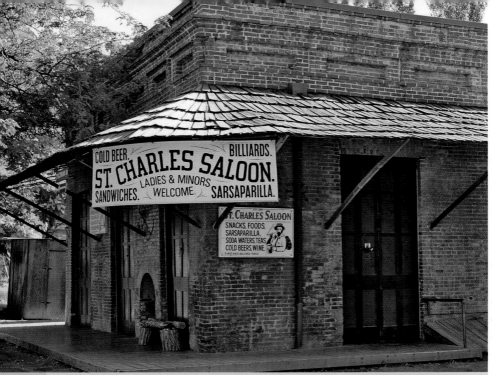

Columbia's St. Charles Saloon still offers alcoholic beverages, but its clientele is now considerably more family-oriented than it was during the gold rush. *Philip Varney*

million in gold had been shipped from the Gem of the Southern Mines.

Columbia retains its gold rush atmosphere better than any other sizable Mother Lode town. One reason is that automobiles are not allowed within its interior streets. Another is that shops selling wares are not permitted to display gaudy, touristy signs.

A third reason Columbia is so delightful is that it is a living history museum (with no admission fee) where shopkeepers dress in period attire, a strolling folk singer plays traditional instruments while singing nineteenth-century songs, and a blacksmith uses hundred-year-old tools to create his wares. You can ride in an authentic stagecoach, watch a play, or stay the night in the 1856 City Hotel.

Columbia has too many attractions to list them all, but I found the most enjoyment in buildings in which there was little or nothing for sale, such as the 1858 Wells Fargo Express Building on the south end of Main Street, which has a chalkboard announcing the stages "arriving" and "departing" as well as freight ready to be "shipped."

You need to explore Columbia carefully to see more than the obvious attractions. For example, hidden behind the Wells Fargo Building is a well-equipped assay office that would be easy to overlook.

An often-overlooked building is the 1860 two-classroom Columbia Schoolhouse. An enjoyable way to reach it is on foot, taking the Old School Trail from Pacific and Columbia Streets. The attractive two-story brick building last saw students in 1937, when it was deemed unsafe should an earthquake occur.

Behind the schoolhouse are three of Columbia's four cemeteries: the public cemetery (with "In God We Trust" on a wooden arch over the entrance) and adjacent graveyards for the Masons and Odd Fellows. (The fourth, a Catholic cemetery, stands south of town next to St. Anne's Catholic Church on Kennebec Hill.)

The Columbia Schoolhouse has an outside staircase, barely in view on the far right, to reach a second-story classroom. *Philip Varney*

The first-floor classroom of the Columbia Schoolhouse shows a map of the Americas—and a dunce cap awaiting an unprepared student. *Philip Varney*

WHEN YOU GO

From downtown Murphys, head east on Main Street for 0.4 of a mile to its junction with California Highway 4. Follow that highway for 3.3 miles and turn left on Parrotts Ferry Road. That road will take you to Columbia in 9.8 miles.

CHINESE CAMP

Chinese Camp is the other true ghost town in the Mother Lode, along with Campo Seco (see page 18). For that reason alone, it is well worth a visit. In addition, its Main Street absolutely invites a sketchpad.

Chinese Camp was the oldest town populated by Chinese, settled in 1849 at a place first known as Washington Camp. Later called Chinese Diggings and then Chinese (or even Chinee) Camp, it received its post office in 1854. By that time, it had a population of five thousand, as many as half of them non-Asian.

Although the Chinese were targets of discrimination, that did not mean they were always a united people. Secret societies called "tongs," based upon one's home area in China, were prevalent where there were large numbers of Chinese.

Two of those tongs had a violent skirmish near Chinese Camp in 1856, apparently caused by a large rock rolling from one group's diggings into the other's. The subsequent Tong War, as it came to be known, involved over two thousand men wielding daggers, axes, spears, and even a few muskets. Four men died during the resulting mayhem, and 250 were jailed afterward.

Placer mining at Chinese Camp lasted into the 1870s and yielded an estimated $2.5 million in gold. The town also served as an important transportation hub.

Chinese Camp today consists of almost a dozen buildings in various states of decay among a proliferation of *Ailanthus* trees—the traditional Chinese Tree-of-Heaven, a highly invasive species that is difficult to control or eradicate.

The Chinese Camp Store stands prominently near the intersection of High-

Chinese Camp's St. Francis Xavier Catholic Church, built in 1855, features a cemetery with about a dozen old graves, most for natives of Ireland. *Philip Varney*

way 49 and California Highway 120. Go south from the store to a historical monument and park there, as the town's Main Street is around the corner.

The first commercial building on the north side of the street is the 1854 Timothy McAdams Store, which served as both a general store and the post office.

Next door to the McAdams Store is a two-story wooden residence that was a doctor's home, office, and boarding house. Across the street is one standing wall of the 1849 office of the Adams Express Agency, later Wells Fargo.

Next door to the doctor's house is a brick building with iron doors that was a foundry and blacksmith shop. John Studebaker, who later made wheelbarrows for miners in Coloma and Placerville before becoming an Indiana automobile builder, learned his trade in that shop, according to a town resident.

Across the street from the foundry is the Buck Store, a stone building with a wooden false front. Next door is a large, two-story, wood-frame structure on the corner of Main Street and Red Hills Road that was a fandango parlor and house of prostitution.

East of Highway 49 on Main Street is the attractive 1855 St. Francis Xavier Catholic Church and Cemetery, with about a dozen old graves, most for natives of Ireland.

Although Chinese were the town's principal residents, one would not expect to find graves of Chinese there: it was tradition to return their remains to their native land. California law, however, required their burial for sanitary reasons. The remains had to stay buried for three years, but for a four-year period after that, the remains could be disinterred and shipped to China. During that four-year time frame, Chinese societies and organizations, including the tongs, made certain that remains were properly disinterred and returned to China.

WHEN YOU GO

From Columbia, follow Parrotts Ferry Road south for 1.9 miles until it meets California Highway 49. Continue 2.3 miles into Sonora. Chinese Camp is 10.2 miles southwest of Sonora on California Highway 49.

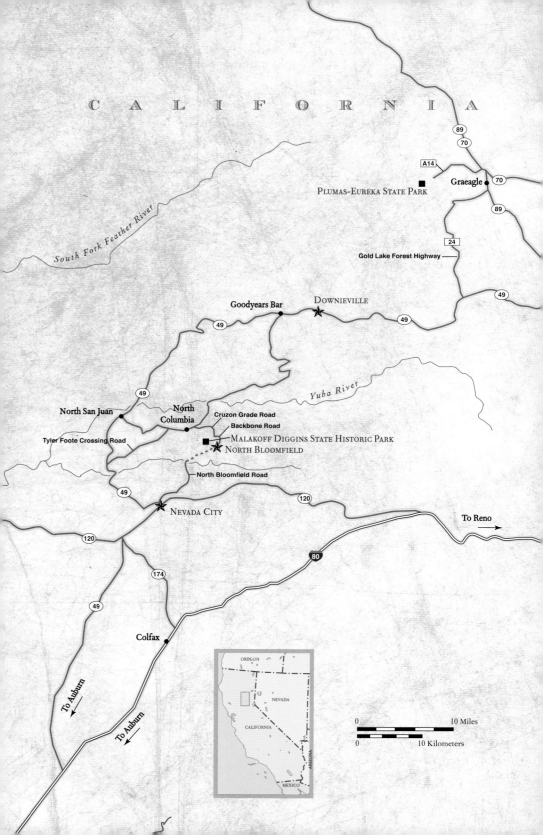

When an unknown prospector found placer gold where Nevada City would later stand, he named his spot Deer Creek Dry Diggings. Later it would be called Caldwell's Upper Store for Dr. A. B. Caldwell's trading post. Finally it became Nevada and then, when it was incorporated in 1851, City of Nevada. By 1858 it was widely known as Nevada City.

Nevada City likely provided the name for California's eastern neighbor, as Nevada Territory was named in 1861, long after Nevada City was already a thriving community. Furthermore, it was Nevada City miners who started the Washoe silver rush by venturing east over the Sierra Nevada and bringing back ore samples. When "Nevada" was finalized for the new state, Nevada City residents protested, saying they had the name first.

According to the 1850 census, Nevada City had a population of 1,067. But by the end of that year, it had risen to 6,000 citizens as miners flocked to an area where gold veins did not pinch out as usual but rather widened into remarkable primary deposits. Miners would burrow into the hills, in a process that became known as "coyoteing" after the digging prowess of that canine.

The town's population rose to ten thousand by the late 1850s, when Nevada City was "Queen of the Northern Mines" and the third-largest California

Nevada City's Nevada Theatre featured performances by such notables as Mark Twain and Jack London. *Philip Varney*

Nevada City women staged a grand ball to raise money for the construction of Pennsylvania Engine Co. No. 2, which was finished in 1861. *Philip Varney*

The National Hotel in Nevada City claims to be the oldest continuously operated hotel in California. Note the lovely wrought iron railings on the third-floor balconies.
Philip Varney

city. But Nevada City was already in decline by the end of the decade, with many prospectors heading east to the silver excitement of the Nevada Territory's Comstock Lode.

Nevada City's entire downtown business section is now a National Historic District. The primary street to explore is Broad Street, but a good place to start a walking tour is at the Chamber of Commerce, located one block north of Broad Street where Commercial, Main, Union, and Coyote Streets all converge. There you can obtain a free walking-tour guide.

A logical second stop is a few doors northwest on Main at the 1861 Nevada Hose Company No. 1, a graceful two-story structure, with delicate carpenter's lace gingerbread trim, that currently operates as a museum.

On Broad Street you will find the largest concentration of interesting buildings, beginning with the 1856–1857 National Hotel,

The New York Hotel in Nevada City displays its delicate latticework and elegant wood trim.
Philip Varney

Nevada City's 1864 Methodist Church has an offset bell tower. Note how the window above the entrance is echoed in design by the window in the bell tower itself. *Philip Varney*

an elegant amalgamation of three three-story brick buildings on the east end of the business district. Up the street stands the 1859 Nevada Theatre, where such notables as Mark Twain and Jack London appeared. Across the street are the 1861 Firehouse No. 1 and the 1880s New York Hotel, now a series of shops.

The lovely 1864 Methodist church stands where Broad Street begins a turn to the northwest and becomes West Broad Street (with East Broad Street branching from it about 300 feet north of the church). Beyond that church 0.3 of a mile on West Broad Street is St. Canice Catholic Cemetery, which features excellent marble headstones, many for natives of Ireland and Italy. Immediately south of that graveyard is the 1851 Pioneer Cemetery.

WHEN YOU GO

evada City is 4 miles north of Grass Valley on California Highway 49 and California Highway 120. Take the Broad Street exit.

NORTH BLOOMFIELD AND MALAKOFF DIGGINS STATE HISTORIC PARK

North Bloomfield is the premier ghost town of the Northern Mines. Now a state historic park, it moves at a much slower pace than the other three more famous state park mining towns: Coloma, Columbia, and Bodie. Some Gold Country tour books consider North Bloomfield a "side trip." Not so—it is the destination.

Early prospectors in the North Bloomfield area were disappointed in their findings along a stream and so named it Humbug Creek. When a camp formed nevertheless, the community was called Humbug. Despite the moniker, the town prospered. When a post office was granted, the town was hardly a "humbug," and citizens chose Bloomfield as its name. The US Postal Service required the addition of "North," because another Bloomfield already existed in California (and it still does, southwest of Santa Rosa).

The reason the camp went from a "humbug" to a town of two thousand citizens was the invention of hydraulic mining. In 1853 local prospector Edward Matteson used a rawhide hose and a wooden nozzle to wash gold-laden ore from a bluff. Matteson's invention drastically changed the gold mining industry. His wooden nozzle was refined into a metal cannonlike contraption called a

A hydraulic monitor, also known as a "giant," sits in the bottom of Malakoff Mine. *Philip Varney*

This view of Malakoff Diggins clearly shows where the hydraulic monitors washed the hillsides, releasing a fortune in gold—but causing environmental havoc downstream. *Philip Varney*

"monitor" or "giant" that propelled water with incredible force into gravel banks containing gold. The gold was exposed and separated, while the water, which eventually was brought to North Bloomfield through 43 miles of flumes and ditches, washed away the waste.

As a result, gold that had been impenetrably locked in gravel became highly profitable to mine. An estimated $4.5 million in gold was retrieved from only two of the area's many mines. At one of them, the Malakoff, gold was smelted on site. The largest bar weighed 510 pounds and was valued at $114,000, the richest bar ever shipped from Nevada County.

The process was almost too easy—if it had not been for hydraulicking's aftereffects. The mines themselves were denuded of vegetation, and enormous amounts of waterborne detritus created environmental havoc downstream. Silt in rivers caused floods, killed fish and riparian wildlife, destroyed farmlands, and hampered navigation as far away as San Francisco Bay.

For ten years, concerned Californians waged a legal battle against powerful financial interests to halt the devastation. In 1884 a federal court finally ordered a halt to the wholesale dumping of

This ghostly interior photo of St. Columncille's Catholic Church in North Bloomfield was taken through one of its windows. *Philip Varney*

North Bloomfield's McKillican and Mobley General Merchandise was the social center for the town. It also housed the post office, which closed in 1941. *Philip Varney*

The McKillican and Mobley General Merchandise featured everything from household items to livery equipment. *Philip Varney*

tailings, effectively eliminating most hydraulic mining—and effectively emptying North Bloomfield.

North Bloomfield today is a picturesque town of picket fences, shade trees, small but pleasant single-story clapboard homes, and several attractive wood-frame commercial buildings.

Park headquarters is Cummins Hall—a former dance hall and saloon, containing a well-stocked museum and an informative video on hydraulic mining. Here you pay a modest admission price to the park.

Next door is the reconstructed Kallenberger Barber Shop and, beyond, the tiny King's Saloon, built in the early 1870s. Next door to the saloon is a reconstruction of the two-story Masonic Lodge with the Smith and Knotwell Drugstore on its first floor.

Across the street stands the 1870 McKillican and Mobley General

The King's Saloon was erected in the early 1870s. The Smith and Knotwell Drugstore, with a Masonic Lodge on the second floor, is a reconstruction of the original. *Philip Varney*

Merchandise. This building contains new-old-stock items and the town's post office, featuring a convenient outdoor mail drop.

West of town 0.4 of a mile is the 1860 St. Columncille's Catholic Church. It originally was located northeast of French Corral, now a minor ghost town about 13 air miles southwest of North Bloomfield. In its original location, it first served as the Bridgeport Union Guard Hall before becoming a church in 1869. It was moved to this location, the site of an earlier Catholic church, in 1971.

King's Saloon in North Bloomfield extols its honesty with a sign at the rear of the establishment: "This is a square house. Please report any unfairness to the proprietor." *Philip Varney*

Next door to St. Columncille's is the 1872–1873 North Bloomfield School, a large, two-room L-shaped building that allowed for a teacher's nightmare: about forty desks are set up in one of the rooms. The school last had students in 1941.

Behind the church is a small, well-kept cemetery. Across the street from the church is a path that takes you a short distance through a manzanita grove to an overlook of the Le Du hydraulic mine.

But that view pales in comparison to the sight that awaits you 0.4 of a mile west of the church and school at Malakoff Diggins. Park your car and take the 240-foot trail to the overlook.

A five-minute walk beyond that overlook gives you an even better view of the "diggins." The colors of the denuded hills range from slate gray to tan to tawny brown. If it were natural, we'd think it was beautiful, because it has an otherworldly appearance, rather like Utah's Bryce Canyon. We are reminded that this is unnatural, however, by a stream running through the diggins with water disturbingly darker than it should be.

Beyond the main diggins site 0.2 of a mile on North Bloomfield Road is the West Point Overlook, where a short hike takes you down to a water pipe and its monitor. This short but somewhat steep trail goes into the mine itself, giving you a genuine feel for how the hydraulicking process can alter the environment.

WHEN YOU GO

From Grass Valley, go 4 miles north on California Highway 49 and California Highway 120 and take the Broad Street exit into Nevada City. From Nevada City, head to California Highway 49, which you can do by simply driving north from the Nevada City cemeteries on West Broad Street for about 0.2 of a mile. Turn left on Highway 49 and drive for 10 miles to Tyler Foote Crossing Road. Turn right and proceed for 8.1 miles to North Columbia, which features a delightful former schoolhouse. A mile and a half beyond North Columbia, turn right onto Cruzon Grade (it becomes the main road and Tyler Foote Crossing the lesser). Cruzon Grade will dovetail into Backbone Road. In 5.7 miles from North Columbia, turn right on Derbec Road, which in 0.7 of a mile will meet North Bloomfield Road. Turn right and proceed 1.3 miles to North Bloomfield. That's a total distance of almost 28 miles from Nevada City.

DOWNIEVILLE

uring the week, Downieville is a somnolent, delightful community replete with friendly people, well-kept historic buildings, good restaurants, and enjoyable accommodations. On weekends, something always seems to be happening—mountain bike festivals, fly-fishing activities, kayaking expeditions, motorcycle rallies, E Clampus Vitus "doins"—you name it. But whether the place is sleeping or jumping, there is one constant: the entrancing sound of rushing water from either the Downie or the Yuba River, which have a confluence right in town.

Lizzie Campbell's headstone lies in the grass of Downieville Cemetery. *Philip Varney*

That confluence of the Yuba and a then-unnamed river yielded placer gold in the fall of 1849. The settlement that grew at the discovery site was variously called Jim Crow Diggins, Washingtonville, Missouri Town, and The Forks. The community settled on the name Downieville for Scotsman William Downie, its leading citizen. On Christmas Day of that year, Downie, who had proclaimed himself a

Just beyond the St. Charles Place Saloon in Downieville, California Highway 49 turns into one lane as it crosses the Downie River. *Philip Varney*

Downieville's cemetery has dozens of exceptional grave markers of antiquity.
Philip Varney

major, climbed onto a cabin roof armed with a flag and a pistol. The major later wrote, "I made a short speech, waved the flag, and fired a few shots and finished up by giving three cheers for the American Constitution." Merry Christmas!

By May of the next year, Downieville had fifteen hotels and gambling houses along with four butcher shops and four bakeries. By the next year, it had five thousand citizens.

Placer mining yielded to quartz and even hydraulic mining, but the excitement was over by 1867. One exception was the Gold Bluff Mine, which was worked sporadically into the 1950s, producing about $1.5 million in gold.

You will likely be coming into Downieville from the west, and that's too bad, because the far more pleasant entrance is from the east. When you enter town coming from Sierra City, you slowly pass attractive residences, an 1850s Protestant church, and an 1864 Masonic Lodge—and then you stop to check traffic from the opposite direction, because the highway narrows for a one-lane bridge as you cross the Downie River. This is the only place I know that Highway 49 goes to one lane, and the effect is absolutely charming.

But coming from the west has its allure as well. You will not have seen a business establishment for quite a while on Highway 49, and suddenly a roadside diner appears. Then you come to Cannon Point at a turn in the road, where a cannon believed to have been hauled from San Francisco sits. No one seems to be certain why it was brought to the community. It once was located near the

The former 1864 I.O.O.F. Hall now serves as Downieville's library. *Philip Varney*

Catholic church in town, where it was fired in celebration for the first time. Two gentlemen wanted to fire it again, but they were told not to because it needed to be cleaned after every firing. They set it off anyway, and both died from the experience. Celebration over.

Downtown Downieville meets at Main and Commercial Streets. On the southeast corner stands the 1852 Craycroft Building, a brick and stone structure with an overhanging porch. A plaque states the building was famous for its seventy-foot-long basement bar, made from a single rip-sawn board.

Across the street on Main stands another excellent antique structure, the 1852 Mackerman Building. According to its historical marker, it has been a brewery, a drugstore, and a meat market. Currently it houses the state's oldest weekly newspaper, *The Mountain Messenger*. Its wooden false front is deceiving, because the building has 3-foot-thick stone side walls and a 4-foot-thick mud and brick ceiling.

Visible on a hill behind the Mackerman Building is the unusual steeple of the 1858 Immaculate Conception Catholic Church. Worshippers and visitors access the very narrow church from the side, thus preventing people from entering and exiting the church amid Downieville's considerable "traffic."

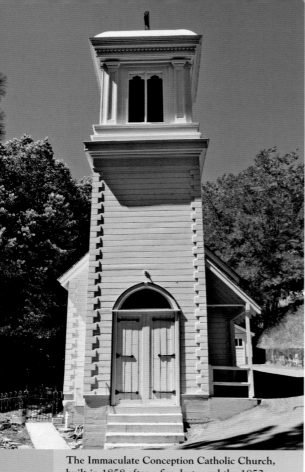

The Immaculate Conception Catholic Church, built in 1858 after a fire destroyed the 1852 original, is one of the narrowest churches in northern California. *Philip Varney*

To reach the cemetery, only 0.6 of a mile from downtown, continue east on Main from Commercial and follow the road as it climbs through a neighborhood. Just after Oxford Mine Road goes left, veer left down onto Gold Bluff Road when Main drops to the right. The cemetery will be in view on your left. A sign states that this graveyard, dating from around 1876, was the second burial ground in Downieville. An earlier cemetery was being "disturbed by greedy miners," so the graves were disinterred and brought to this site.

For yet another Downieville historic spot, turn south from Main onto Nevada Street. You will cross a bridge and then come to a reproduction of the Sierra County Sheriff's Gallows, the site of the 1885 hanging of James O'Neill. That was the only time it was used, and that was the last legal execution in the county.

According to the historic marker, the 1852 Mackerman Building has been a brewery, a drugstore, and a meat market, and now it is home to *The Mountain Messenger*. *Philip Varney*

WHEN YOU GO

From North Bloomfield, head northeast out of town, following North Bloomfield Road for 1.4 miles. Turn left on Derbec Road and go 0.8 of a mile to Backbone Road and turn left. This will dovetail into Cruzon Grade Road and take you to North Columbia in 5.7 miles. By the time you reach North Columbia, Cruzon Grade Road will have dovetailed into Tyler Foote Crossing Road. Follow Tyler Foote Crossing Road from North Columbia for 4.6 miles to Oak Tree Road. Turn right and follow it for 2.6 miles to California Highway 49, which you will reach 0.2 of a mile north of the gold rush town of North San Juan. I suggest taking a small detour to explore that community.

Downieville is 28 miles northeast of North San Juan on Highway 49.

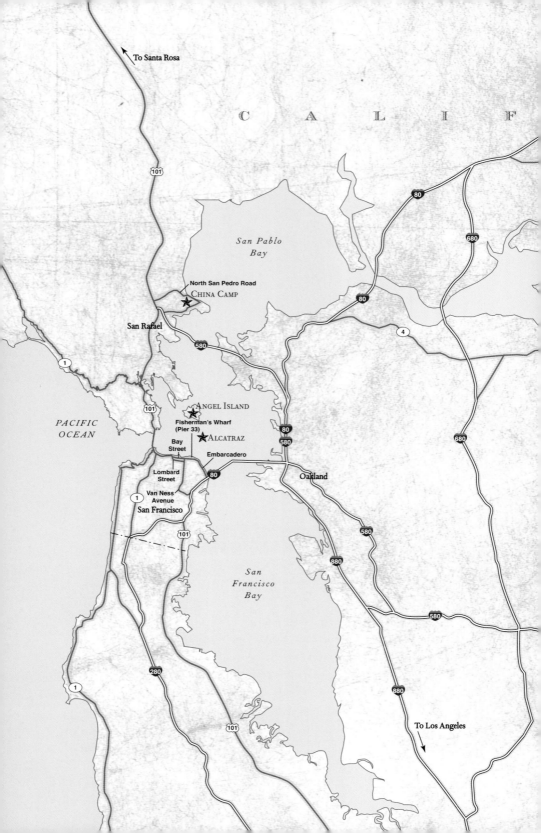

To Santa Rosa

C A L I F

101

San Pablo Bay

80

680

North San Pedro Road
CHINA CAMP ★

San Rafael

80

4

580

PACIFIC
OCEAN

1

ANGEL ISLAND ★

101

Fisherman's Wharf
(Pier 33)
★ ALCATRAZ

Bay
Street

Embarcadero

80

580

680

Lombard
Street

Oakland

Van Ness
Avenue

1

San Francisco

580

101

880

*San
Francisco
Bay*

280

580

1

101

880

To Los Angeles

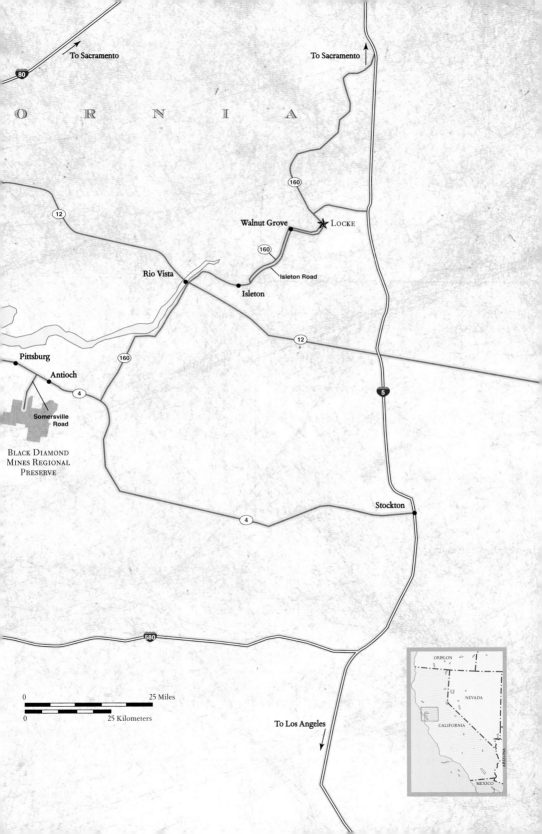

ALCATRAZ

lcatraz was "a small town with a big jail," according to former head guard Philip Bergen. In addition to its "big jail," Alcatraz was home to about three hundred civilians who shopped in the small store, received mail at the post office, and attended events in a social hall that featured a bowling alley. Among those civilians were sixty to eighty children who played on a concrete playground (no cap pistols or rubber knives, however) and were ferried daily to school in San Francisco, a mere 1.25 miles away. Bergen's daughter remembers fondly, "It was a great place to grow up. . . . There were parties for kids, formal dances for the teens. We were within steps of the prison, but no one locked their doors."

Those children and their parents have gone, and Alcatraz is now a small ghost town with a big ghost jail. It is also one of the West's most fascinating places to visit.

Isla de Alcatraces (Spanish for "Pelican Island") was the name bestowed in 1775 on what is now known as Yerba Buena Island in San Francisco Bay. The name was transferred in 1826 to the place now popularly called "The Rock."

The gold rush made Alcatraz important. The amazing Mother Lode brought hundreds of ships with tens of thousands of people to San Francisco through the Golden Gate, and Alcatraz had the Pacific Coast's first lighthouse, built in 1854,

The Parade Ground stands on the south end of Alcatraz. It was here that the children of guards played. The overgrown piles of rubble in the center and right are all that is left of the family housing, leveled in 1972. In the background is San Francisco, with the Bay Bridge extending toward Oakland. *Philip Varney*

Built by the army in the 1920s on top of the Alcatraz Island guardhouse and sally port, this building has always been known as "The Chapel," although there is no record of its ever being used for religious purposes. Its principal function during both military and prison duty was as quarters for single men, although it served for a short time, during the military phase, as a schoolhouse. *Philip Varney*

The Recreation Yard, adjacent to the Cell House, has been used in several motion pictures about life on Alcatraz. *Philip Varney*

to usher them in safely. When the Civil War broke out, San Francisco's enormous gold supply (and silver supply from Nevada's Comstock Lode) tempted the Confederacy, but by that time Alcatraz also was the Pacific Coast's first permanent military outpost, with 111 cannons and rows of gun emplacements. The strength of Alcatraz and other fortifications deterred the Confederacy, and not one shot was fired from the battlements. (That might have been fortunate, because during an 1876 centennial celebration, a ship was towed into range for Alcatraz's mighty cannons to obliterate. They failed.)

In 1907 Alcatraz was deemed no longer necessary for defense, and it was converted to a full-time military prison. Construction began in 1908 on the huge cell house that still dominates the island, a structure that was at the time the world's largest steel-reinforced concrete building. It was designed so cells had neither an outside wall nor an outside ceiling—escaping one's cell would still leave the inmate within the building's walls. The prisoners who helped construct the cell house were its first occupants when it was completed in 1912.

The federal penitentiary that gave the island its notoriety was opened in 1934 as a place to house inmates whose behavior at other federal prisons made them particular risks. Alcatraz was for many of them the end of the prison line. Among the most infamous were Al Capone, "Machine Gun" Kelly, and Robert Stroud, the "Bird Man of Alcatraz," who in fact had birds at Leavenworth penitentiary, but not at Alcatraz.

The residence for the warden of Alcatraz was burned during the American Indian occupation in 1970. It was built in the 1920s for the commander of the military prison.
Philip Varney

The food was good and prisoners were not mistreated physically, despite Hollywood's various depictions. But there was one cruel punishment: the proximity of the lights and sounds of San Francisco. As one inmate reported, "There was never a day when you couldn't see what you were losing." On New Year's Eve, it was said that inmates could even hear champagne corks popping at shoreline clubs.

Alcatraz closed in 1963 because buildings were deteriorating and the prison was overly expensive to run. Of the 1,545 men who did time over those twenty-nine years, eight were murdered, five committed suicide, seven were killed attempting to escape, and two were eventually executed at the prison at San Quentin for killing two Alcatraz guards. No successful escape is known, although five inmates were presumed drowned in San Francisco Bay. One inmate in 1962 actually made it to rocks near the Golden Gate Bridge, but he was too exhausted to climb to dry land and was apprehended.

After Alcatraz's closing in 1963, the island was uninhabited, except for a caretaker, until November 1969, when fourteen Native American students invaded the island. Eventually a group calling itself the "Indians of All Tribes" claimed possession of Alcatraz under a Sioux treaty of 1868 guaranteeing that abandoned federal lands would revert to Indians. The occupiers sardonically claimed that the island would be an ideal place for Indians since it was isolated from modern facilities and had inadequate sanitation, high unemployment, and no educational facilities. It was also a place where the population had always been held as prisoners and kept dependent upon others. The federal authorities were not amused and eventually cut off electricity and water supplies before evicting the Indians in June 1971.

Scars of that occupation remain on Alcatraz. A fire on June 2, 1970, destroyed the lighthouse keeper's home, the once-lovely warden's residence, and the Post Exchange.

I suggest, when you arrive at Alcatraz, to try to forget the prison's cinematic portrayals and see it for what it was, because former inmate Jim Quillan worries that movies, books, and legends have glorified the prison. He reminds us that Alcatraz was "about isolation, sadness, anger, and death." Glenn Williams, another inmate, says simply: "This was a horrible, horrible place."

Understanding Alcatraz's reality is much easier if you do two things: buy an inexpensive brochure detailing the layout of the island and take the excellent recorded tour of the cell house. The tour is narrated by former guards and inmates and features the sounds of clanging doors and the echoes of men's voices. The effect is mesmerizing.

After the headphone tour, be sure to walk everywhere you are permitted to go. Make a thorough exploration of corridors and walking paths, and be certain to visit the Recreation Yard. From there you can see the prisoners' views of the Bay Area, so close but so distant.

Most of the ghost prison is still standing, but little of the ghost town. On the island's southeast end, you can look down to a large parade ground that served as the playground for the town's children. Here is a memory from Jolene Babyak, who grew up on the island: "This two-acre slab of concrete was our batting field, our skating rink, our tennis court, our touch football gridiron." Adjacent to that space is the rubble of the families' apartments, which were bulldozed in 1972.

WHEN YOU GO

Ferries leave San Francisco's Fisherman's Wharf (Pier 33) to Alcatraz Island on a frequent basis, but advance reservations are essential. Incidentally, neither food nor drink is sold on the island.

ANGEL ISLAND

ngel Island offers one of the premier day trips of the Bay Area. Visitors leave behind the human tumult and San Francisco's exorbitantly priced real estate to discover solitude, relaxation, and, yes, even ghost towns— or at least ghost forts.

Isla de Los Angeles was named in 1775 by Lt. Juan Manuel de Ayala, commander of the packet San Carlos, which anchored in the cove that now bears Ayala's name. Angel Island has been the site of Miwok villages, a Spanish rancho, a hangout for thieves and a dueling ground, a Civil War fortification, a sandstone quarry, a military detention center, a quarantine station, an army base, an immigration facility, and even a Nike missile base. Remains of several of these deployments stand on the island today, creating a daylong adventure for naturalists, photographers, and ghost town enthusiasts.

You will dock at Ayala Cove, which, beginning in 1891, housed a quarantine station where foreign ships were fumigated and possibly contagious immigrants were isolated. A two-story attendants' quarters from that era now houses a museum.

A tram that circumnavigates the island leaves from Ayala Cove, and I took it once simply to be able to report about it. If, however, you want more than a cursory glance at the highlights of the island, I cannot recommend it. It stops for only a few minutes at the island's major attractions, which would be very frustrating for a photographer, for example. But it certainly is the easiest way to enjoy the island and the only option for some. A newer way to go is a Segway tour, but, again, you cannot venture out on your own or set your own timetable.

Camp Reynolds's officers' quarters—boarded up, grayish-white, two-story wooden residences— appear to be standing at frozen attention beside the parade ground on Angel Island. *Philip Varney*

Camp Reynolds's warehouse, with its old wharf piling rotting in San Francisco Bay, stands at the base of the parade ground. *Philip Varney*

If you really desire to investigate Angel Island, I recommend walking or, as I did on two visits, riding a mountain bicycle. These are not easy options, as the perimeter road of the island is 5 miles around, and it is very hilly in places. In addition, to visit the great ghost forts you must descend from the perimeter road almost to the shoreline and then, alas, venture back up. This is much more than a mere walk or ride in the park. You also must pay attention to the time of day, as you don't want to miss that last ferry.

Your first ghost fort is southwest of Ayala Cove. Camp Reynolds was established in 1863 to repel a potential Confederate attack on San Francisco and its enormous gold and silver supply. More than a dozen buildings stand near a parade ground sloping toward the bay. Most of the structures are officers' quarters—boarded-up, two-story wooden residences that appear to be standing at frozen attention beside the parade ground. Near the shore stands a large brick warehouse built in 1909 that housed camp supplies and ordnance for the island's gun emplacements. The Commanding Officer's Quarters, standing at the top of the parade ground, is occasionally open for tours.

Angel Island's Fort McDowell features an Officers' Row of elegant, sturdy residences topped with mission tile roofs. *Philip Varney*

The Artillery Barracks, seen in both a back and front view, housed six hundred soldiers at Fort McDowell's military induction center. *Philip Varney*

On the southeast end of Angel Island are the considerable remains of Fort McDowell. Begun in 1899 as a detainment facility for soldiers returning from the Spanish-American War who had been exposed to contagious diseases, the facility became known as Fort McDowell two years later when it became a discharge center for the same war. In 1910, Fort McDowell was greatly enlarged and became a military induction center. During World War II, the fort was a crucial point of embarkation for troops bound for the Pacific.

Most of Fort McDowell's buildings date from the 1910 enlargement. You will enter along Officers' Row, a stately procession of two-story, red-tile-roofed residences, some of which house park employees. The major structures of Fort McDowell are down the road: a chapel, a combination mess hall and gymnasium, a supply store, artillery headquarters, an administration building, and a hulking six-hundred-man barracks.

Ghost town enthusiasts are accustomed to the partial remnants of buildings that were flimsy when built and meant to last only for a bonanza's duration. Fort McDowell is different. It looks as if it could withstand anything on the Richter scale that San Francisco could take.

On the north side of Angel Island is the least ghostly of the installations on the island, an immigration station that began operation in 1905. Unlike New York's Ellis Island, this facility was not built to welcome and process immigrants but rather to attempt to exclude them, as most arriving at the station were Chinese during a period of anti-Asian sentiment, although many other nationalities also were processed there, such as Mexicans, Latin and South Americans, Australians, New Zealanders, and Canadians. Immediately prior to World War II, more than eight thousand Jewish and Russian immigrants arrived, spurred to action by the rise of Nazism. But the primary would-be immigrants were Chinese, and only those who could prove they had relatives in this country could enter, a process made trickier when the 1906 earthquake and subsequent fire destroyed immigration records. The station closed in 1940. The main attraction is the barracks building, which houses an informative museum with often touching displays, such as mournful, desperate poems carved into the walls by detainees. Not far from the barracks is a marker in memory of the 175,000 Chinese who were detained here.

WHEN YOU GO

Visit Angel Island by ferry from San Francisco or Tiburon, or by private boat. Ferry reservations are recommended, especially on holidays or summer weekends.

China Camp, a small fishing village that is now part of a beautiful state park on the shores of San Pablo Bay, tells an important story about the Chinese in the San Francisco area.

In 1879, John McNear leased twelve acres of land on the shores of the bay to Richard Bullis, who in turn sublet the land to Chinese shrimp fishermen. The settlement that became known as China Camp was one of five fishing villages that grew around Point San Pedro, north of San Rafael. Because maritime regulations decreed that only white men could be captains of ships 40 feet or longer, Bullis made weekly voyages to circumvent the law for his Chinese lessees, who eventually made up a camp of 469 people, all adult males except 50 and all from Kwantung Province in China.

The camp featured a school, a barbershop, three mercantile stores, and a marine supply store. Within five years, the shrimping operation was extremely successful, with the fishermen using efficient bag nets that utilized the actions of the tides. Between 1885 and 1892, the average annual catch for the entire bay was 5.4 million pounds of shrimp, virtually all of it dried and exported to China. China Camp was one of the leading producers of bay shrimp.

Shrimping became an important California industry, but the Chinese fishermen were attacked on two fronts: by white fishermen who resented their hardworking rivals and by conservationists who feared that the bay was being severely overfished.

In 1901, the California legislature passed a law banning fishing during the height of the season and in 1905 passed another prohibiting the exportation of dried shrimp, effectively crippling the industry.

In the following year, two disasters hit the Chinese living in Northern California. The first was a suspicious fire that destroyed Pacific Grove's

The pier extending from China Camp is usually closed to the public, but I was able to get this shot because a lone fisherman was tending his boat and the gate was open.
Philip Varney

The shrimp-drying shed at China Camp contains items common to the town's fishermen. The signs read, left to right, "Safety on Land and Sea," "Get What You Wish," and "Peace and Prosperity." *Philip Varney*

From this pier in San Pablo Bay the China Camp fishermen launched the most successful shrimping operation in Northern California—so successful that the California legislature passed laws restricting their trade. *Philip Varney*

Chinese section, and the second was the great earthquake and fire that destroyed San Francisco. As a result, many Chinese found refuge in a tent city at China Camp, a place largely out of business but, because of its isolation, free from persecution. By 1911, laws were passed prohibiting the use of bag nets and making the possession of dried shrimp unlawful. The industry was moribund for four years and would never fully recover.

In 1915, some restrictions were eased, and China Camp came back to limited life into the 1930s. Eventually only one company remained, operated by the Quan family, who were the last Chinese fishermen on San Pablo Bay. The remains of their company stand at China Camp today.

Those remains consist of almost a dozen buildings under roof. A visitors' center located in a shrimp-drying shed displays memorabilia and photographs. Nearby stands a long brick heater covered by a wooden roof where shrimp were dried using blowing fans (although the process was less efficient than simply sun-drying the catch). The remainder of China Camp consists of a pier, residences, a Flying A gasoline pump (featuring fuel at 49.9¢ per gallon), and a small café. The café formerly offered Tacoma beer ("Best From East to West"), cooked crab, and shrimp cocktail. You can still purchase the latter when it is open on weekends.

WHEN YOU GO

From San Francisco, take US Highway 101 and proceed north, across the Golden Gate Bridge, for 14.4 miles to the North San Pedro Road exit, which has a sign marked for China Camp State Park. Go east on North San Pedro Road for 4.7 miles. There you will find the park office, which has a helpful brochure and map. The village is 0.4 of a mile beyond the park office.

ocke is a town with an unusual history and considerable architectural charm. It came into being in 1916 when a group of Chinese leased land from the brothers George, Clay, and Lloyd Locke to construct residences and businesses after nearby Walnut Grove's Chinatown had burned the previous year. The Chinese could only lease land because California's Alien Land Act, passed in 1913, prohibited Asians from owning land. (Incredibly, that law was not repealed until deemed unconstitutional in 1952.)

The community known as Locke (pronounced by non-English-speaking Chinese as "Lockee") was built in less than a year using Chinese capital but white carpenters. With a resident population of about six hundred, and about one thousand more during various crop-growing seasons, Locke contained every imaginable legitimate business—grocery stores, shoe repair shops, slaughterhouses, canneries, and gambling halls. The gambling halls were considered quite respectable, as they also served as social halls and a place to secure laborers. But there were many illegitimate enterprises as well: opium dens, brothels (run and staffed by whites), and speakeasies, which flourished during Prohibition in hidden back rooms and second stories of otherwise legal enterprises. Locke had no official law enforcement.

The citizens of Locke were primarily agricultural workers who traveled among neighboring farms harvesting a variety of crops, with asparagus and Bartlett pears prominent among them.

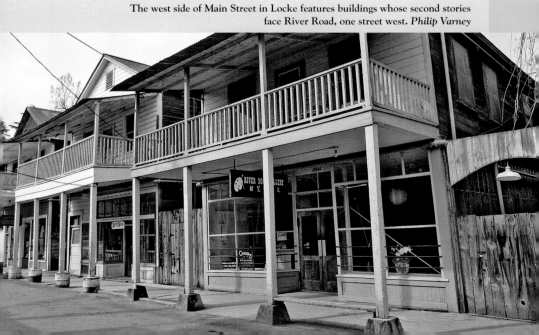

The west side of Main Street in Locke features buildings whose second stories face River Road, one street west. *Philip Varney*

Most of the town's remaining Chinese residents have lived long lives in Locke, but the younger generation has largely left for more lucrative opportunities elsewhere. Locke was placed on the National Register of Historic Places in 1971 and remains the last rural Chinese town in the United States.

When you arrive in Locke from the south, you will see a row of wooden buildings on the east side of River Road across from a large warehouse. These are unusual because, as they face west, they are actually the second stories of structures whose first stories face east on Main Street, the next street over. For example, the seventh building from the south once served as a theater for traveling Chinese repertory companies. Its first floor, facing east on Main, was a gambling hall.

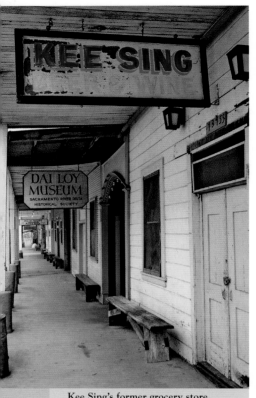

Kee Sing's former grocery store, the Dai Loy Museum (now a museum), and Al's Place, a popular restaurant and bar, stand on Locke's Main Street. *Philip Varney*

Go north to Locke Street, turn right, and park in the nearby lot. Then take a stroll along a street unique in the West, featuring fragile wood structures with overhanging second-story balconies.

The first building of note, the Joe Shoong School, is on the northwest corner of Locke and Main. The 1926 school was funded by and named for the millionaire founder of the National Dollar stores. Students did not attend this school for their regular studies; they would attend classes after returning home from a segregated Asian elementary school in Walnut Grove. At the Joe Shoong School they learned about Chinese art, culture, and language.

The other buildings on the west side of the street are the ones whose second stories you saw one block west.

The business that is likely to be the center of activity when you visit, especially if it is a weekend, stands in the middle of Main Street's east side. It is Al's Place, built in 1916 as Lee Bing's Restaurant. It was purchased by Al Adami in 1941 and has been known by the wonderfully politically incorrect name of "Al the Wop's" ever since. Have you ever slathered peanut butter on a steak? It is de rigueur at Al's (and delicious).

Locke's most fascinating building is the Dai Loy ("Big Welcome") Gambling Hall, home of Locke's museum. In addition to historical photos, the museum features gaming tables, lottery baskets, and other gambling paraphernalia. The Dai Loy has a wonderful, dark, even mysterious mood about it.

The museum sells a booklet, "Discovering Locke," which has a helpful map for exploring the town, along with a brief history of the community. For more information, consider purchasing *Bitter Melon*, which contains interviews with Locke residents. From that volume comes a simple, telling reason to explore this picturesque town: "Locke is the most visible monument to the extraordinary efforts made by the Chinese to develop agriculture in California and establish communities in rural America."

The former Locke China Imports faces River Road, while its first floor serves as a commercial building on Main Street.
Philip Varney

WHEN YOU GO

Locke is about 82 miles east-northeast of China Camp. From China Camp, return to US Highway 101 and proceed south to San Rafael. Take Interstate 580 southeast over the Richmond Bridge for 8.7 miles to Richmond. Take the Cutting Boulevard/Harbour Way exit and drive 2.4 miles east on Cutting Boulevard to the Interstate 80 onramp. Take Interstate 80 going northeast toward Sacramento for 8 miles until you see California Highway 4 exiting toward Hercules and Stockton. Take Highway 4 for 29 miles through Concord, Pittsburg, and Antioch until California Highway 160 branches off to the northeast. Stay on Highway 160 for 16.9 miles to Isleton. Shortly beyond Isleton, Highway 160 crosses the Sacramento River, but you can stay on the southeast bank, which is Isleton Road, to Walnut Grove, 9.3 miles beyond Isleton. (Both Highway 160 and Isleton Road go to Walnut Grove.) Locke is 0.6 of a mile north of Walnut Grove. Incidentally, both Isleton and Walnut Grove are interesting communities worthy of your inspection.

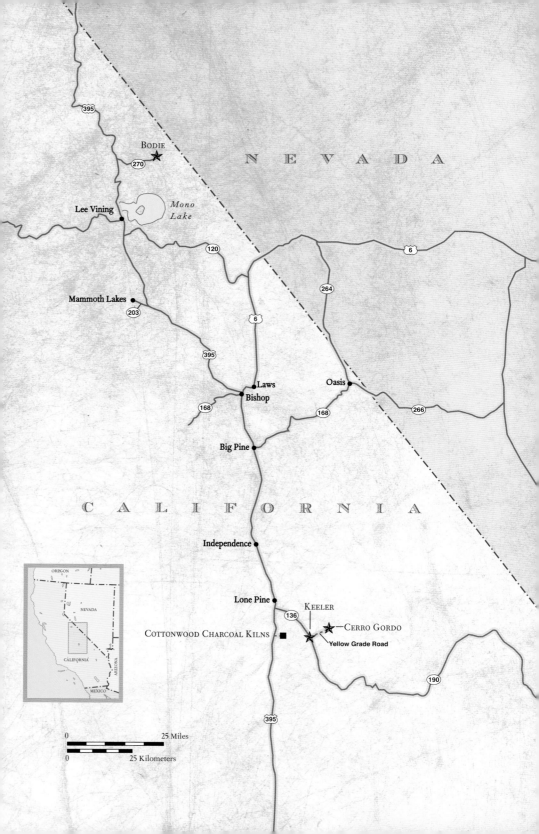

BODIE ★
270

N E V A D A

395

Lee Vining ●
Mono
Lake

120

6

264

Mammoth Lakes ●
203

395

Laws ●
Bishop ●
Oasis ●

168
6

168
266

Big Pine ●

C A L I F O R N I A

Independence ●

Lone Pine ●
KEELER ●
136
★ Cerro Gordo
★ Yellow Grade Road

Cottonwood Charcoal Kilns ■

395

190

OREGON

NEVADA

CALIFORNIA

ARIZONA

MEXICO

0   25 Miles

0   25 Kilometers

odie is one of a kind. No ghost town has as much remaining from its heyday, and no place is maintained like Bodie. Now a state park, it is kept in a state of "arrested decay," which means that it is not being restored to its original condition but rather preserved in its present shape. When shingles or windows need replacement, they are identical to the original. Many buildings that have a charming lean are actually braced from within by specially trained carpenters.

And what buildings they are! Almost 170 remain, most of them made of wind-battered and sun-bleached wood. Although the majority are residences, Bodie also has a variety of commercial and mining-related structures. As many buildings as there are, they represent only one in twenty of Bodie's total number, as fires in 1892 and 1932 ravaged the town.

Although Bodie is a state park, it does not feel like one; there are no tourist concession stands, no multimedia presentations, and no modern automobiles. There are also no food stands, so bring your own fare to eat. And you will need sustenance, because you will want to spend at least three hours in Bodie. In fact, if you hope to see most of it, I rec-

Buildings at Bodie often lean at precipitous angles, but many are propped or braced to keep them standing. *Philip Varney*

ommend staying all day (or spend parts of two days). I have visited more than six hundred ghost towns in twelve states, and this one is the best.

Only four years after the discovery of gold, the Mother Lode was saturated with argonauts. Late entrants found little opportunity for success and so ventured elsewhere. One of those disappointed prospectors was Waterman (or William—accounts differ) S. Body (also spelled "Bodey"), who came from Sonora to the Eastern Sierra after gold was discovered in Mono County in 1857. In 1859, Body and a partner, E. S. "Black" Taylor, headed into the hills and found gold in Taylor Gulch, named for the partner, where they built a cabin.

Body, from Poughkeepsie, New York, never saw the glory of their discovery, as he died the next year in a snowstorm while bringing supplies to the cabin.

A mining district was formed, including Taylor Gulch, on July 10, 1860.

EVELYN,
BELOVED
DAUGHTER OF
FANNIE J.
& ALBERT K.
MYERS,
BORN MAY 1, 1894,
DIED APRIL 5, 1897.

A beautiful headstone for the beloved Evelyn, at Bodie. *Philip Varney*

The first recorded spelling of the camp as "Bodie" appeared in October 1862. Emil Billeb, a Bodie resident for decades, says the name was spelled that way because of a careless sign painter, but others claim it was a deliberate change because, spelled "Body," people were pronouncing it "bah-dee," not "boh-dee."

The 1879 Bon Ton Lodging House became Bodie's schoolhouse after a delinquent burned down its predecessor. *Philip Varney*

The bonanza began in 1874, and two years later a cave-in at the Bunker Hill Mine exposed a rich concentration of gold ore. In 1878, a huge strike at the Bodie Mine brought $1 million worth of ore in only six weeks. In that year, Bodie's population reached about three thousand people. Two years later, the population had more than tripled.

Building a metropolis at an elevation of more than 8,000 feet was no simple matter. The Bodie area is virtually treeless. Lumber for buildings and wood for fuel were freighted from a forest 32 miles away, south of Mono Lake, creating a lumber boomtown there called Mono Mills. In 1881 a narrow-gauge railroad from Mono Mills to Bodie made wood shipments cheaper and more reliable. It was a good thing, too, because Bodie's mines and mills consumed forty-five thousand cords of wood annually.

The only way to visit Bodie's Standard Mine and Mill complex is to take an informative tour. *Philip Varney*

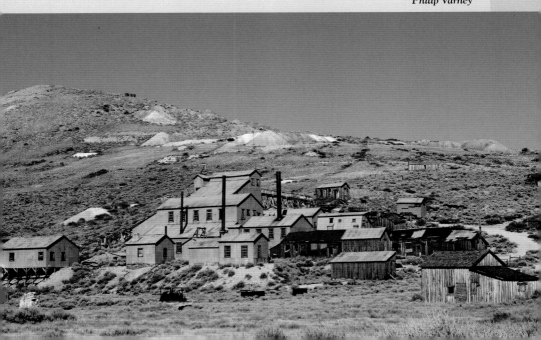

Mono Mills's lumber created a boisterous Bodie, with sixty-five saloons and gambling halls, seven breweries, and a red-light district on Bonanza Street, which was facetiously known as Maiden Lane or Virgin Alley. The jail was conveniently located immediately east of Bonanza. A minister in 1881 proclaimed the place "a sea of sin, lashed by the tempests of lust and passion."

But that is only one version of Bodie. Popular histories tend to emphasize, even glorify, the violent and tempestuous nature of bonanza camps, as if drunken, bawdy, and murderous behavior was both accepted and the norm. It was neither. Grant H. Smith, later a respected mining attorney, came to Bodie at age fourteen in 1879 and served as a telegraph messenger boy. As a result, he entered every imaginable social and business situation. He counters Bodie's scurrilous reputation, saying, "These men, as a rule, were virile, enthusiastic, and free-living, bound by very few of the rules of conventional society. However, they had an admirable code of ethics: liberal-minded, generous to a fault, square-dealing, and completely devoid of pretense and hypocrisy. . . . A friend in Bodie was a friend for life."

But Bodie's reputation, Smith's efforts notwithstanding, will forever be tainted toward its lawless side by one famous quote, uttered by a little girl whose family was moving from nearby Aurora, Nevada, to the infamous town. In her evening prayer, she was overheard by her parents saying, "Goodbye, God, I'm going to Bodie." Aurora journalists used the prayer to ridicule Bodie, but Bodie journalists, in a rejoinder, insisted that the tone and punctuation were vastly different. What the little girl had actually said was "Good! By God, I'm going to Bodie!"

The door is open at the 1882 Methodist church in Bodie, one of only a few buildings you can actually enter. *Philip Varney*

The Dechambeau Hotel, the I.O.O.F. Hall (with the Bodie Athletic Club downstairs), the Miners Union Hall, and the town morgue stand left to right along Bodie's Main Street. *Philip Varney*

Bodie's boom times lasted a mere three years. During its peak, almost fifty mines were producing ore that was fed to ten mills with a combined 162 stamps. By 1882, however, the population had dropped drastically from about ten thousand to less than five hundred. In 1883, Bodie mine stocks crashed. The town was virtually lifeless.

During the bonanza years, an estimated $21 million in gold had been extracted. Naturally, some refused to believe that Bodie's glory days were over, and one of those became the person crucial to Bodie's present-day state of preservation—James Stuart Cain.

Jim Cain came from Canada in 1875 at age twenty-one looking to find his fortune in Carson City, Nevada, just when the Comstock Lode was in

The billiard table inside the Wheaton and Hollis Hotel in Bodie, with elegant lions supporting it, leans to give a house player a true advantage. The photo was taken through the glass of the front window. *Philip Varney*

Another photo taken through glass shows the interior of Bodie's Boone Store and Warehouse. Notice the shelves that feature merchandise ready for "sale." *Philip Varney*

decline. Like many others, he went on to Bodie, arriving in 1879.

Cain began in the lumber and freighting businesses. As Bodie boomed, he supplied much of the wood, transporting it across Mono Lake by barge. As he prospered, he diversified by investing in mines and leasing the Bodie Railroad and Lumber Company, which replaced his barge. When Bodie plummeted, Cain stayed, buying bargain-rate mines and the Bodie Bank.

In 1890, Cain brought to Bodie the then-new cyanide process to treat previously worthless tailings. To lower costs at the highly successful cyanide plants, he brought electric power to Bodie, the first use of electricity generated over

James B. Perry's stone is one of the most artistic I have seen. From quarried stone evolves a kind of parchment announcing that he was a native of Ireland and served as Supervisor of Mono County. Note that the "parchment" even is rolled at the bottom and has a turned "edge" at the upper right. *Philip Varney*

long-distance lines (the hydroelectric plant was 13 miles away). The technology was so untested that power lines were laid in a straight line, for fear that if the line curved, the electricity might jump off into space.

The successful use of long-distance electricity at Bodie caused a revolution in the way mines were powered and changed the way the world produced ore.

The cyanide tailings process kept Bodie profitable into the early twentieth century, but Cain was convinced that Bodie would have another windfall from new gold deposits.

One constant in all these dealings was Cain's Bodie Bank. Although he was a banker, Cain hardly fit the stereotype. His bank, for example, had calendars featuring pinup girls on its walls.

Cain operated the bank for forty years, until 1932. He would open every weekday at 10:00 a.m. to no customers. In that year, a boy playing with matches started a fire that leveled about two-thirds of Bodie's largely vacant business district. The fire consumed Cain's bank, although the vault held and the safe inside protected its contents. In that same year, Cain left Bodie for good, moving to San Francisco where he died in 1939 at age eighty-five.

But Cain's legacy did not die. He had the foresight to hire a watchman to protect the town, and in 1962 Bodie became a state park. Because of Jim Cain, Bodie stands as a monument to the rush for riches in the American West.

An outstanding brochure you can purchase when you enter Bodie suggests a logical walking tour. Remember to peer into every building through as many windows as you can to study its contents.

For example, if you gaze into the living room window of the Metzger House on Fuller Street, you will see a dusty old doll carriage, a wooden sled, and a small toy dog for a child to sit on and rock, like a hobby horse.

A comment I have heard several times on my visits to Bodie is that it is unfortunate that we can only gaze through the windows of most buildings. But if we could step inside, floors would have to be reinforced, valuable objects would have to be placed out of reach, and the whole feeling of Bodie—that people up and left in a moment—would be seriously compromised. The town is much more genuine because we cannot enter most structures.

In the center of town, on Main Street south of Green Street, stands the 1878 Miners Union Hall, which houses the park's interesting museum. While in the hall, consider purchasing tickets to one of the park's outstanding tours.

The most frequently offered tour is of the huge 1899 Standard Mill, east of town on the slopes of Bodie Bluff. Tours are given as if you were a 1905 prospective employee, a delightful illusion that makes the experience more genuine.

Two other tours go into otherwise closed-off areas, including the train depot and mineshafts. They do not run daily, however, and are given but once a day when offered, so inquire before you visit.

The 1879 Bodie Schoolhouse, on Green east of Main, offers one of the most fascinating glances into Bodie's past. Originally the Bon Ton Lodging House, the building was pressed into educational service when a delinquent burned down the first school. When you peer through the windows, notice textbooks on desks and a wooden globe whose maps have peeled off, leaving it merely a large wooden ball. A wall clock, appropriately, has no hands.

Bodie's cemetery (actually three adjoining graveyards) is 0.3 of a mile southwest of town. The site is well worth exploring, and not just because of its many interesting headstones. It also features an overview of Bodie, making it a natural stop for photographers. An informative cemetery guide is usually available at the gate for purchase or loan.

After you have completed your tour of Bodie, you might recall those journalists who doctored the little Aurora girl's prayer. In a way, they were speaking for present-day ghost town enthusiasts—Bodie has become our mecca, and now we can justifiably say, "Good! By God, I'm going to Bodie!"

WHEN YOU GO

From Lee Vining, drive 18.3 miles north on US Highway 395. Turn east on California Highway 270 and proceed 12.3 miles to Bodie State Historic Park. All but the last 2.7 miles are paved. In good weather, even motor homes traverse the route.

CERRO GORDO

erro Gordo is, like Bodie, one of the best ghost towns in the American West. Bodie (see previous entry) has many more buildings, but it also has something Cerro Gordo does not—many more visitors. Cerro Gordo's structures are photogenic, the artifacts are plentiful, and the twisting, steep road to the site has only been marginally improved since the 1870s. The total experience of visiting Cerro Gordo rivals any site in any of my ten ghost town books.

The silver and lead bonanza in the mountains high above Owens Lake made Los Angeles a city. If that seems like an impossible exaggeration, consider the *Los Angeles News* in 1870: "To this city, the Owens River trade is invaluable. What Los Angeles is, is mainly due to it."

In 1865, Pablo Flores and two other Mexicans found rich silver ore deposits near Cerro Gordo Peak (*cerro gordo* means "fat hill" in Spanish, referring either to the rounded shapes of the mountains or, more likely, that they were "fat"—meaning "rich"—in ore). Because of the size and depth of the vein, a shipping route was established through the Owens Valley that gave the sleepy Pueblo de Los Angeles ("City of the Angels") the bulk of its transportation and supply business. Los Angeles didn't just grow; it exploded: hence the remark in the *Los Angeles News*.

In 1867, the Lone Pine Mining District was formed, which included Cerro Gordo. Two years later, San Francisco mining engineer Mortimer Belshaw

The former company store at Cerro Gordo now serves as a museum. *Philip Varney*

One of the two Cerro Gordo assay offices stands to the left of a crib for Lola Travis's House of Pleasure. Behind stands the trestle for a tramway that extends all the way to Keeler. *Philip Varney*

arrived at Cerro Gordo, assessed the enormous profits to be made at the site, and took steps to make sure that much of those profits would be his. Shipping silver ore is much more expensive than shipping pure silver. That means smelting the ore at or near the site will increase profits. Smelting of silver requires lead, which is found in galena, which was in abundance at Cerro Gordo. As a result, Belshaw invested heavily in the Union Mine (for silver and lead) and eventually owned two of the three smelters near the mines. Perhaps the smartest thing he did was tactical: he constructed a toll road following the only practical access route (which is still used today), thus controlling the only way between Cerro Gordo and the logical shipping point at the base of the mountains. That meant he also controlled something even more precious than silver: the supply of water to the mines—and to the miners.

Victor Beaudry had arrived in Cerro Gordo before Belshaw and owned the principal store there. He saw that Belshaw was the ticket to riches at the site and became his partner. The two dominated the short but extremely prosperous life of Cerro Gordo. How prosperous? Between 1868 and 1875, approximately $13 million in silver-lead bullion was shipped from the smelters, making the Cerro Gordo mines the greatest producers of those metals in California's history. For seven years, California had its own Comstock Lode.

Getting the bullion to market was the responsibility of Remi Nadeau, whose mule-team freight wagons, about eighty in number, worked their way down the steep and treacherous Yellow Grade Road (Belshaw's toll road), so named for the area's yellow shale. From there they skirted the north shore of Owens Lake, headed across the Mojave Desert into Los Angeles, and finally unloaded their treasure at that city's port of San Pedro. The journey took about fifteen days each way.

The only problem was that there was too much silver to haul. The smelters were producing a staggering four hundred ingots, weighing about eighty-five pounds each, in every twenty-four-hour period, and Nadeau's freight teams could not keep up. At one point, thirty thousand bars had accumulated on site, and miners stacked them to make cabins—no doubt the most expensive shacks ever built.

By 1877, however, the mines began to play out. The last load of bullion was shipped the next year. In 1883, by the time a railroad reached Keeler (see page 72), the prosperity was over and the reason for a railroad long past. The town's post office somehow hung on until 1895.

Cerro Gordo was not quite done yet. In 1911, Louis Gordon discovered enormous zinc deposits up in the mountains, and the once-great silver and lead producer became the principal source of high-quality zinc in the United States. Two aerial tramways were constructed to transport the ore, one from the Union Shaft at Cerro Gordo all the way to the Southern Pacific tracks

The Cerro Gordo townsite spreads out before you, with the Owens Valley and the Sierra Nevada behind. *Kerrick James*

at Keeler, a distance of more than 4 miles. The other tram ran just over a mile from the Morningstar Mine, south of the townsite, to a terminus on the Yellow Grade Road. Neither tramway required power, because the weight of the ore going down was heavier than any supplies loaded into the buckets heading back up.

The zinc operations lasted into the 1930s, when the town that built Los Angeles and gave California its own "Comstock" withered into obscurity.

The house of Billy Crapo, who shot the town postmaster and then fled, stands to the left of Cerro Gordo's American Hotel. *Michael Moore*

Over the decades, the town was subjected to repeated vandalism and theft despite efforts by occasional caretakers, but Cerro Gordo seemed to have a solid, steady future when Jody Stewart purchased it in 1985. She was barely forty years of age and had funds available to use to restore the town, which had become a haphazard near-junkyard despite its remarkable, historic buildings. She was joined by Mike Patterson, three years her junior, as her general manager, helpmate, and, eventually, her husband. They made enormous progress over the next several years, clearing the property, shoring up buildings, and generally bringing the site back to life.

However, in 2001, Jody Stewart, then Jody Stewart-Patterson, died at age fifty-seven. Mike Patterson continued to work on Cerro Gordo until 2009, when he also died. I tell you this principally because I would be remiss if I didn't acknowledge my friends' enormous contributions to this marvelous ghost town. They saved Cerro Gordo so there is still a town for you to enjoy and explore. But their deaths may also have an effect upon your ability to visit Cerro Gordo. At this writing, the future of the town is uncertain: volunteers are attempting to protect the site and continue the work that has been sustained since the mid-1980s. I have provided a website address at the end of this entry; I hope it will still be current when you read this so that you may ascertain how to visit Cerro Gordo.

As you enter Cerro Gordo, the first structure will be on your left—the stone chimney of Victor Beaudry's smelter. Beyond it on the same side of the road stands what once served as a shop and/or a garage, now fashioned into a chapel, and behind it, the bunkhouse and what likely was an assay office.

The 1911 trestle of a tramway that sent zinc all the way to the railroad at Keeler stands above Cerro Gordo. *Michael Moore*

To your right will be a string of classic Western buildings on a rise just above the road: an icehouse, a screened-in coolhouse for outdoor food storage, and the wonderful 1871 American Hotel. Next to the hotel is the former residence of Billy Crapo, who killed Postmaster Harry Boland by shooting him from behind in 1893. Crapo bolted from town and was never captured. On the hills behind the hotel stand several miners' shacks.

Of these first several buildings, the American Hotel is the treasure. The two-story wooden structure features a bar, tables, a card room, a working kitchen, and furnished upstairs rooms.

The road you came in on forks beyond those first buildings. Directly in front of you on the right is the home of the town's original tycoon, Mortimer Belshaw, built around 1868. Behind his residence is a shack believed to have been the home of Belshaw's Chinese cook. Across the street from that shack is the beautifully restored 1909 home of Louis Gordon, the man who brought Cerro Gordo back to prosperity with his discovery of zinc.

Across the street from the Belshaw house is the tin-covered former general store, now a museum. When I first saw it, the store was so thoroughly surrounded by junk and trash that it was difficult even to approach. Now it features a spacious front deck.

Up the hill from the store is an odd pairing of wooden structures. One is believed to have been a crib for Lola Travis's House of Pleasure, a dance hall that stood behind the crib. This is the only crib still standing, although at least one other is believed to have existed next to it. Immediately adjacent to the crib is a second assay office, an unusual use of a building so close to a brothel.

The most dramatic structure in town is the trestle of the Union Shaft, the one that was built during the zinc operation that began a tramway that extended all the way to Keeler. I was standing on that trestle in 1982 when I had the most terrifying experience in all my years of ghost town exploring. I was peering through my telephoto lens down to the Owens Valley, when suddenly into focus came the nose of a jet fighter heading straight at me as it careened up the canyon. I could, for an instant, see the helmeted pilot in the cockpit. It screeched over the townsite and left me gasping and holding on to the shaking trestle. I have returned to Cerro Gordo three more times, but, strangely enough, I have not ventured again out onto that trestle. It is also much more rickety now, and you shouldn't go out there either.

The Union Shaft hoist house, the Morningstar Mine, and all mine tunnels are, at this writing, off-limits to visitors.

WHEN YOU GO

From Lone Pine, head south on US Highway 395 for 1.9 miles to the junction with California Highway 136 (the location of the informative Eastern Sierra Interagency Visitor Center). Drive 12.4 miles to the town of Keeler (see following entry). Just beyond the main part of Keeler is a dirt road that heads north into the mountains. A sign there indicates that it is the route to Cerro Gordo. The 7.6-mile drive up the Yellow Grade Road is, in places, very, very steep, as Cerro Gordo, at an elevation of 8,500 feet, is almost 5,000 feet above Keeler. It is often impassable in bad weather. I strongly recommend a high-clearance truck, preferably with four-wheel-drive.

NOTE: Cerro Gordo is privately owned. You can get information about exploring the town at www.cerrogordo.us, which currently refers you to the email address of the current owner. When you do visit the town, be sure to take your own water, as it still must be trucked up from the valley below. I also suggest a generous contribution if admission is not required.

As a railroad town, Keeler was, quite literally, the end of the line. Today, with the railroad long gone, it has a dusty, forlorn look that also gives it an end-of-the-line feeling.

In the 1870s, what is now called Keeler was known as Cerro Gordo Landing, the shipping point to cross Owens Lake for the silver and lead ore that was coming out in astonishing quantities from the mountains above town (see Cerro Gordo, the preceding entry).

The "end of the line" refers to the terminus at Keeler of the Carson & Colorado Railroad. The plan was for the narrow-gauge rail line, which was begun in 1880, to extend from one river to another, accounting for its name: from Mound House, Nevada, on the Carson River, to Fort Mohave, Arizona, on the Colorado River. The plan was to have a rail stop at Cerro Gordo Landing, which was renamed Keeler (for mill owner and entrepreneur Julius M. Keeler), so that the great wealth of the Cerro Gordo mines could then be shipped from Keeler north to San Francisco, eliminating the route taken by boat and then pack train south to Los Angeles. Unfortunately, by the time the railroad was completed to Keeler in 1883, production at Cerro Gordo had ceased. When financier Darius O. Mills traveled along the route of his Carson & Colorado Railroad that same year for the end-of-track inspection, he looked at the empty scene at Keeler and somberly intoned, "Gentlemen, we either built it three hundred miles too long or three hundred years too soon." Mills sold the 293-mile-long white elephant to the Southern Pacific at a tremendous loss in 1900.

A tramway was constructed from Cerro Gordo to Keeler beginning in 1911, when zinc deposits were found in the old silver and lead mines, which resulted in a modest rebirth at Keeler and a legitimate purpose for the railroad. When the zinc operations shut down in the 1930s, the town headed

The deteriorating Sierra Talc Company is Keeler's most prominent building. You can just barely read the word "Sierra" on the two-story middle structure. *Philip Varney*

toward ghost town status. The last train from Keeler left in April 1960, and the town truly was at the end of its line.

Keeler has three fine buildings worth examining. The most prominent is the Sierra Talc Company plant, a favorite subject of artists. Unfortunately, the painted sign on the western face of the building has faded significantly since I first photographed it in the early 1980s.

The depot at Keeler served as the Carson & Colorado Railroad. This is a building well worth restoring, or at least preserving. *Philip Varney*

West of the talc company is the Keeler School, obscured by foliage. A photo I have seen of students in front of the school is dated from the 1930s, so the school is obviously at least that old.

The two-story Carson & Colorado depot, which badly needs propping up or restoration, is the most intriguing building in town. At this writing, it is thoroughly boarded up, so one cannot even peer into its recesses.

To the east of the depot is an E Clampus Vitus historical plaque on Keeler's "end of the line" status, and south of the depot is a foundation with its western wall touting "Famous ABC Beer." I guess fame is relative.

Near the shore of Owens Lake, now mostly dry, is the Keeler swimming pool, fenced, locked, also waterless, and abandoned. I have seen a photo from the 1930s of bathing beauties posing on its deck.

Finally, on the north side of the highway just east of town stands the barren Keeler Cemetery.

A concrete wall in Keeler touts "Famous ABC Beer." *Philip Varney*

WHEN YOU GO

Keeler is at the base of the Yellow Grade Road, the route to Cerro Gordo (see preceding entry), and 14.3 miles southeast of Lone Pine on California Highway 136.

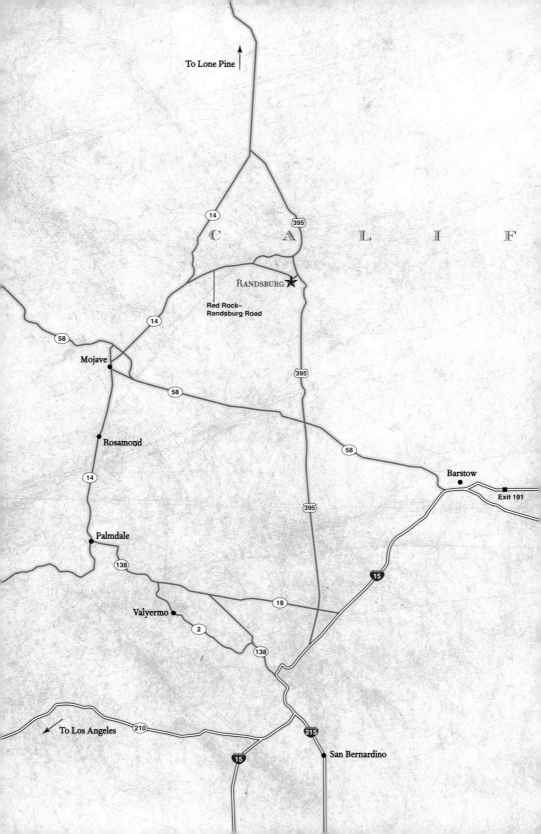

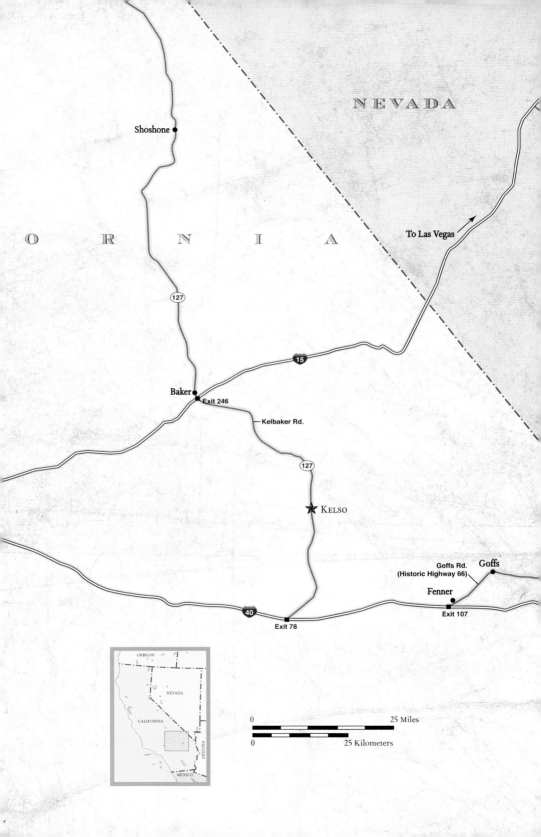

NEVADA

Shoshone ●

O   R   N   I   A

To Las Vegas →

(127)

(15)

Baker ●
■ Exit 246

Kelbaker Rd.

(127)

★ KELSO

Goffs Rd.
(Historic Highway 66)
Goffs ●

Fenner
■ Exit 107

(40)
■ Exit 78

0 _____ 25 Miles

0 _____ 25 Kilometers

OREGON

NEVADA

CALIFORNIA

ARIZONA

MEXICO

RANDSBURG

Most of the historical accounts in this book are about men, simply because most of the towns included here were settled early on by an almost entirely male population. In addition, the heads of mining companies were traditionally male, as were the leaders of expeditions. If you are looking for a story of a strong-willed, intelligent, highly educated woman who was prominent in her town's history and success, you have found it.

Dr. Rose Burcham's husband, Charles Austin Burcham, had a bad case of gold fever. To appease it, Dr. Burcham, a respected general practitioner in San Bernardino, had grubstaked her husband for two years' worth of prospecting in the desert. The time had almost expired when Charles and his fellow adventurers John Singleton and Frederic Mooers made claims near Goler Wash in April 1895. In a clever ruse, the three filled a wagon full of their "find" and visited a nearby camp. Miners there peered under the tarp, saw worthless quartz, and dismissed the three prospectors as ignorant fools. What they did not realize was that the "fools" knew perfectly well that their load was worthless—nor did the other miners realize that the real ore of the trio's claims would yield a true bonanza—the Rand Mine.

The mine was named in hopeful emulation of a huge gold strike in South

Randsburg's Butte Street contains several of the best ghost town buildings in Southern California. Here you see the General Store, the adobe former post office, and the former union hall with its corrugated false front. *Philip Varney*

Africa, Witwatersrand (commonly known as the Rand). The town that grew up around the California mine was originally Rand Camp, later Randsburg. The name of the mine itself became the Yellow Aster, the title of a book Mooers had been reading.

Charles Burcham and his male partners were almost immediately offered quick money to sell the claims; fortunately, there was a fourth partner. Rose Burcham insisted that the four retain total control of the mine, refusing all outside capital. This was a woman who had already broken barriers, practicing medicine in a virtually entirely male profession. Many a potential investor walked away from the Yellow Aster muttering about "that woman," but her intransigence paid off. They all became millionaires.

Randsburg grew as the Yellow Aster prospered. In the summer of 1896, only a little more than a year after the discovery, the camp had a population of about a thousand. Within three years, the population more than tripled.

By 1899 the Yellow Aster had a payroll exceeding $13,000 per month, paid to a hundred and fifty workers. A one-hundred-stamp mill processed the ore. Dr. Burcham, who in the earliest days kept the books and

The Randsburg City Jail is a stout and incommodious building. Imagine occupying one of the two cells in the Mojave Desert's summer heat. *Philip Varney*

cooked the meals, became the dominant partner. Marcia Rittenhouse Wynn, who grew up in Randsburg and wrote about the early days, described Dr. Burcham as a "brilliant, business-like, crisp, hard-working, exacting person." Her presence was felt in every detail of the operation: for example, the Yellow Aster's stamp mill—usually a dark and dingy place—was kept spotless, with a potted palm residing in the main engine room.

Within five years of the discovery of the Yellow Aster, an estimated $3 million had been taken from the district's mines, the largest amount from the Yellow Aster itself.

Because it was primarily a company town, Randsburg was hardly the raucous place some mining towns were. It was spirited, but not rowdy, and its small

Randsburg's White House Saloon, still very much in operation, is rumored to have had a tunnel that led toward the Yellow Aster Mine, perhaps to aid in the high-grading of ore. *Philip Varney*

jail had only two cells. But Randsburg was the site of union strife. When an attempt was made to make the Yellow Aster a fully unionized mine, a strike resulted that lasted from 1902 until 1916. Production continued, however, with nonunion miners. The town was divided in its sympathies: on Saturday nights, two dances were held, union and nonunion, and girls who were observed at one dance were not welcome at the other.

The Rand District's mines produced on a large scale until 1918, with an estimated total of $20 million, $12 million of which came directly from the Yellow Aster. In addition to gold, smaller amounts of silver and tungsten were also extracted. Smaller-scale mining continued into the 1930s and 1940s, and no doubt someone is still digging in those hills. The Rand District was the largest producer of gold ore in Southern California.

If you are coming from Keeler, the previous entry in this chapter, you will enter Randsburg from the north. As the main road takes a bend, you will see the stark, two-cell jail on your left. Read the historical plaque and then take a look inside. Consider how incommodious the cells would be in the summer heat of the Mojave Desert.

Now continue south into the heart of Randsburg, where you will see some of the finest historic buildings in central or Southern California. In the middle of three of the best along Butte Street is what once served as the post office, made of adobe to withstand fires. Adjacent to the post office on the right is the corrugated false front of the former union hall, headquarters for the union movement during the labor troubles. It also served for a time as the post office. On the left of the adobe building is the town's general store, now the hub of activity in Randsburg. Three other false-front commercial buildings are adjacent to these first three.

Across the street is the White House Saloon, which features a long bar created to accommodate thirsty miners. A door in the basement of the saloon once opened into a tunnel that led toward the Yellow Aster Mine. Local lore says that it was used occasionally for high-grading the mine. Several other businesses make up the remainder of the Butte Street area, as well as the informative Randsburg Desert Museum (open on Saturdays, Sundays, and holidays—except Christmas and New Year's), which features a display of mining equipment, including a five-stamp mill.

Continue east on Butte until it intersects Lexington. On the northeast corner stands the board-and-batten 1904 Santa Barbara Catholic Church. Take Lexington around to the west to see a series of residences and the 1934–1935 Community Methodist Episcopal Church.

The Yellow Aster Mine, which was the original reason for the Rand District excitement, stands on a hill south of town and is closed to the public.

In addition to Randsburg, several lesser sites make up the Rand District. East of Randsburg is Johannesburg, whose primary historic remnant is its cemetery, which is southwest of the commercial area at Mountain Wells Avenue and Ophir Street. Directly behind the graveyard is the King Solomon Mine.

South of Johannesburg 1.5 miles on US Highway 395 is Red Mountain, whose historic school has been restored as a senior center. Atolia is 2.9 miles south of Red Mountain. Scattered mining debris marks the site.

WHEN YOU GO

From Keeler, drive 5.1 miles southeast on California Highway 136 to California Highway 190. Turn right and head southwest for 15 miles to a junction with US Highway 395. Stay on US 395 for 70 miles to Johannesburg. When you leave Johannesburg, turn left off US 395 after 1 mile and take the Redrock–Randsburg Road for 1.1 miles into Randsburg. Signs clearly show the turnoff.

Many of the graves in the Roslyn, Washington, cemeteries are for miners who came from eastern Europe. *Philip Varney*

WASHINGTON

CHAPTER 2

Your Washington ghost town adventures include five sites within day trips of Seattle: a delightfully preserved former lumber town, three former coal communities, and a failed mining town. Because these sites are in the most populous areas of Washington, they are not as "ghostly" as many others in this book, but each displays only vestiges of its former life.

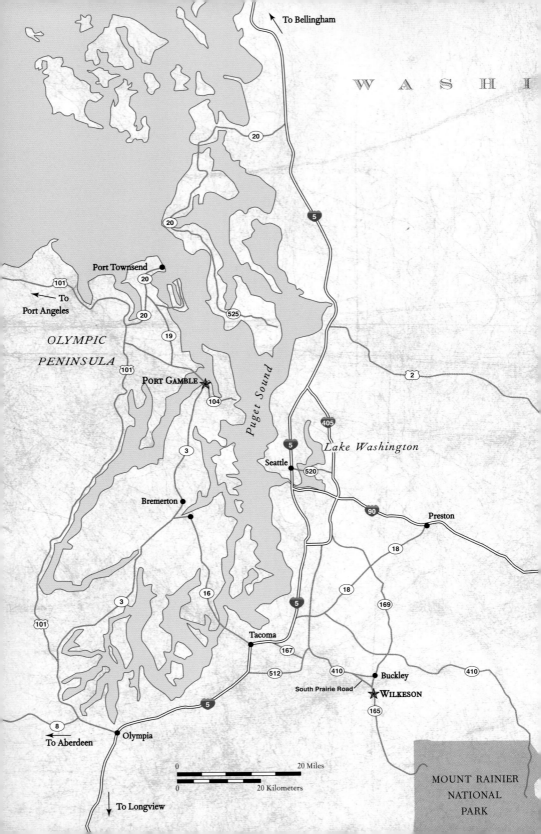

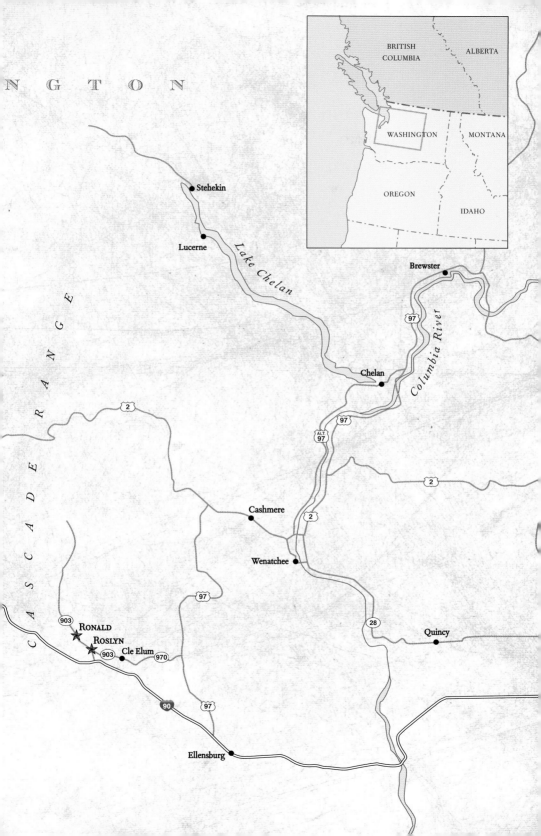

PORT GAMBLE

Port Gamble is one of the Northwest's most delightful communities. It was created as a company town in 1853 by Pope and Talbot, a lumber and shipping company originally formed in December 1849.

The year 1849 was, of course, the beginning of the California gold rush, which was to yield the largest concentration of gold in the history of the world. A. J. Pope, Captain William C. Talbot, and Cyrus Walker, natives of Maine, saw in the gold rush an opportunity for more than mineral wealth. They realized that San Francisco, the center of commerce for that rush, was about to surge in growth and prosperity. In 1853, Talbot and Walker led a maritime expedition up the Pacific Coast, eventually coming across huge supplies of timber, along with water deep enough for a sizable port, in Puget Sound. Pope and Talbot became experts at providing lumber for the booming economy in northern California. Pope handled sales and merchandising in San Francisco, while Talbot was almost constantly at sea, bringing Puget Sound lumber to the port of San Francisco.

Before Pope and Talbot invested in Puget Sound, a small settlement existed where Port Gamble would eventually develop. That community was originally known as Teekalet, a word meaning "brightness of the noonday sun" in the

Port Gamble's 1906 community center and post office is still the center of the action in town. *Philip Varney*

language of the S'Kallam tribe. Port Gamble was named in honor of Lieutenant Robert Gamble, a naval officer wounded in the War of 1812. The Pope and Talbot company town that grew on the site in 1853 was constructed to resemble East Machias, the hometown of the three Maine natives. The maple trees that line the main streets of Port Gamble today were brought as seedlings from East Machias.

Port Gamble was the site of Washington's oldest continuously operated sawmill until it closed in 1995. Today, only concrete foundations remain, and logs are merely shipped out by truck. Technically speaking, Port Gamble is no longer a "port."

The largest building in downtown Port Gamble today is the 1906 community hall, which once housed the post office, the telegraph and telephone headquarters, the doctor's and dentist's offices, a barber shop, and an upstairs movie theater. The post office is still in operation.

South of the community hall stands the 1872 Franklin Lodge, which is the oldest active Masonic lodge in Washington, having been chartered in 1859. The building was never turned around when it was moved across the street in 1907, so its original front is now in the rear.

The most interesting building in town is the Port Gamble General Store and

Built in 1916, Port Gamble's general store sells merchandise and houses two interesting museums. *Philip Varney*

Even the company-owned row houses are immaculately maintained in Port Gamble, one of Washington's best-kept communities. *Philip Varney*

Port Gamble's St. Paul Episcopal Church was modeled after a Congregational church in East Machias, Maine. *Philip Varney*

Office, which dates from 1916. A plaque in front of the store states that this was actually the fifth general merchandiser in Port Gamble but the first in this location. The previous four were along the shore, because customers, such as settlers, Indians, sailors, and loggers, commonly arrived by boat.

In its present incarnation, the store not only sells merchandise, but it also contains two museums. The Of Sea and Shore Museum, located on two mezzanines above the first floor, offers a display of seashells and other marine items. In the basement, the Port Gamble Historic Museum chronicles the history of Pope and Talbot.

Port Gamble's 1856 Buena Vista Cemetery, located west of the business district, does indeed have a "good view," as it stands on a hill offering a panorama of the town.

On the south end of town stand several company houses and the community's loveliest building, the 1879 St. Paul's Episcopal Church, modeled after a Congregational church in East Machias. The church features a tall, graceful steeple with elaborately jigged woodwork.

WHEN YOU GO

Port Gamble is 24.5 miles north of Bremerton. Drive north from Bremerton on Washington Highway 3. When it intersects with Washington Highway 104 at the Hood Canal Bridge, go northeast on Highway 104 instead of crossing the bridge. You will enter Port Gamble in 1 mile. You can also reach the site by taking the Edmonds ferry to Kingston. Port Gamble is 8 miles northwest of Kingston on Highway 104.

Wilkeson is a reminder that not all mining towns exist because of precious metals. The town was founded in 1876 when the Northern Pacific Railway laid tracks to extensive high-grade coal deposits discovered two years earlier. The community was named for Samuel Wilkeson, secretary of the railroad's board of directors. Mining began in 1879, and in 1885 the Tacoma Coal and Coke Company built 165 brick ovens to heat coal into hotter-burning coke.

A second industry began when the railroad started quarrying sandstone for use as ballast. The sandstone later was used for buildings after it was discovered that the stone did not absorb water, unlike virtually all sandstone. The quarry provided blocks for numerous structures, includ-

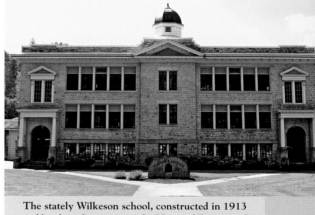

The stately Wilkeson school, constructed in 1913 of local sandstone, is on the National Register of Historic Places. *Philip Varney*

ing the dome of the Washington State Capitol in Olympia.

The nation's declining demand for coal and coke led to Wilkeson's decline in the 1930s.

Two large sandstone columns—with a huge log sitting atop them, stretching across the road—welcome you to the quarry and coal town of Wilkeson. The community's center features several attractive brick buildings, including the Wilkeson Grocery, which resembles the stores of California's 1849 gold rush with its porch over the sidewalk.

Other historic buildings include the brick, two-story 1910 Carlson Block, and a two-story 1910 brick structure that houses the Fraternal Order of Eagles.

Also note the single-story 1923 sandstone edifice that serves as a combination city hall and library and also the attractive Washington Hotel across the street.

At the south end of the business district stands the 1913 Wilkeson School, a large, three-story sandstone building featuring a cupola and two stately columned entrances. It is on the National Register of Historic Places.

Wilkeson's cemetery, with its many concrete borders, has a distinctly European look to it. *Philip Varney*

Beyond the school, the remains of fifty-two coke ovens remain in two back-to-back rows behind a set of bleachers. Encroaching blackberry vines make the ovens almost disappear.

The residential section of town features the 1910 Holy Trinity Orthodox Christian Church. Its graceful blue "onion dome" reflects the architecture of eastern Europe.

The small community of Carbonado, another coal mining company town, is 2 miles south of Wilkeson on Washington Highway 165 and is worth a visit.

The 1880 Washington Hotel in Wilkeson was at one time a brothel. It also served as a gin mill during Prohibition. *Philip Varney*

WHEN YOU GO

Wilkeson is 18 miles southeast of Puyallup. From Puyallup, head north on Washington Highway 167 until Washington Highway 410 branches off heading east toward Sumner and Yakima. Follow Highway 410 for 5.9 miles and turn right on South Prairie Road East. You will drive for 4.1 miles, just skirting the small town of South Prairie. Turn left on Pioneer Way East and go for 2.1 miles. When it intersects with Washington Highway 162, keep right. Keep right when Washington Highway 165 goes south only 300 feet from your last turn. Follow Highway 165 for 2.7 miles to Wilkeson.

Roslyn is a very charming town. So charming, in fact, that it had its own television show. From 1990 until 1995, Roslyn posed as Cicely, Alaska, on the quirky series *Northern Exposure*. Even a cursory visit to the town reveals why it was selected as the location; a longer look will convince you that this is one of Washington's genuinely special communities.

Roslyn came to life in 1886 when the Northern Pacific Railway began mining the area's abundant coal. Logan M. Bullitt, vice president of the railroad's subsidiary coal company, supposedly chose the town's name because a woman he was trying to impress lived in Roslyn, New York.

The former city hall and library, with the former fire department located in the basement in between them, combine into a kind of governmental triplex. *Philip Varney*

The railroad's mining company recruited extensively in Europe for experienced miners, and over time people from twenty-eight nations settled in Roslyn. In 1888, hundreds of African Americans were brought in from the southern and eastern United States to mine coal. What these new workers did not know was that they were being used as strikebreakers, and their arrival generated hard feelings that lasted for many years. Despite the initial hostilities, many African Americans remained in the area, and tensions eventually subsided. In fact, in 1975 Roslyn became the first town in Washington to elect an African American mayor.

In the peak coal production years, from 1901 until the 1920s,

Unrestored, original residences from Roslyn's coal-mining days are getting harder to find. Only a few remain. *Philip Varney*

These three false-front buildings in Roslyn, built in about 1890, are classic examples of commercial structures from that era in the American West. *Philip Varney*

Roslyn mines surpassed two million tons per year, and the town's population exceeded four thousand people. But in the 1930s, more widely available electricity and fuel oil lessened the demand for coal, and production began to decline. Mines began closing in 1936, and by 1949 Roslyn was quietly heading to ghost town status. The last mine held on until 1963. Today it is estimated that 283 million tons of coal, four-fifths of the original seams, still remain.

The quiet community of Roslyn became a National Historic District in 1978. The old company store, which operated from 1889 until 1957, stands on the northeast corner of Pennsylvania and First. A sign on the brick-and-wood-truss building says "Northwestern Improvement Company," referring to the firm that purchased Roslyn and the coal mines in 1898.

Across the street from the company store stands the former Cle Elum State Bank, built in 1910, which now houses Roslyn's government offices. There you may obtain a flyer with directions for a helpful walking tour of the town and a second sheet that highlights the locations used in *Northern Exposure*.

Standing across First Street from the old bank is the 1899 Brick Tavern, reportedly Washington's oldest operating saloon. One of its highlights—if that's the right word—is a "gutter" spittoon with running water.

Across the street from the tavern are three wooden, false-front commercial buildings followed by another group of three, all constructed roughly between 1888 and 1890.

An unusual combination city hall–fire station–library stands on First Street south of Pennsylvania Avenue. The 1902 building is a kind of government triplex, with identical stairways for the former city offices and the library—between them sits the basement fire department and its driveway.

The residential areas of Roslyn are graced by many restored former company homes. Mixed into the neighborhoods are attractive churches, including the 1887 Immacu-

Roslyn's City Cemetery features fine old headstones and elaborate wrought-iron fences. *Philip Varney*

late Conception Catholic Church and the 1900 Mount Pisgah Presbyterian Church.

The remarkable Roslyn cemeteries comprise one of the finest historic graveyards in this book. The expanse of these cemeteries, twenty-five in all with an estimated five thousand graves, is simply staggering. To reach these exceptional graveyards, take Pennsylvania Avenue west to Fifth Street, which leads to Memorial Avenue.

You can explore the City Cemetery, the oldest graveyard, dating from 1887; two areas for veterans; and many fraternal graveyards, such as Moose, Eagles, Odd Fellows, Knights of Pythias, Red Men, Foresters, and Masons. There are several cemeteries for immigrant lodges, which were formed to provide accident and death benefits as well preserve the heritage for citizens of Italian, Croatian, Lithuanian, Polish, and Serbian backgrounds.

WHEN YOU GO

Roslyn is 94 miles northeast of Wilkeson. From Wilkeson, follow Washington Highway 165 for 4.3 miles north to Buckley. Continue north on Washington Highway 410 for 3 miles to Enumclaw. From Enumclaw, take Washington Highway 169 to Maple Valley, a distance of 15 miles. Head northeast on Washington Highway 18 for 12 miles to Interstate 90. Turn onto I-90 heading southeast and drive 55 miles to Exit 80. Go north for 3.1 miles, where you will enter a roundabout onto Washington Highway 903, which leads you to Roslyn in 1.2 miles.

RONALD

onald is an often-overlooked community northwest of Roslyn. Although Ronald cannot compare to its more luminous sister, it remains well worth exploring. The town was named for Scotsman Alexander Ronald, one-time superintendent of the coal mines of the Northwestern Improvement Company. The town shares much of its history with Roslyn, because many of the coal mines were located between the two communities.

A local resident who grew up in Ronald during its heyday reported that during Prohibition the miners made more money in the bootlegging business than in their mining jobs. He said the Slovaks were the whiskey providers, while the Italians were specialists in winemaking. He related that once a still blew up and took out an entire block. He also mentioned that his grandfather didn't receive an actual check for wages for several years because he was always in hock to the company for his house, groceries, and other necessities. It reminds us of the famous line from the song "Sixteen Tons": "Saint Peter, don't you call me, 'cause I can't go / I owe my soul to the company store."

Ronald's schoolhouse features covered staircases leading to the main entrance on the second floor. *Philip Varney*

This one-time company house in Ronald stands in its original, unrestored condition. It was last occupied in the 1950s. *Philip Varney*

Ronald features some company houses similar to those in Roslyn, a one-stall firehouse with a cupola, and a large, two-story community center. The best building in town is the tan, two-story clapboard schoolhouse, which features matching covered staircases that students would take up to the elevated main entrance at the center of the building. The school offered grades one through eight. Northwest of the school on Third Street are several company houses, including one on the southwest corner of Third Street and Pacific Avenue that has remained unoccupied and virtually unchanged from Ronald's mining days.

WHEN YOU GO

onald is 1.8 miles northwest of Roslyn on Washington Highway 903.

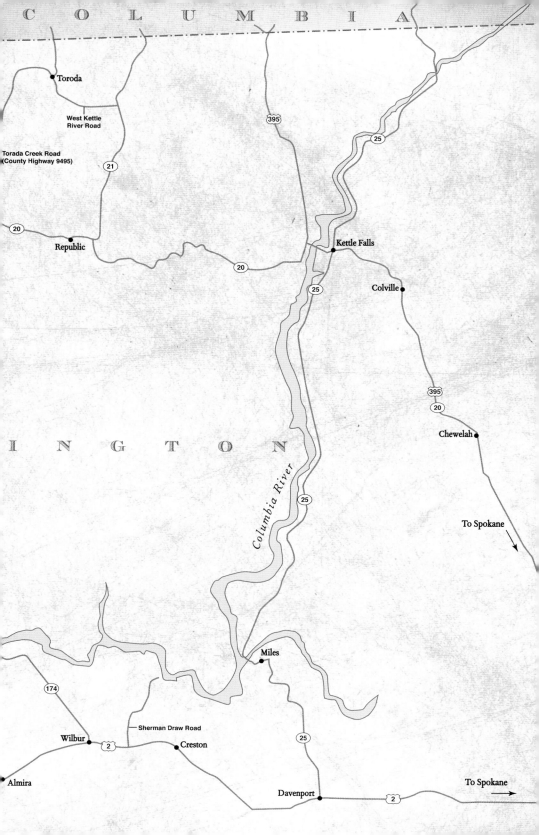

The Molson State Bank contains teller cages, a safe, and, oddly, a printing press. The downturned horseshoes indicate Molson's luck has run out. *Philip Varney*

Molson was founded as a mining and speculative enterprise in 1900 by promoter George Meacham with the financial backing of Montreal banking and brewing entrepreneur George Molson. The community, which Molson himself never saw, almost died within a year, but homesteading pioneers resurrected the site. When a farmer claimed that the whole town was part of his homestead, Molson was moved 0.5 of a mile north. The arrival of the Great Northern Railway in 1906 further legitimized the town.

Molson, which had a peak population of about seven hundred, became a trading and commercial center, serving not only north-central Washington but also south-central British Columbia. It once featured hotels, five churches, three fraternal organizations, a café, a confectionery, and two pool halls.

When area mines played out, Molson's decline began. When the railroad tracks were taken up in 1935, the town's demise was assured. The town lost its post office in 1967, its final step toward becoming a ghost town.

The southernmost part of Molson today is actually Old Molson. The Molson State Bank, which features an angled front door, tellers' cages, and a 1906 safe made in Cincinnati, is the best of several historic buildings grouped closely together.

Northeast of Old Molson is Central Molson, where the 1914 former schoolhouse, now a museum, is the principal attraction. The building served grades

Molson is a little more than a mile south of the US-Canadian border, and this old sign in Molson sternly reminds us of that. *Philip Varney*

one through twelve from 1915 until 1962, when high school students were bused to Oroville. The school closed entirely two years later. Take your time walking through this wonderful museum, because much of the school looks as it did when it closed in 1964.

Across from the schoolhouse stands a tidy brick building with a sign proclaiming it "Molson Trading Company, Gen'l Merchandise." The store has a clever mural painted on its front showing the reflection of a street scene.

The tiny Molson Cemetery stands on a hill 0.7 of a mile south of Old Molson.

A classroom inside the Molson schoolhouse has many delightful touches, including three vintage lunchboxes, two (foreground and center) featuring Mickey Mouse and Goofy in a school bus, and one (far right) made to look like a television set with Bugs Bunny and Sylvester on the screen. *Philip Varney*

The Molson Trading Company has a creative mural featuring "townspeople" inspecting the "merchandise" in the "windows." *Philip Varney*

WHEN YOU GO

Molson's closest town of size is Oroville. In Oroville, go north on Main Street (Washington Highway 97 in town) to Central Avenue. Turn right on Central and proceed 0.3 of a mile to Cherry Street. Cherry Street becomes Chesaw Road in 0.2 of a mile. Follow Chesaw Road for 9.1 miles and turn left on Molson Road. From that point, follow Molson Road for 4.9 miles to Old Molson, on your right.

NOTE: Chesaw Road was formerly called Oroville–Toroda Creek Road and is still so labeled on some maps.

The Flora Cemetery in Flora, Oregon, features a beautiful metal arch over its gate. *Philip Varney*

OREGON

3

The ghost towns of Oregon featured in this book all have a distinctly "yesterday" look to them, and all but one, Sumpter, are mostly deserted. But Sumpter makes up for its bustle with two wonderful attractions—a steam train and an antique dredge.

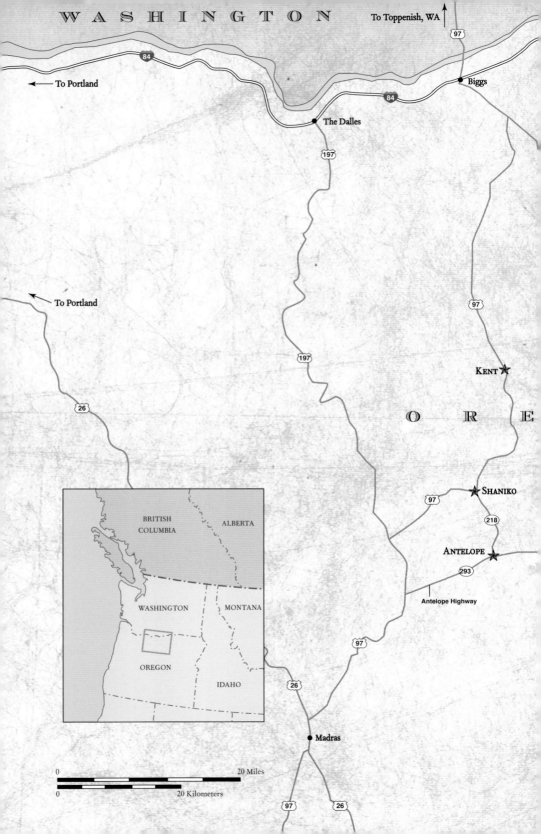

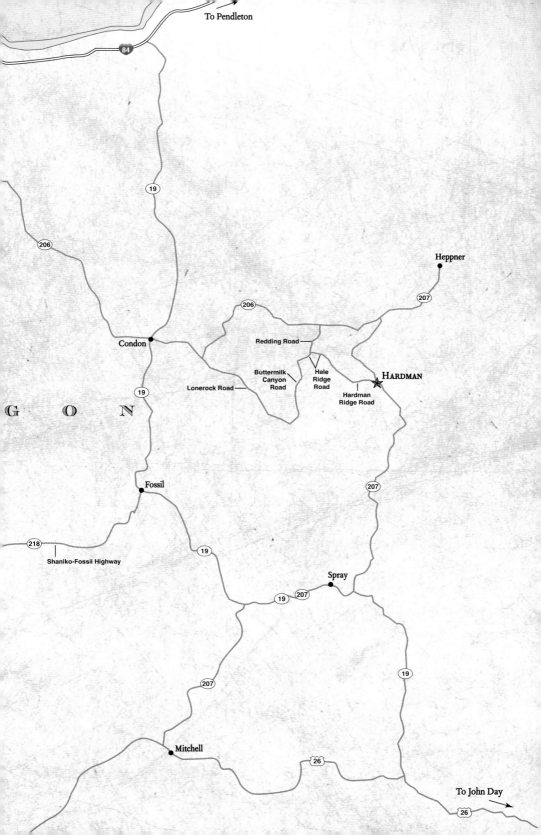

To Pendleton

84

19

206

Heppner

207

206

Condon

Redding Road

Buttermilk
Canyon
Road

Hale
Ridge
Road

HARDMAN

Hardman
Ridge Road

Lonerock Road

19

G   O   N

Fossil

19

207

218

Shaniko-Fossil Highway

19

Spray

19   207

19

207

Mitchell

26

To John Day

26

KENT

With its two grain elevators standing like sentinels on the prairie, Kent is visible from miles away. The town was settled in the 1880s, receiving its post office in 1887. Its name reportedly was drawn out of a hat, submitted by a citizen who thought it was "nice and short." The Columbia Southern Railroad laid tracks to Kent in 1899, and for a short time the town boomed as the terminus of that railroad. When the tracks were extended to Shaniko, however, Kent fell into decline, although it remained significant for its grain elevators, from which stored wheat was shipped north by rail to Biggs Junction. When the tracks were washed out in 1964, Kent, along with Shaniko, headed toward becoming a ghost town.

Kent today has several historic buildings. On the north end of town stands an empty combination café and gas station (possible motto: "Eat Here, Get Gas"?) advertising petrol at the bargain price of 66.5¢ per gallon.

Immediately across the street from the service station is a beehive stone structure with a metal cap. It was built in the 1930s to house a generator that produced electric power to the gas station and to the station owner's home, which stood west of the generator.

Kent's combination gymnasium and auditorium is one block east of the

A former gas station and café on the north end of Kent attests to the fact that plastic deteriorates less quickly than wood, paint, and shake shingles. *Philip Varney*

Phillips 66 gasoline sold for 66.5¢ per gallon when this gas station and café closed in Kent. *Philip Varney*

An odd, beehive-shaped concrete and stone structure, across the street from the gas station and café in Kent, once housed a generator that gave power to the station across the street and to the station owner's house. *Philip Varney*

Two dilapidated false-front commercial buildings stand along Dobie Point Road in Kent. *Philip Varney*

service station. A large, extraordinarily plain school built in 1902 that once stood north of the gym is now merely a concrete foundation, having burned in the mid-1980s after about twenty years of disuse.

South of the gymnasium stand those dramatic grain elevators, one made of concrete and the other of wood. The six-story-tall wooden grain elevator, made of two-by-six-inch boards laid flat, is especially eye-catching.

Several other wooden buildings can be found on Dobie Point Road leading to the elevators. One of these buildings once had an exterior staircase to the Independent Order of Odd Fellows (I.O.O.F.) Hall on the second floor. Across the street are two wooden false-front buildings. When I first photographed them in 1982, one of them had a sign proclaiming it to be the Smith Store, selling "hardware, groceries, and implements." The sign has since completely faded and is now illegible.

A sign over the cemetery 1.4 miles north of town declares it to be the Kent Cemetery, but a US Geological Survey topographic map indicates that it was previously known as the Odd Fellows Cemetery.

WHEN YOU GO

Kent is 143 miles southeast of Portland via Interstate 84 and US Highway 97.

SHANIKO

or about a decade, Shaniko could boast that it was the largest wool-shipping center in the world. The town came into being in 1900 as an important stop on the route of the Columbia Southern Railroad. It turned out to be the railroad's southern terminus. Serving as the center of commerce for a 20,000-square-mile area of central Oregon, Shaniko was the place where ranchers and farmers took sheep, wool, cattle, and wheat to market.

The town's name comes from a mispronunciation of the last name of August Schernechau, who owned a stage stop at nearby Cross Hollows, south of present-day Shaniko. When the railroad came to Shaniko, virtually everything in Cross Hollows was moved to the newer community. By 1900, Shaniko had a population of 172, most of them construction workers building themselves a town.

In the banner year of 1903, more than 1.1 million bushels of wheat were sold, and wool sales in excess of $3 million made Shaniko the "Wool Capital of the World." Wool sales are believed to have topped $5 million in 1904.

The decline of Shaniko began in 1911, when a competing railroad, the Oregon Trunk, was completed along the Deschutes River to Bend, which then linked central Oregon south to California markets. Shaniko was merely the terminus of a dead-end railroad. A fire that same year consumed many downtown buildings, which were never rebuilt.

The demand for Oregon wool declined after World War I as Australia and New Zealand began producing less expensive wool, further reducing Shaniko's importance. The town's reduction to ghost town status was assured by 1942, when the railroad tracks were taken up to Kent. The town's progress was also slowed by the fact that it did not have electricity until the mid-1940s.

Incidentally, the town is located virtually on the forty-fifth parallel, making it equidistant between the North Pole and the equator.

The Shaniko Hotel has always been the anchor of Shaniko. Built around 1900 as the Columbia Southern Hotel, the two-sto-

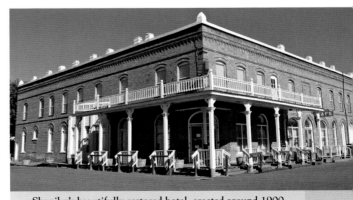

Shaniko's beautifully restored hotel, erected around 1900, stands empty and for sale at this writing. *Philip Varney*

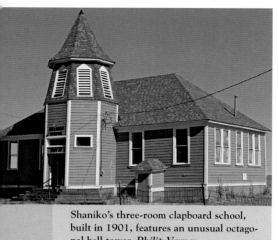

Shaniko's three-room clapboard school, built in 1901, features an unusual octagonal bell tower. *Philip Varney*

ry brick edifice has not only offered pleasant lodgings, but it also has had a very good restaurant and a gift shop. Unfortunately, the hotel is closed and up for sale at this writing. The town will continue to fade away unless the hotel reopens. One can only hope for a positive resolution so that Shaniko can reclaim its place as one of the best ghost towns of Oregon.

Across the street from that now-shuttered hotel to the south are several clapboard false-front structures, including the former Gold Nugget Saloon, built in 1901.

At the rear of the 1901 city hall, which stands east of the hotel, is the town's three-cell jail, a wooden structure with boards laid flat, stockade-style, for stoutness. The cells were given names by early occupants: "The Snake Pit," "The Bum-Lodging," and "The Palace-Sleeper." The building also served as the town's firehouse.

The largest structure in Shaniko is the tin-covered wool shed, which stands east of town. The railroad tracks ran immediately east of the structure, and the depot stood north of the shed.

The 1901 water tower, northwest of the business district, is Shaniko's most imposing structure. Water was pumped from a spring south of Shaniko to two ten-thousand-gallon wooden tanks located 70 feet up inside the tower.

East of the water tower is the three-room, clapboard 1901 school, which has an unusual octagonal bell tower.

Shaniko, surprisingly, has no cemetery. The ground was too hard for one.

About 0.5 of a mile south of Shaniko on the road to Antelope, a double-cupola barn on the west side of the road stands as the last remnant of the area's original town, Cross Hollows.

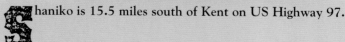

WHEN YOU GO

Shaniko is 15.5 miles south of Kent on US Highway 97.

ANTELOPE

ntelope Valley was named in 1862 by freighters of a supply train who saw herds of pronghorn (colloquially known as "antelope") while carrying goods to the recently discovered gold fields at what would become Sumpter, Granite, and Bourne, all now ghost towns in northeastern Oregon. The town that developed in Antelope Valley took Antelope as its name when a post office was granted in 1871. It became a commercial center for ranchers and sheepherders until the Columbia Southern Railroad extended tracks south from Biggs Junction and Shaniko came into being. The new town took most of the commerce from Antelope.

When I first visited Antelope in 1982, it was a place of both peace and turmoil. The peace came from the apparent—and the key word is apparent—bliss experienced by the majority of the town's population, who were followers of Bhagwan Shree Rajneesh. The turmoil came from the resentment felt by residents who had lived there before the arrival of the Bhagwan and his devotees in 1981. They watched Antelope being taken over and radically changed. The town's name became Rajneesh, and the only restaurant/store became Zorba the Buddha Restaurant. The town was featured on national news programs as the silent Bhagwan's spokesperson, Ma Anand Sheela, defended the cult's policies. She eventually fled the country, allegedly with considerable amounts of money, and the Bhagwan himself was deported in 1985 on charges of immigration fraud. With the departure of the Bhagwan and his followers, the town unanimously voted to return the town's name to Antelope and then promptly disincorporated to avoid a recurrence.

The vacant Antelope Garage features ornamental tin on its front and sides. *Philip Varney*

Antelope's 1897 Methodist church.
Philip Varney

Antelope today has returned to its pre-Bhagwan existence. It consists of several very photogenic buildings, the most striking of which is the 1897 Methodist church one block east of downtown's Main Street.

On Main Street, south of Union, stands the tiny former office of Antelope's newspaper, *The Herald.* Across the street from the newspaper is an old Shell station with its signature white, yellow, and red banding below its windows. South of the Shell station stands the two-story Ancient Order of United Workmen (AOUW) Hall, built in 1898. South of the

Antelope's Ancient Order of United Workmen Hall, built in 1898, appears at this writing to be a private residence. *Philip Varney*

AOUW Hall is the former Antelope Garage, which features a tin false front with several hard-to-read signs, one bleeding into the other, except for one that establishes clearly that it was a Union 76 station.

The Antelope Cemetery is quite large but rather sparsely populated, as if townspeople expected Antelope to be much bigger than it turned out to be.

The compound that Bhagwan Shree Rajneesh built for his followers is now the Washington Family Ranch, a Young Life Christian camp. As one local resident told me, "That place has gone from very bad to very good—but then so has the town."

WHEN YOU GO

ntelope is 7.9 miles south of Shaniko on Oregon Highway 218, the Shaniko–Fossil Highway. The cemetery is 0.4 of a mile east of town, off of Union Street.

HARDMAN

Hardman is one of Oregon's most picturesque towns, a prairie ghost of several dozen wonderful, weathered, wooden buildings—fewer than half of them in use—surrounded by wheat fields and grasslands.

Dairyville was a small stop along a popular stage and freight route in the 1860s. Popularly known as Raw Dog, the town even had a small rival up the road, known as Yallerdog. The two towns eventually combined into one, informally called Dog Town. A nearby farmer named David Hardman had been operating a

Across the street from the community center in Hardman stands a former grocery store and gas station. *Philip Varney*

small post office from his home, and when he moved into town, he brought the post office with him. Dairyville–Raw Dog–Dog Town became Hardman.

Hardman developed as a milling center for area wheat farmers, and the popular freight route brought hotels and modest prosperity in the early 1900s. But no railroad reached Hardman, and the town went into a gradual decline.

The keystone building in Hardman today is the 1870 community cen-

Immediately north of Hardman's community center is the former post office, along with the mailboxes of the town's few residents. *Philip Varney*

The Hardman Community Center was originally the I.O.O.F. Hall, built in 1870. Notice the elaborately jigged ornamental brackets that decorate the building's cornice. *Philip Varney*

ter, formerly the I.O.O.F. Hall. The structure features a stage at the back and an attached kitchen. The building is used for wedding receptions and other social occasions. Several photographs hang on the walls, including one of an overview of Hardman taken in about 1900.

Smaller structures stretch north from the hall, the first of which was the former post office. Attached to it is a deserted residence with a string of rural postal boxes extending north along the highway. A one-time gas station and grocery store stands across the street. Residences are scattered on back streets on both sides of the highway.

The cemetery is on a hill 0.2 of a mile southwest of the community center. In it stand five headstones in a large, fenced-off area. One of the graves is for Sina Emry, who died on November 19, 1892, in her forty-first year. Buried next to Emry—with a headstone so close that at first it appears attached to hers—is her infant son, who died the day before she did. In 1892, being pregnant at age forty was perilous indeed.

A second cemetery, the I.O.O.F., is 4.1 miles northwest of town on Hardman Ridge Road. The graveyard is off to the left of the road.

WHEN YOU GO

ardman is 19.6 miles southwest of Heppner on Oregon Highway 207.

In 1862, five southerners found gold in Oregon's Blue Mountains. They named the town that grew near their claims Fort Sumter, after the site of the first Confederate victory in the Civil War. Early placer deposits were modest, and success was sporadic until the 1880s, when hard-rock mining began. When a post office was granted in 1883, officials in Washington likely surmised the Confederate origins of the name, because "Fort" was dropped and the spelling was altered to "Sumpter."

The Sumpter Valley Railway, known affectionately to locals as the Stump Dodger, reached the town from Baker City in 1896. Sumpter's population peaked at about 3,500, and by 1899 it featured eleven hotels, eleven general mercantile stores, and seventeen saloons, along with various other enterprises.

By 1906, mines began to close, and prices of real estate in town plummeted. A smelter that was erected in 1903 shut down in 1908. The town seemed doomed, but only five years later, the seemingly moribund outpost found new life when dredging operations began and, except for being shut down during World War II, lasted until 1954, greatly prolonging the life of Sumpter.

Sumpter is currently home to almost two hundred people. Mill Street, the main street through town, contains several historic buildings and many modern ones. Actually, "historic" is relative; few buildings date to the town's origins, since eleven city blocks, including nine brick buildings, burned in 1917.

Heisler locomotive No. 3 sits at the depot in Sumpter. Built in 1915, the engine served the W. H. Eccles Lumber Company on branch lines off the Sumpter Valley main line. *Philip Varney*

The Sumpter Municipal Museum is one of the more photogenic structures on Mill Street. Formerly Sumpter Supply, it is housed in two side-by-side brick buildings.

Near the north end of town stands the two-story, brick Sumpter Trading Post, which originally was Basche's Hardware. Built in 1899, it burned in the fire of 1917 but was rebuilt four years later.

Another historic building, one block east of Main on Columbia Street, was built in 1900 as the Sumpter General Hospital; it is now

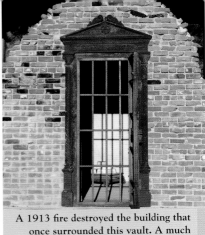

A 1913 fire destroyed the building that once surrounded this vault. A much larger fire destroyed most of downtown Sumpter in 1917. Notice the cache of "gold" stashed inside. *Philip Varney*

a bed and breakfast. The two-story clapboard structure survived the great fire only because the conflagration was contained across the street. Masons purchased the building in 1918 because their lodge had perished in the fire. They used the former hospital as a lodge for fifty-five years.

Sumpter features two enjoyable tourist attractions. One is the Sumpter Valley Railway, a steam-powered narrow gauge line that runs between Sumpter and McEwen on weekends and holidays from Memorial Day through September. The line's 1915 Heisler locomotive is one of very few operating

The Sumpter Municipal Museum and public library is housed in the former Sumpter Supply Building. *Philip Varney*

Sumpter Dredge No. 3, abandoned in a pond of its own making in 1954, has become a major tourist attraction in the Sumpter Valley. *Philip Varney*

wood-burning engines in regular service in the United States today.

The other attraction stands at the south end of town: Sumpter Dredge No. 3, a 1,250-ton behemoth that remains where it was abandoned in 1954. It was launched in 1935, built primarily from parts salvaged from earlier dredges that had been idle for a decade. These dredges traveled more than 8 miles in their mining efforts and reclaimed between $10 million and $12 million in gold from the riverbeds. Dredge No. 3 is more complete than most, because abandoned dredges were salvaged for scrap, many during World War II. This one is not, however, entirely complete: For example, the electric motor that powered the digging winch is missing. Despite its idleness, the dredge still smells of grease and fuel. (There is no charge to tour the dredge, although donations are accepted.)

Since dredges are so rare, and there are only two featured in this book, here is a primer on the subject: A dredge is a digging apparatus located on a flat-bottomed boat. It is constructed on land and then launched into a pond created for it. It then digs its way along, floating on the extended pond it creates with its massive buckets. Each of Dredge No. 3's buckets, seventy-two in number, weighs one ton. They are

John Beardsley's tree stump headstone in Sumpter's Blue Mountain Cemetery establishes that he was a member of the Woodmen of the World, a fraternal organization. *Philip Varney*

Sumpter General Hospital, built in 1900, now operates as a bed-and-breakfast inn.
Philip Varney

connected to a huge "digging ladder" that scoops into the pond. Through an elaborate screening process, gold-bearing sand or gravel is separated from rock, and the detritus is sent out the rear of the dredge, creating enormous piles behind the contraption.

Though not exactly a tourist attraction, Sumpter also has an interesting graveyard, the Blue Mountain Cemetery. Those of us who wander through old cemeteries are accustomed to reading stones that pose more questions than they answer. I found one headstone near the northern boundary of the Blue Mountain Cemetery most disturbing. It has the names of three people: Clara E. (born in Posen, Germany), Willy Gustav, and Ella M., wife and children, respectively, of Ernst Maiwaldt. Clara, his wife, was thirty-four. Willy never saw his third birthday. Ella lived for little more than two months. They all died on the same day: April 26, 1895. Illness? Fire? Buggy accident? One tries to imagine the husband and father's grief.

WHEN YOU GO

Sumpter is 29 miles southwest of Baker on Oregon Highway 7 and Oregon Highway 410. If you wish to visit Sumpter's Blue Mountain Cemetery, take Mill Street to Austin Street. Head southeast for 1.4 miles on Austin, which becomes Sumpter Cemetery Road.

G ranite came into being when a party led by Albert Gallatin Tabor and scout Robert W. Waucop found gold in a gulch on July 4, 1862. Tabor appropriately named his claim the Independence, and the town that grew at the site took the same name. When a post office was granted in 1876, an Independence, Oregon, already existed near Salem, so the town's name was changed to Granite. A. G. Tabor served as the first postmaster.

By 1900, Granite consisted of a drugstore, three other stores, five saloons, and two hotels, including the three-story Grand Hotel, which had dining facilities, a bar, and forty-two rooms. Many Civil War veterans and citizens originally from Italy, France, the Netherlands, Sweden, and Ireland populated the town. Ladies in town formed the Daughters of Progress, which created a library and helped form religious societies.

The Cougar–Independence and Buffalo mines were solid gold producers for decades. The town at first flourished—but eventually only subsisted—as the supply center for area mines into the 1950s. The Grand Hotel served meals into the late 1930s but was demolished in about 1943 as Granite slid into decline. The post office closed in 1957.

The J. J. O'Dair Store in Granite would be a fairly standard clapboard, false-front building were it not for its front door set jauntily on the diagonal. *Philip Varney*

The first building you see as you enter Granite today is Allen Hall, a board-and-batten combination city hall and one-room school. The bell tower of the building is unusual because it is only framework rather than an enclosed structure. A larger school closed for lack of students in the 1940s and burned in the 1950s.

Up the street stands the J. J. O'Dair Store, a large general merchandiser with a white, clapboard false front and a front door on the diagonal. An advertisement in the local newspaper, the *Granite Gem*, touted the store in 1900: "Sells the cheapest. Carries a full line of groceries and dry goods. New goods constantly arriving and we are prepared to fill any and all orders."

A cabin in Granite features logs with chinking for the main part of the structure, but a board-and-batten addition makes up the rear of the building. *Philip Varney*

South of the O'Dair Store on the opposite side of Main Street is the boarded-up dance hall and saloon, featuring an unusual shingle pattern under the cornice and decorative trim on the second-floor windows. The elegant Grand Hotel formerly stood across the street.

Across the street east of the O'Dair Store stands the 1901 drugstore, now a residence. The former Catholic church, across from the drugstore, is also a residence. Down the hill behind the former church is the attractive cemetery, which features dozens of well-carved headstones of antiquity, including one for gold discoverer A. G. Tabor. As mentioned before, he made his gold discovery on Independence Day. Coincidentally, he also died on that day—in 1892.

WHEN YOU GO

Granite is 16.5 miles northwest of Sumpter on Oregon Highway 220, the Granite Hill Highway, which is the main street heading out of Sumpter.

Granite's Allen Hall has a belfry that is unusual in that it is only framework rather than being enclosed.
Philip Varney

FLORA

Once a town of 1,200, Flora currently has a population of seven. Flora is one of Oregon's most delightful ghost towns, containing some extremely photogenic buildings.

Originally called Johnson Meadow for pioneer homesteader Frank Johnson, the community became Flora when a post office was granted in 1890. It was named for then-six-year-old Flora Buzzard, daughter of the first postmaster, Adolphus Buzzard.

The Flora School, built in 1915, now serves as the Flora School Education Center, primarily for adults. *Philip Varney*

The agricultural community soon featured a school, a general store, a lumber company, a blacksmith's shop, a hotel, two churches—and no saloons.

The town prospered until after World War I, when its isolation from major markets and the decline of the small family farm caused a population decrease. The post office closed in 1966; the school shut its doors in 1977.

A two-story residence in Flora embodies what people want to see when they visit a ghost town. *Philip Varney*

Flora's 1898 Methodist Episcopal church stands in the foreground with the 1915 Flora School behind it. *Philip Varney*

The two most striking structures in town today are the 1898 Methodist Episcopal church and the Flora School, which stand near each other on the north side of town. The two-story clapboard school, erected in 1915, has a shingled bell tower topped with a flagpole. It now serves as the Flora School Education Center, which has programs in folk arts and historic agriculture, centering on skills that were crucial to the original homesteaders in the area.

One rather curious thing about the Flora Cemetery, west of the main part of town, is that most of its headstones face west, with graves east of them. Therefore, instead of standing at the foot of a grave to read the stone's inscription, you must stand behind the head of the grave to read it.

WHEN YOU GO

From the town of La Grande, take Oregon Highway 82 northeast to Enterprise, a distance of 63.3 miles. In Enterprise, go north on Oregon Highway 3 for 33.6 miles, where the turnoff to Flora is clearly marked.

A miner's cabin hides among the turning aspens at Miner's Delight, Wyoming, a tiny community that likely never reached a population of one hundred citizens. *Philip Varney*

WYOMING

CHAPTER 4

The word "Wyoming" comes from a Dakota word meaning "large plains." A state couldn't be more aptly named. The three ghost towns in this short chapter lie along a route taken by more than three hundred thousand emigrants as they traversed the Wyoming Territory on the Oregon Trail, which extended 2,000 miles from the Missouri River to Oregon City, Oregon. Southern branches of that trail led Mormons to their Zion and argonauts to their gold-filled California dreams. Later, the Oregon Trail became the course for the transcontinental telegraph and, for the westernmost Wyoming portion of the trail, the path of the Transcontinental Railroad—the means of transportation that made all the trails and routes obsolete.

Near South Pass City, the best ghost town in Wyoming, is South Pass, used by the Oregon Trail pioneers because it was the gentlest ascent over the great mountains of the West. Two lesser sites, Atlantic City and the true ghost town of Miner's Delight, stand near South Pass City.

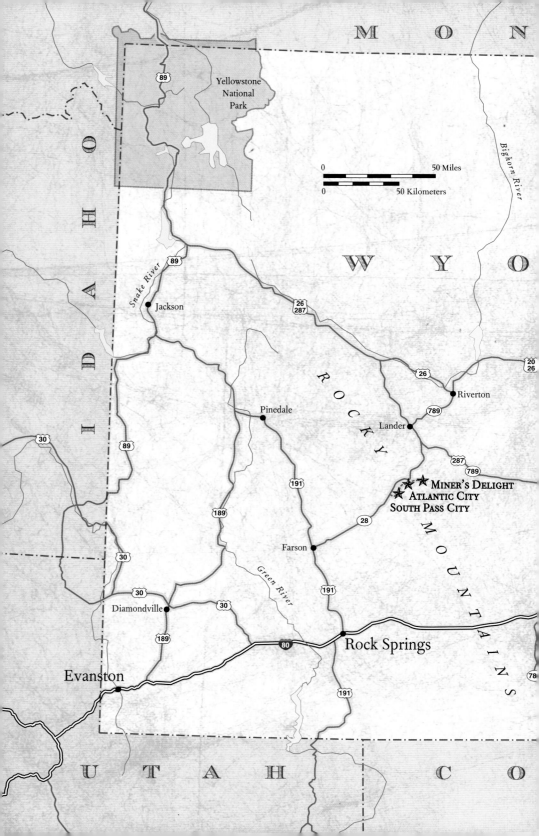

SOUTH PASS CITY

The Oregon Trail traversed the Continental Divide at South Pass, Wyoming, because it was a gentle ascent and descent over what was known as "Uncle Sam's Backbone." After the 1848 discovery of gold in California, hundreds of thousands of the trail pioneers headed over South Pass with dreams of getting in on the stories of incredible riches. They did not realize that they were practically tromping on a field of gold as they passed.

Although modest quantities of gold were discovered near South Pass as early as 1842, it wasn't until 1867 that a group of Mormon prospectors (or Fort Bridger soldiers—sources disagree) found what would become the Carissa Mine. Others rushed to the area and founded South Pass City near the site of an 1850s stagecoach stop and telegraph station. Founded at about the same time were two other smaller communities, Atlantic City and Miner's Delight. As many as three thousand citizens packed the three towns and the surrounding hills searching for gold—or in support, in one way or another, of those who were.

By 1868, the arrival of families had made South Pass City, despite its early rowdy reputation, a fairly civilized place. The men, women, and children of South Pass City enjoyed a main thoroughfare of hotels, general stores, butcher shops, a billiard parlor, a bowling alley, a school, and the usual saloons.

South Pass City became the seat of Carter County in Dakota Territory, and when Wyoming Territory was separated from Dakota Territory in 1869, it retained its county seat.

This view of South Pass City shows the Carissa Mine in the background. *Philip Varney*

The big rush was remarkably short. The federal census of 1870 tallied 1,166 people in the entire mining district. By 1872, only a few hundred diehards held on. Subsequent explorations in the 1880s and 1890s brought some people back, followed by another small boom in the 1930s, as the Great Depression forced hundreds of former prospectors and miners to rework, in desperation, older diggings across the American West.

On your way to South Pass City, you'll pass the enormous workings of the Carissa Mine, the principal reason for the existence of the town. The mine closed for a final time in the 1950s. The State of Wyoming purchased the mine property in 2003 and now offers a tour of the mill. Most of the buildings at the Carissa, which produced somewhere between 60,000 and 180,000 ounces of gold, date from the 1930s.

South Pass City's Carissa Saloon served thirsty patrons sporadically until 1949. Behind is the cabin in which Barney Tibbals, manager of the Carissa Mine, lived. *Philip Varney*

The Smith-Sherlock Company Store was built in 1896 using logs salvaged from the 1870 Episcopal church. The Sherlock family operated the general mercantile store until 1948. *Philip Varney*

South Pass City State Historic Site, just down the road from the Carissa, is now a quiet village that once pulsed with a much more vibrant heartbeat. At the visitors' center, located in an 1890s dance hall, you will receive an informative brochure that takes you through the almost three dozen standing buildings

In the foreground stands the Exchange Saloon and Card Room. Next door is a restaurant erected by Janet Sherlock Smith in 1899 to support her neighboring South Pass Hotel. *Philip Varney*

and ruins of South Pass City. The town is a classic example of a place whose structures were built of crude logs and hand-adzed beams on three sides, but with more genteel (and expensive) sawed boards as a false front. Of particular interest are the 1890s Carissa Saloon, the 1868 South Pass Hotel, an 1870s mercantile store (now housing a gold mining exhibit with some life-size dioramas), and the 1890s schoolhouse. The school last served students in 1948. West of the schoolhouse is the Wolverine Mine, which features a ten-stamp mill.

Up the hill from the parking lot 0.3 of a mile is the South Pass City Cemetery, which consists of two headstones, two wrought-iron fences, and, very likely, many unmarked graves.

WHEN YOU GO

South Pass City, Atlantic City, and Miner's Delight are south of Lander. From Lander, head southeast for 8 miles on US Highway 287 to the intersection with Wyoming Highway 28. The turnoff to the South Pass City area is clearly marked near milepost 43, about 29 miles from that intersection.

ATLANTIC CITY

tlantic City was founded during the same mining boom that created South Pass City. It became a solid community with the usual businesses and services, including one truly sophisticated touch: a cigar store.

Like its neighbor, Atlantic City was mostly dead by the 1870s, but a resurgence took place in 1884 when French mining engineer Emile Granier attempted to use hydraulic mining to tap the riches of Rock Creek. After an investment of $250,000, the project failed in 1902.

In 1960, United States Steel opened the Atlantic City Iron Ore Mine, which gave a modest rebirth to the community that accounts for several modern structures in town. That mine ceased production in 1983.

St. Andrew's Episcopal Church is one of two excellent buildings in Atlantic City. This photo was taken in August 2000.
Philip Varney

Atlantic City Road lacks the charm of South Pass City because of many modern elements amid the historic structures—and a certain amount of clutter. The best building in town, and the center of activity, is the Atlantic City Mercantile, built in 1893 by German immigrant Lawrence Giessler of adobe brick with a pressed-tin false front. Within its current incarnation as a steakhouse and bar, you can examine the mercantile building's historic interior, complete with old photographs, various articles of antiquity, and a small museum.

Another fine building is the 1913 St. Andrew's Episcopal Church, which was carefully restored between 1965 and 1967. Inside is attractive wainscoting matching the wooden ceiling. Both the church and the mercantile store are on the National Register of Historic Places.

A tiny private cemetery sits just west of Dexter Street on the west side of town. The public cemetery is east of town up on the hill as Atlantic City Road turns northeast toward Miner's Delight.

WHEN YOU GO

o reach Atlantic City from South Pass City, retrace your route past the Carissa Mine for 0.6 of a mile and turn right. Atlantic City is 3.7 miles down that road.

MINER'S DELIGHT

Miner's Delight is one of the least known, most overlooked, and most rewarding ghost towns in this book. It is an unexpected delight.

A camp called Hamilton City began with the discovery of the Miner's Delight Mine in 1867. When that mine produced a modest bonanza of at least $60,000 in gold within two years, the camp appropriated the name of the mine. (A note about the apostrophe: The name probably should be "Miners' Delight," as it was meant to convey "the delight of miners." The topographic map eliminates the apostrophe altogether, which implies the US Postal Service did the same thing much earlier. I am choosing "Miner's" because that is the way it most commonly turns up in historic documents and current accounts.)

Miner's Delight's population likely never reached a hundred, peaking before 1882. The camp was deserted and in ruins in 1907, when speculators attempted to reopen the Miner's Delight Mine. The attempt was futile; a 1914 geologist's report noted that the mine was abandoned and flooded. During the Depression, several cabins were occupied, as in South Pass City and Atlantic City, by unemployed miners hoping to eke out a living.

To visit the townsite, you will park your car adjacent to the tiny Miner's Delight Cemetery, with its solitary marker and three wrought-iron fences, and

One of the wonderful rewards to taking the walk down the path to Miner's Delight is seeing an abandoned community with something else: absolute solitude. *Philip Varney*

Many of the Miner's Delight cabins appear unstable, but they are propped up from within.
Philip Varney

take a five-minute walk down a well-marked trail to see a true, abandoned ghost town listed on the National Register of Historic Places. The Bureau of Land Management protects eight log cabins, propped up from within and held in a state of arrested decay. Nearby are the remains of a small stamp mill. The townsite sits amid a grove of aspens, which adds to the charm and solitude of this small treasure.

WHEN YOU GO

ead east and then north for 2 miles on the main road leading out of Atlantic City. Turn right and proceed for 2.8 miles to a sign directing you to the parking area for Miner's Delight.

The Empire Saloon now serves as the visitors' center and park headquarters at Custer. Eventually, the building will be restored as a historic saloon. *Philip Varney*

IDAHO

This chapter will take you to eight ghost towns, all but the first related to mining. Gold was originally discovered in 1862 near what became Idaho City, and gold fever spread throughout the Idaho Territory, although it was later strikes of silver that made Idaho's fortune. Incidentally, the nickname the Gem State initially had nothing to do with minerals or precious stones: "Idaho" was a made-up word coined by those who for political reasons wanted an Idaho Territory proclaimed by Congress.

They claimed Idaho was a Shoshone word meaning "gem of the mountains." The name stuck, the nickname survived, and only much later did mineral wealth make the nickname a fact.

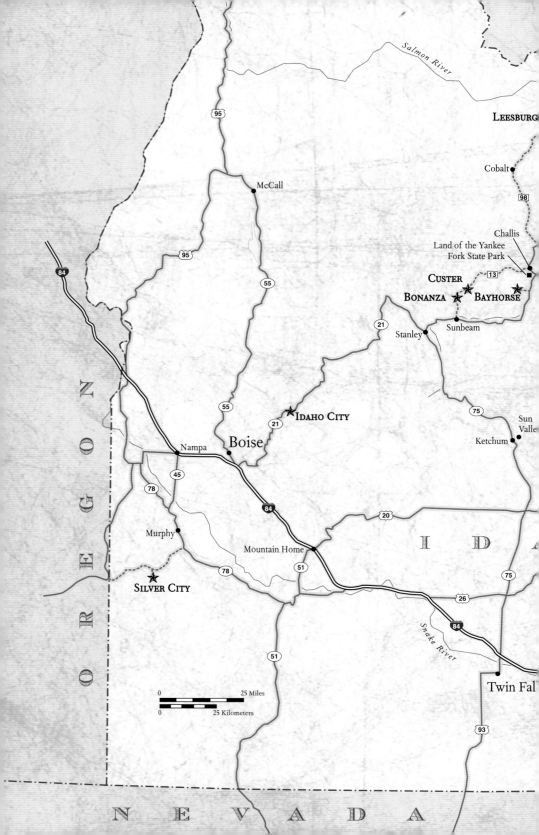

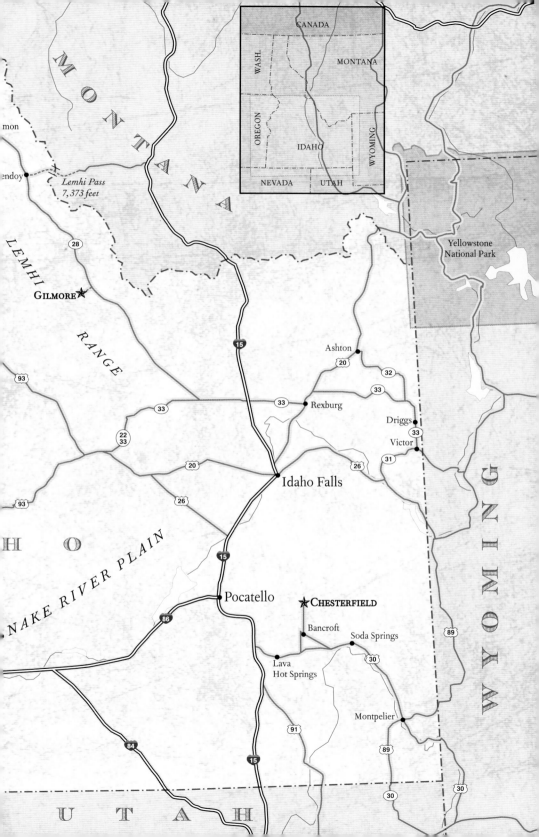

CHESTERFIELD

In 1879, Mormons Chester Call and his nephew, Christian Nelson, came to southern Idaho with three hundred grazing horses because land in northern Utah was becoming scarce. Other members of the Church of Jesus Christ of Latter-day Saints joined them, and within two years the community of Chesterfield (named either for cofounder Chester Call or because it reminded a Mormon official of Chesterfield, England) was thriving, eventually reaching a population of more than four hundred. The selection of property lots was originally by lottery.

In addition to agriculture, the town served as a supply point along the Oregon Trail, which was still in limited use in the 1870s. The town's prosperity lasted for only a couple of generations. For one thing, the site was isolated, with a railroad and major roads bypassing it, making the winters difficult. For another, large-scale farming techniques doomed hundreds of rural communities across America by the end of World War II, and Chesterfield was one of them. The town's last business, the Holbrook Mercantile, somehow hung on until 1956. But unlike many villages that simply disappeared as huge farming conglomerates engulfed them, Chesterfield has survived.

Chesterfield today contains almost two dozen historic buildings, fifteen of which are being or have been restored. Farm fields extend both north and south from the town boundaries.

The meeting house in Chesterfield was constructed between 1887 and 1892 of local brick crafted by hand. *Philip Varney*

Originally built by Nathan Barlow and Judson Tolman in about 1903, Chesterfield's Holbrook Mercantile closed in 1956 with Chester Holbrook as owner. *Philip Varney*

As you enter the community, listed since 1980 on the National Register of Historic Places, you'll see several austere brick or log residences and the brick Call-Higginson-Muir Store (the bricks of Chesterfield were crafted locally). Another building of note is that last business in town, the brick Holbrook Mercantile, built about 1903 (and featuring two old gas pumps of different eras). On the northern fringe, as you head out of town down a short hill, stand two deserted log cabins and their outbuildings.

The 1892 Meeting House (or church), now a museum, stands on a hill on the west edge of town, where you can obtain a brochure for further explorations. Next door is a 2003 reconstruction of the 1895 Amusement Hall, a community center. A roofless brick shell east of the hall is the remains of the 1922 schoolhouse, which burned in 2000 after being struck by lightning. South of the Meeting House 0.7 of a mile is the town's well-tended cemetery, still in use, which includes the graves of many founding families of Chesterfield.

East of the Meeting House area is a second group of homes, including a few that are often open for visitation with volunteer docents. One pleasant residence is the Tolman-Loveland house, built by Bishop Judson A. Tolman in 1896 and purchased by Bishop Carlos Loveland in 1898. A small, wooden balcony projects from the second story. Across the street stands the tiny, two-room, brick tithing office, where financial matters of church members were settled.

The Tolman-Loveland home in Chesterfield, like the Meeting House, was constructed of homemade brick. Note the second-story wooden balcony. *Philip Varney*

One place easily overlooked is the Higginson-Holbrook property, because all that is visible of it from most of town is its windmill. When you take a dirt road that climbs a hill and passes in front of that windmill, you'll see a seven-gabled, two-story home, built about 1903. The rest of the buildings in Chesterfield are sturdy and solid—but staid. This alone has a stylish grace. One wonders if any Chesterfield residents considered it a bit "showy."

WHEN YOU GO

The town of size nearest Chesterfield is Pocatello, Idaho. Take Interstate 15 south from Pocatello for 22 miles to Exit 47, US Highway 30. Follow that highway east through Lava Hot Springs for 18.8 miles to the turnoff to Bancroft. Turn north (left) and proceed 9.4 miles to the townsite.

GILMORE

ilmore features the largest remnants of a silver and lead mining boom that began in the 1870s and ended in the 1920s in the Birch Creek Valley. Originally known as Horseshoe Gulch, the settlement began as a cluster of cabins near the early diggings in the late 1880s. A stagecoach line connected Horseshoe Gulch to the outside world, and in 1902, the town's citizens elected to change the community's name to honor Jack T. Gilmer, one of the owners of the stage company. The US Postal Service approved the name but accidentally spelled it "Gilmore." Townspeople apparently decided to accept the error rather than fight the federal bureaucracy.

Gilmore's impressive general mercantile should look considerably better in the future. The Lemhi County Historical Society intends to restore the ravaged building. *Philip Varney*

The town was moved in 1910 from what is still known as Horseshoe Gulch to its present location when the Gilmore & Pittsburgh Railroad—a branch line beginning at Armstead, Montana (now submerged beneath Clark Canyon Reservoir, southwest of Dillon)—arrived in that year. The G&P Railroad was known derisively as the "Get off and Push." With the arrival of the railroad, town honoree Jack Gilmer's stage line was obsolete.

Gilmore's Pittsburgh-Idaho group of mines (financial backing came principally from Pennsylvanians) continued into the late 1920s, second only in production to the Coeur d'Alene silver mines in northern Idaho. Gilmore's prosperity ended when a power plant explosion and resulting fire in 1927 ended large-scale mining after producing $11.5 million in silver and lead. The railroad ceased service, and the rails were sold for scrap in 1940. The post office somehow hung on, perhaps by federal indifference (after all, they got the name wrong in the first place), until 1957.

As you head from Idaho Highway 28 up into Gilmore, you will see the old roadbed from the G&P Railroad as you cross it. More than two dozen buildings, ranging from habitable to tumbledown, remain at the town.

At the main intersection in Gilmore, you will be facing the very long, one-story, wood-frame general mercantile store, which is covered with ornamental tin. The false front has three messages, the top bleeding into the middle, as they were painted in different years: The top reads "US Post Office." Halfway underneath is "Gilmore Mercantile," with "general merchandise" below that. Painted in large letters on the north side of the building's roof is the town's name. The store was built by the Ross brothers in 1910, the year the railroad came to Gilmore. (The Lemhi County Historic Preservation Committee and the Lemhi County Historical Society and Museum have purchased the building for preservation and restoration.)

In addition to several log cabins and wood-frame residences is a two-story wood building, now painted red, that served as the automobile repair shop. It stood adjacent to the rail line, where new autos shipped to the Birch Creek Valley could be unloaded and serviced on the spot. The second floor had living quarters.

Up the road beyond the townsite 0.4 of a mile are several deteriorating log cabins. A large log structure, which might have been the base of an ore hopper, is just beyond. This is Horseshoe Gulch, the original townsite.

Continue uphill on the road beyond the gulch. In 0.3 of a mile, an unmarked road, definitely not for passenger cars, takes a sharp turn up to the left. This leads in 0.1 of a mile to the town's cemetery, which contains several markers in two sections.

WHEN YOU GO

 ilmore is 64.3 miles southeast of Salmon, Idaho, on Idaho Highway 28.

LEESBURG

Leesburg came to life in 1866 after Frank Sharkey and his party found placer gold in nearby creeks. Named by Confederate sympathizers for Robert E. Lee, Leesburg might have become just another quickly abandoned mining site with rich but shallow prospects. But in addition to placer gold, primary deposits were found in the hills, and hard-rock mining eventually brought three thousand gold seekers to the town. Eventually, nearly a hundred businesses were established, including a newspaper. A competing town, named Grantsville by those who favored the Union side in the recently ended Civil War, developed east of Leesburg, but only the name Leesburg stuck.

As primary deposits waned, hydraulic operations began in the presumably played-out placer deposits, and new fortunes were made. Supplies came from newly opened routes from Boise through Idaho City to Salmon, where pack trains kept Leesburg alive, even requiring sleighs and dogsleds during the winter months. We think of stagecoaches as being relics that were retired in the late 1800s, but, amazingly, until a truck road was completed in the early 1930s,

Leesburg's main street features, from left, a butcher shop, a post office, a schoolhouse, and the tax assessor's office. *Philip Varney*

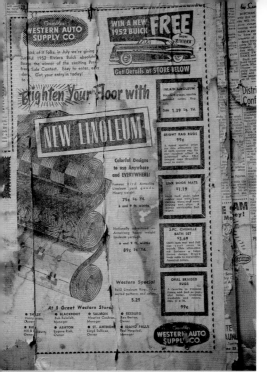

The inside of the former post office is insulated, if that's the right word, with newspapers from the 1950s. *Philip Varney*

Leesburg was served by four or five stages and freighters daily, according to Salmon resident Jim Caples, who rode the stage each summer from 1926 until 1930.

Despite the road, Leesburg was moribund after World War II when the diggings finally gave out, but not before producing an estimated $40 million in gold.

The site includes residences, an 1890s tax assessor's office, a 1935 schoolhouse, Mike and Maude Fraker's 1937 post office (which has old newspapers glued to the walls for insulation), a 1902 butcher shop, an 1890s Chinese laundry (Chinese made up almost half the population in 1880), the stagecoach office, an 1870s stable that later became a saloon, a boarding house, the Leesburg Hotel, and more. The hotel once had a very genteel feature: it offered a covered walkway to the other side of the street.

You passed the entrance to the cemetery on your way to town. From the parking lot, head back down the road 0.3 of a mile, where you will see on your right a walkover across a buck-and-rail fence. Five headstones, a metal fence, and a couple of wooden fences make up the graveyard.

WHEN YOU GO

Leesburg is 31.6 miles northwest of Salmon. From Salmon, head south on US Highway 93 for 5.1 miles to Forest Road 021 and turn west. In 13.4 miles, you'll come to an intersection at a summit, but continue straight on Forest Road 021. In another 2.8 miles, there's another intersection: Forest Road 021 continues to Cobalt and Forest Road 098 goes right to Leesburg, now 10.3 miles away. The entire route is a wide, smooth road, because it is the haul road for the Beartrack Mine, which is adjacent to Leesburg. Ignore the turnoff to the Beartrack Mine 0.3 of a mile before the townsite. Forest Road 098 dead-ends at the Leesburg parking area.

Bayhorse will look markedly different on your visit than it does in this book's photographs, and that will be good news. For decades, Bayhorse was privately owned and off-limits to visitors. The best one could do was to gaze and photograph from across Bayhorse Creek, trying to get a good look through the trees and brush.

The Idaho Department of Parks and Recreation, however, now owns the site, and in 2009 Bayhorse was opened to the public after an extensive cleanup of mine tailings, a slag dump, and even the town itself, which was poisoned with arsenic, among other dangerous elements. You cannot actually enter the buildings at this point because they are unsafe after, in some cases, more than a century of neglect.

The most-repeated version of the naming of the mining district, the creek that runs through it, and the town that grew there is that a single prospector worked the area in about 1864 with the assistance of two bay horses. Other area prospectors couldn't remember his name, so he was identified as "the fellow with the bay horses."

Beginning in 1872, other prospectors working along Bayhorse Creek found promising silver deposits, but the real rush to the area didn't occur until Tim Cooper and

The State of Idaho's Department of Parks and Recreation is shoring up all the buildings at Bayhorse, including the enormous Bayhorse Mill. *Philip Varney*

Charley Blackburn discovered their Ramshorn claim in 1878. They sold it to others for a rather modest price because they lacked the capital to develop a mine in such a remote location.

As other deposits were discovered, the mining camp of Bayhorse (likely shortened to one word by the US Postal Service) grew on a flat area along the

The charcoal kilns at Bayhorse were built using mortar from the tailings pile of the Bayhorse Mill. *Philip Varney*

north side of the creek. By 1882, a stamp mill and a smelter were built immediately west of town. Coke to fuel the smelter was initially shipped all the way from Pennsylvania, but the completion of six charcoal kilns on the south side of the creek later that same year created a less expensive local supply of fuel.

In that same year, Bayhorse had about three hundred citizens and featured several saloons, boarding houses, a meat market, and a general store. The peak years were the 1880s, but dropping silver prices, culminating in the Silver Crash of 1893, led to the town's decline, despite limited mining efforts between 1902 and 1918. The post office managed to hang on until 1927.

You'll be parking atop the old smelter's slag dump, which has been capped because of hazardous materials beneath. You'll be able to see, on the west end of town, the huge Bayhorse Mill, built in 1882 by John Gilmore and O. J. Salisbury. The stamp mill was remodeled in 1919 to become a flotation mill and plant.

East of the mill is the 1880s stone Wells Fargo building with its heavy iron doors, followed by several cabins and outbuildings, and the two-story 1880s Bayhorse Hotel, the only hotel remaining of several that once stood in town. Across from the hotel are the collapsed remains of the so-called tin can building, a log, false-front, tin-covered structure that probably served as a livery stable and perhaps later as a garage.

Other buildings and remnants are farther down the street. On the south side of Bayhorse Creek are several other attractions, beginning with the six partially dismantled charcoal kilns (mislabeled on the topographic map as "coke ovens"), made of uncut stone and mortar.

These kilns are the first ones featured in this book, followed by ones at Frisco, Utah. They converted wood to charcoal by heating wood in a controlled-burn process. Wood was loaded into a ground-level opening. First dry wood, followed by green wood, was stacked as high as possible. A higher door in the rear of the kiln, which was reached through a ramp, was used to finish filling the kiln. The doors were closed and sealed, the wood set afire, and the air within the kiln carefully regulated through vents that were alternately opened and sealed.

This slow "cooking" process would take about ten days. At that time, the kilns were opened and the fire was doused with water. The charcoal was removed and, after cooling, taken to the nearby smelter.

The process was very similar when coal was converted to coke. Such kilns, when using coal, are called "coke ovens."

Beyond the kilns are the ruins of a miner's log cabin.

West of the kilns 0.1 of a mile, up to the left along the road, is the tiny Bayhorse Cemetery with eight dilapidated wooden fences for individual graves. There are no markers. One has the feeling, walking around the graveyard, that there are many unmarked graves.

Immediately beyond the cemetery is a large log structure, possibly the base of an ore hopper. You can also see, on the opposite side of the canyon, considerable mining remnants of Bayhorse: the canyon walls are crisscrossed with mining trails and pockmarks of failed adits.

About 3 miles above town, on four-wheel-drive-only roads, are the remains of the Ramshorn and Skylark mines.

WHEN YOU GO

From Challis, which is 60 miles southwest of Salmon, drive southeast on US Highway 93 to Idaho Highway 75, a distance of 2.3 miles. At that junction stands the Land of the Yankee Fork Interpretive Center, which features highly worthwhile exhibits and artifacts, along with knowledgeable personnel. From the interpretive center, turn south on Idaho Highway 75 and proceed 7.9 miles to Bayhorse Creek Road (Forest Road 051). You will cross the Salmon River by bridge and travel 3.2 miles to the site of Bayhorse.

BONANZA, THE YANKEE FORK DREDGE, AND CUSTER

Sylvester Jordan and Captain Dudley B. Varney discovered placer gold deposits in 1870 along a tributary of the Yankee Fork of the Salmon River. (Captain Varney is only the second person with my surname that I have found in my ghost town travels.) That small tributary, later known as Jordan Creek in Sylvester Jordan's honor, enticed a stream of prospectors to descend upon the remote diggings. Securing necessary supplies became an immediate problem. In 1876, the town of Challis was built as a center for the distribution of goods to the Yankee Fork mines. A toll road from Challis to the Yankee Fork area, completed in 1879, provided a link to the outside world.

Bonanza was the first mining camp along the Yankee Fork, founded in 1877 by Charles Franklin to serve the prospectors and miners who had rushed to the

Bonanza's tumbling buildings sit right along the main road, which may partially account for why they are deteriorating so rapidly. *Philip Varney*

The Yankee Fork Dredge is a rarity in the American West. Since it was not salvaged, it sits virtually intact in a pond of its own making. *Philip Varney*

area. A town of more than six hundred people, the community had refinements not often found in placer mining camps: baseball and croquet fields, a watchmaker's shop, an actual street grid, and community wells with a piped water system for drinking and fire protection. That system, however, was not sufficient to protect Bonanza from major fires in 1889 and 1897. After the second conflagration, most people moved to neighboring Custer. When the final mine closed near Bonanza, the town was moribund.

Bonanza today is a minor site with a few standing, leaning, and tumbling cabins. If you follow Forest Road 074 to the west, in 0.5 of a mile you'll arrive at the Bonanza Cemetery. This graveyard features an informative sign that relates how different ethnic groups contributed to the Idaho mining boom. One of those buried in the cemetery is Captain Dudley Varney. He originally came to the West in 1864 with one of Jim Bridger's expeditions before making the claim on the Yankee Fork with partner Jordan.

A second cemetery, Boot Hill, is 0.9 of a mile beyond the first.

The Yankee Fork Dredge stands north of the townsite of Bonanza very near the spot of Varney and Jordan's original find at the confluence of Jordan Creek and the Yankee Fork.

The dredge was constructed about 5 miles downstream at Pole Flat in 1940.

The schoolhouse at Custer would likely have disappeared were it not for Tuff and Edna McGown, who saved it and turned it into a museum in 1960. *Philip Varney*

It worked its way north, creating its own standing pond in the Yankee Fork, chewing through the river bottom and upturning the bed into huge piles of river rock, which you drove through on your way to Bonanza. The dredge operated until 1952, with a hiatus during World War II, when Law 208 made mining of non-war-related minerals illegal. The dredge recovered more than $1 million worth of gold and silver, but it cost slightly more than it recovered to run the dredge. The huge operation, which lasted about eight years, was essentially a wash. But in its day, according to local author-historian Howard A. Packard Jr., it was quite a sight: "The Yankee Fork gold dredge looked like a well-lighted four-story hotel, lost in the mountains."

A self-guided tour of the Yankee Fork Dredge is well worth the modest admission, and because it is self-guided, you may take as little or as much time as you like. Parents with small children may appreciate that option.

Custer was founded in 1879, two years after Bonanza. The town was named for the area's principal mine, the General Custer, which had been discovered in 1876, not long after the famous Battle of Little Bighorn in that same year in which Custer made his last stand.

Samuel L. Holman, a graduate of Harvard Law School who headed to the West shortly after the death of his fiancée, founded the town. He became the first justice of the peace in the recently created community of Bonanza, but he also worked claims along the Yankee Fork. As the General Custer Mine prospered, Holman saw that his claims would be more profitable as city lots, so in 1879, he laid out the town of Custer, which eventually surpassed Bonanza in importance. That occurred after a thirty-stamp mill was constructed north of town to process the estimated nine hundred tons of ore per month that were yielding about $1 million worth of gold annually.

The Yankee Fork's mineral wealth played out in the early years of the twentieth century, and both Bonanza and Custer eventually emptied. Only the Yankee Fork Dredge brought the area back to life beginning in 1940.

Now a state park (donations are accepted, but there is no admission charge), Custer contains several buildings of interest, including one of the more photogenic false-front buildings in Idaho, the Empire Saloon. The structure was built sometime before 1903 and is now used as the park's headquarters. Across the street from the saloon is the 1900 former schoolhouse, now housing a very worthwhile museum. A walking tour brochure will increase your enjoyment of the town.

As you leave Custer heading north, on your right you'll see the stepped-down hillside marking the location of the General Custer Mine's mill, which, like several other buildings, burned in 1986 as the result of a fire caused by a carelessly discarded cigarette.

The Custer Cemetery is 1 mile north of town on the west side of the road. Seven marked graves are at the site, including one of antiquity.

WHEN YOU GO

From the junction of Bayhorse Road and Idaho Highway 75 drive southwest 13.2 miles to the small semi–ghost town of Clayton. From Clayton, drive west on Idaho Highway 75 for 19.7 miles to Sunbeam. Turn north on Yankee Fork Road (Forest Road 013) and proceed 7.8 miles north to Bonanza. Where the road turns from pavement to dirt, you will see extensive evidence of the tailings of dredging operations extending north to Bonanza. In fact, you'll be driving on a smoothed portion of it.

Idaho City has a look of permanence that most mining camps lack. Many buildings are made of brick, and, in fact, several views of the town could be mistaken for some of the better-preserved sites of the California gold rush. In addition to its permanence, the community also has enough life that it should be considered a historic town rather than a ghost town. Idaho City, however, is neither overly touristy nor overly dressed up: parts are almost dowdy, which I find makes it all the more charming and photogenic.

The Boise County Courthouse in Idaho City has served in that capacity for more than a century. Its courtroom, still in use, has been restored to its early-twentieth-century appearance. *Philip Varney*

In 1862, a party of men led by George Grimes and Moses Splawn discovered placer deposits in what later became known as Grimes Creek. The usual rush to the area ensued, and the Boise Basin came alive. The principal town was Idaho City, which had a population of about six thousand within a year. That made the boomtown the largest community in the Idaho Territory, and at one point it was reputed to be the largest city in the northwestern United States, bigger even than Portland, Oregon. The raucous, bustling town of Idaho City began a decline within a few years as miners raced to the next El Dorados at places such as Silver City, Idaho, and Virginia City and Helena, Montana.

The town did not completely wither, however, as area mines continued to produce, albeit in less spectacular amounts. Later hydraulicking of hillsides and dredging of streambeds kept the Boise Basin producing for decades.

A good place to start enjoying this architecturally diverse community is on Main Street, where you will find the 1865 Boise Basin Mercantile on the southwest corner of Main and Commercial Streets. It lays claim to being Idaho's oldest store still in existence.

One block north, on the southwest corner of Main and Wall Streets, stands the 1871 Boise County Courthouse. A single-story brick edifice that was

Idaho City's Masonic Lodge was built in 1865.
It still contains original furnishings. *Philip Varney*

originally built as a general store, it also served as a tin shop, a hardware store, and a hotel, finally becoming a courthouse in 1909. If it's open, be sure to observe its delightful interior, which looks, except for a few modernities, much as it did in 1909.

North of the courthouse is the 1891 city hall, at Main and School Streets, a two-story, wooden structure with an imposing bell tower. The building originally served as the town's school until 1962.

West of Main is Montgomery Street, which features other excellent buildings.

On a hill east of town, on High Street, stand the 1867 St. Joseph Catholic Church and the 1875 Odd Fellows Hall.

Idaho City's Pioneer

The early morning sun touches Idaho City's city hall, erected as the town's schoolhouse in 1891. The building served students until 1962, when they moved to a new school on the north edge of town. *Philip Varney*

Cemetery is west of town on Centerville Road, which is on the north end of town. Go west on Centerville 0.3 of a mile, turn south on Buena Vista Road, and follow the road for 0.5 of a mile around to the right and up a hill.

A sign at the cemetery states that an estimated three thousand people are buried there, but fewer than three hundred have been identified.

WHEN YOU GO

From Bonanza, return to Sunbeam. Drive west for 13 miles on Idaho Highway 75 to Stanley, one of the most spectacularly beautiful spots on Earth. From Stanley, follow Idaho Highway 21 to Idaho City, a distance of 90 miles.

SILVER CITY

Not only is Silver City the ghost town gem of the Gem State, it is one of the very best in the West. The almost seventy buildings of Silver City are occupied and maintained, but they are not overly restored, so the town has a distinctly noncommercial look to it. Many of the structures are wonderful architectural examples of the 1870s. The streets are dirt and uneven. The residents I have met are cordial, perhaps appreciating the fact that anyone arriving there has gone through a certain amount of effort just to see the town. The overall effect: Silver City is one of my favorite ghost towns.

Located in the southwest corner of Idaho, Silver City sits in Owyhee (oh-WYE-hee) County, named, improbable as it may seem, for the Hawaiian fur trappers who explored the area beginning in 1819. The mining history of Owyhee County, however, begins with the mad rush to War Eagle Mountain that created Silver City.

Prospectors had already found placer gold deposits along Idaho City's Grimes Creek in 1862. A party of twenty-nine miners from that area, led by Michael Jordan, decided to head out in May 1863 in search of the fabled (and perhaps mythical) "lost" Blue Bucket Diggings. What they found instead was placer gold along what came to be called Jordan Creek. Quartz ledges of primary gold deposits were discovered two months later. What the party had come upon was the second biggest mineral find in Idaho's history; the largest was found in the Coeur d'Alene area twenty years later. Soon the area was swarming with miners, and freight routes were extended from both year-old Boise City to the north and Oregon's Jordan Valley to the west.

The Stoddard Mansion in Silver City may not compare in size with other mansions in the American West, but it holds its own when it comes to gingerbread trim. *Philip Varney*

Silver City eventually featured a population of around 2,500 people and seventy-five businesses. The hills surrounding town had more than two hundred mines, but it soon became apparent that the real wealth of Silver City lay within the big hill to the east: War Eagle Mountain. The biggest strike there came in 1865 with the discovery of the Poorman Mine, so named because the discoverers knew they lacked

Silver City's Idaho Hotel is a ghost town lover's dream: historic, authentic, and just rustic enough to make a night's stay unforgettable. *Philip Varney*

the capital necessary to work it. The Poorman was unusual in that it yielded an amalgam of both gold and silver chloride, the latter appearing with a crimson tint. The color was dubbed Ruby Silver. Some of the Poorman Ruby Silver crystals were displayed at the 1866 Paris Exposition, winning a gold medal.

Present-day guests at Silver City's Idaho Hotel enter the past even as they check in. The Diebold Safe behind the counter dates from about 1876. The guest ledger on the counter is an original to the hotel. *Philip Varney*

A telegraph line, Idaho Territory's first, was extended to Silver City from Winnemucca, Nevada, in 1874 and from Silver City to Boise a year later. Telephone service came in the 1880s, followed by electricity in 1903. At its mining peak, the Silver City Range contained more than sixty mills processing ore, with an estimated production of at least $60 million, principally in silver, retrieved from area mines.

The peak years were over by the turn of the twentieth century, and the town's population took a dive after World War I, although some mining continued into the 1930s. Silver City's landmark Idaho Hotel shut its doors in about 1942, and the post office closed in 1943. In that same decade, the nearly empty community suffered a nearly fatal indignity: the electrical transmission lines were removed.

Ed Jagels purchased the Idaho Hotel in 1972 and reopened it for business, using a twelve-volt generator for power. He was a complete believer in the renaissance of Silver City and spent the rest of his life making it happen. I first met Jagels in 1998, three years before his death, and his spirit and enthusiasm were infectious. Roger and Jerri Nelson bought the hotel from Jagels and have continued to make improvements to it (such as adding modern toilets with a

The Wells Fargo office inside the Idaho Hotel has, atop the agent's desk, a telegraph key, a jar battery to power the telegraph, a ledger, and a large scale. *Philip Varney*

septic system), without compromising the history or charm of the great building.

Today, Silver City is on the National Register of Historic Places, which means that property owners do not build new buildings and can only make repairs on existing ones in order to avoid jeopardizing that historic status. About fifty families live there in the summer, and in the winter a watchman looks after the town.

You will enter town on Jordan Street after crossing Jordan Creek. On the southwest corner of Jordan and Avalanche Streets is the former Owyhee County Office Building, now a gift shop. Directly across the street is the Idaho Hotel, a rambling structure that is, simply, one of the finest ghost town buildings in the American West. The Idaho Hotel is actually an amalgam of seven different buildings, the oldest of which is the 1866 three-story west wing, which was disassembled and loaded onto skids and sleds and dragged through snow to Silver City from short-lived Ruby City. That town stood where the road now turns toward Jordan Valley 0.5 of a mile west of Silver City. Inside the hotel, open for both meals and overnight accommodations, are a saloon-dining area, a Wells Fargo office, an elegant parlor, and eighteen rooms for guests, including the luxurious Empire Room, where I enjoyed a night surrounded by the nineteenth century.

Behind the hotel and straddling Jordan Creek is the 1869 Masonic Hall, a two-story structure that was originally built as a planing mill.

If you walk south from the hotel's porch, you'll be on Avalanche Street, which features the aforementioned former county office building, the Knapp Drug Store, and, on the corner of Avalanche and Washington Streets, the Lippincott Building, which contained a doctor's office. More of the town's enchanting buildings extend down Washington, including the former Odd

One of the most graceful churches in the Mountain West, Silver City's Our Lady of Tears Catholic Church has undergone extensive renovation. *Philip Varney*

The rear section of the Getchell Drug Store features a fully equipped dentist's office. *Philip Varney*

Fellows Hall; the Getchell Drug Store and Post Office, which has a fully equipped dentist's office in the rear; and, across the street, the 1866 furniture store and vegetable market, which is a wooden building covered in pressed tin that has also served as a brewery and soda works (there's a natural spring in the basement); a bowling alley; and the Sommercamp Saloon.

On the north side of town off of Morning Star Street are three more of Silver City's best buildings: the 1892 Idaho Standard School, the 1898 Our Lady of Tears Catholic Church (which served as St. James Episcopal Church until it was sold to the Catholic Diocese of Boise in 1928), and the 1870 Stoddard Mansion, which features an almost stupefying amount of gingerbread trim.

The two Silver City cemeteries, one public and the other for Masons and Odd Fellows, stand west of town on a steep hill. The route is quite rough and definitely requires a high-clearance vehicle, but the distance is only 0.2 of a mile, so you can easily walk there from town, starting three buildings west from the former county building. A sign points the way.

WHEN YOU GO

Silver City is 67 miles southwest of Boise. From Idaho City, proceed 36 miles southwest to Boise via Idaho Highway 21. From Boise, take Interstate 84 west 16 miles to Nampa. Follow Idaho Highway 45, which joins Idaho Highway 78, south from Nampa for 27 miles to Murphy. Southeast of Murphy 4.5 miles is Silver City Road, which in 18.8 miles takes you to a junction only 0.5 of a mile from Silver City. Turn left (a right takes you to Jordan Valley, Oregon) and proceed into town, passing two stone powderhouses on your left.

NOTE: The last 12 miles are on a twisting, mountainous road. In dry weather, the road is quite good, but I would nevertheless recommend a high-clearance vehicle.

The Bannack Masonic Lodge and schoolhouse, one of the first Masonic temples erected in Montana, was built in the Greek Revival style. The Masons offered the lower floor to the people of Bannack as a schoolhouse, and the citizens gratefully accepted. *Philip Varney*

MONTANA

Montana is the nation's fourth-largest state. Fortunately, the best ghost towns are all situated in its southwestern quarter. That's also the location of some of the state's most scenic areas. Montana comes from a Latin word meaning "mountainous," which aptly describes the section you'll be exploring.

Montana was admitted to the union in 1889, eight months prior to Idaho and Wyoming. Its state motto is "Oro y Plata," Spanish for "Gold and Silver," although much of the state's wealth came not from those minerals but from copper. When inventions such as the telephone created numerous uses for copper, Montanans found their real bonanza.

Montana's ghost towns range from the protected (Bannack and Garnet) to the commercial (Nevada City) to the almost deserted (Comet and Elkhorn). Each is a delight to visit and photograph.

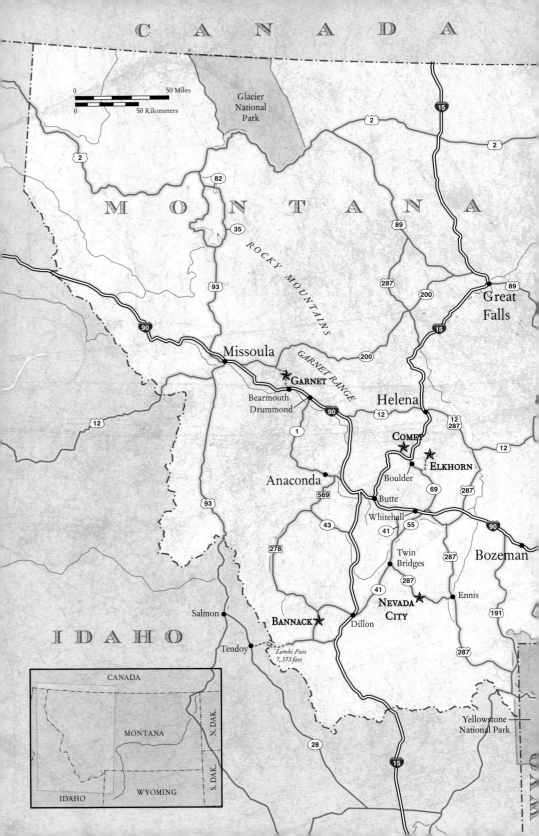

BANNACK

Bannack is one of the Mountain West's great ghost towns, featuring more than four dozen well-preserved buildings, some of which contain artifacts of antiquity.

The town of Bannock was born not long after a group of Colorado-based prospectors (called Pikes Peakers), led by John White and William Eades, found gold along Grasshopper Creek in July 1862. It was named for the nearby Bannock Indians, but the US Postal Service, when granting a post office the following year, mistook the "o" for an "a," and "Bannack" it became. The community, which reached a population of four hundred in a matter of weeks, was the first major gold camp in Montana, with an estimated $500,000 of ore shipped by the end of 1862.

Bannack's prominence was challenged in 1864, when promising gold strikes were found along Last Chance Gulch (later Helena) and Alder Gulch (later Virginia City). Bannack and Virginia City, a mere 50 miles apart as the crow flies, became inextricably linked early in their history by the Vigilance Committee and the Innocents.

When twenty-first-century people think of "vigilante justice," it usually carries a negative connotation. And "innocents"? Certainly they must be law-abiding people. In Bannack and Virginia City, those notions were reversed completely.

Henry Plummer came to Bannack in its earliest days. Appearing to be a trustworthy and earnest fellow, Plummer was selected by townspeople as sheriff. What they did not know was that Plummer was only three years out California's San Quentin prison. He organized a group of similar chaps into a clandestine gang of road agents, or highwaymen, named the Innocents, so called because they swore to their guiltlessness of any wrongdoing. This gang of blackguards began a reign of terror in both Bannack and Virginia City, particularly on helpless travelers en route between the two towns. They are believed to have robbed and/or murdered more than a hundred people in eight short months.

In response to this mayhem, a secret band of stalwart citizens, calling themselves the Vigilance Committee, or the Vigilantes, vowed to restore order and justice. They pursued the road agents and, within a little more than a month, caught, "tried," and hanged twenty-four of them, including, as the result of a condemned man's testimony, Sheriff Henry Plummer himself. When Sidney Edgerton, appointed by President Abraham Lincoln to be Chief Justice of the Idaho Territory (which then included Idaho and Montana), arrived in Bannack two months after the hanging spree, he concluded that the Vigilantes had done exactly what was necessary at the time. A year later, Bannack citizens, now four thousand strong, chose Edgerton to journey to Washington, DC, to petition for a division of the Idaho Territory. Not only was he successful, but also he became the first governor of the Territory of Montana. Legal authority was firmly in place in Bannack, the territory's first capital.

Bannack, however, held that distinction for only seven months, when the first territorial legislature voted in December 1864 to move the capital to Virginia City. Bannack was on a slow path of decline, as other gold strikes eclipsed Montana's first rush.

Mining at Bannack was primarily of secondary deposits—the retrieval of gold from streams and riverbanks. This was done first by panning, then by

The Hotel Meade was erected in Bannack in 1875 as the Beaverhead County Courthouse. It became a hotel in 1890, nine years after the county seat was moved to Dillon, 25 miles east of Bannack. *Philip Varney*

hydraulic mining, and finally by dredging. Each technique is, in a way, a bit more desperate than the method before, since gold seekers are essentially going over the same area, with newer technology, trying to find the precious metal that the previous attempts missed. The easy placering was over in a couple of years. Hydraulicking continued into the turn of the twentieth century, and dredging operations, the first in the United States, lasted from 1895 until about 1905. Small-time hard-rock operations kept Bannack alive into the 1940s, after which the town was essentially abandoned.

Although some subsequent vandalizing took place in Bannack, con-

The winding staircase of Bannack's county courthouse (later the Hotel Meade) was used in August 1877 when women and children were sent inside "the fortress" because of a feared Nez Perce attack. Children were rumored to have been ready to hide in the courthouse's large safes. The attack never occurred. *Philip Varney*

cerned Montanans began to work to save the townsite not long after it became a ghost. When the town was finally turned over to the State of Montana in 1954, a principal stipulation was that it was to be preserved as a relic, not turned into a tourist mecca. You will be pleased at what remains.

Bannack today has a true feel of entering the past. You will pay a park fee and be given a walking tour brochure, which is free unless you decide to keep it.

You can go inside most of the structures; you just have to turn the doorknobs. Park rangers merely ask you to close the doors behind you.

Since you'll have a walking tour brochure, I'll mention only a few highlights. One is the unusual 1874 Masonic Lodge. The Masons helped the community by donating the ground floor of their lodge to serve as a public school and had their meetings on the second floor, which still features Masonic paraphernalia, which you can view through glass partitions.

Across the street from the schoolhouse/lodge is the most impressive structure in town, the two-story brick 1875 Beaverhead County Courthouse, which served until 1881, when the county seat was moved, after a contentious election, to Dillon, where it still resides.

After almost a decade of standing empty, the courthouse was remodeled into the Hotel Meade by Dr. John Singleton Meade. This upscale hostelry operated off and on during every period of Bannack's prosperity until the 1940s.

Next door to the courthouse/hotel is Cyrus Skinner's saloon, a favorite hangout of Henry Plummer's road agents. After the Vigilantes dispatched the highwaymen, Skinner too was hanged for his association with Plummer and his gang. Later, the building became a general mercantile store.

Across the street and down a bit from Skinner's Saloon is Chrisman's Store and, behind it, Bannack's two jails, the first ever constructed in Montana. From the smaller of the jails, one can look through the bars to see, up Hangman's Gulch north of town, a reconstruction of the gallows that Sheriff Henry Plummer ordered built—the same gallows from which he eventually swayed when discovered to be a leader of the Innocents.

If you walk up to those gallows, you can take a path over to the Pioneer Cemetery, used from 1860 until about 1880. A later cemetery, containing more than sixty graves and many wooden fences, is 0.4 of a mile beyond the turnoff to Bannack on the east side of the road to Dillon.

On the east side of Bannack are two more buildings of note. The first is the 1877 Methodist church, Bannack's first house of worship. It was constructed as a result of the determination of William Van Orsdel, known affectionately as Brother Van, who charmed and cajoled Bannack's citizens into contributing funds to erect his church.

Immediately west of the church stands the 1866 or 1867 Roe/Graves House, the first frame house built in Bannack. It is also the town's largest house, with a dozen rooms.

WHEN YOU GO

Bannack is 25 miles west of Dillon. Take Interstate 15's Exit 59, which is 4 miles southwest of Dillon's Exit 63, and follow Montana Highway 278 west for 17 miles to a junction with Bannack Bench Road, where a sign directs you to Bannack, 3.7 miles south.

NEVADA CITY

Lovers of Western history in general and ghost towns in particular owe a tremendous debt of gratitude to Charles and Sue Bovey. In 1944, they bought more than one hundred Virginia City buildings in an effort to save the historic frontier town. As a result of their efforts, the town was designated a National Historic Monument in 1961. Virginia City is a delightful tourist mecca and is well worth walking around, but the town with the more authentic ghost town feeling is just down the road to the west.

Nevada City shows even more evidence of the efforts of Charles and Sue Bovey than Virginia City. While the Boveys were purchasing portions of that town in the 1940s to preserve it, they were also buying a series of buildings in various old towns and ranches and having them placed on the fairgrounds of their hometown of Great Falls, Montana. When that community needed more fairground space, the Boveys had their entire "Old Town" exhibit moved, in 1959, to their latest acquisition, Nevada City.

In the 1860s, Nevada City was essentially a suburb, at about one-fifth the size, of Virginia City. They were linked by the same source of income, Alder Gulch. People moved freely from one town to the other for commerce, entertainment, and services; they also suffered the same violence brought on by Bannack's Henry Plummer and had the eventual retribution by the Vigilance Committee. When Alder Gulch mining faded by 1868, Nevada City virtually disappeared, while Virginia City merely declined to a shell of its former self. The second life

From 1867 to 1873, this tiny schoolhouse served Twin Bridges, northwest of Nevada City. Note that one of the vocabulary words on the blackboard is, appropriately, "Vigilante." *Philip Varney*

The Elkhorn Barber Shop (left), now located in Nevada City, once stood across the street from the two halls still standing in Elkhorn. Next door is Sullivan's Saddlery, where renowned Western artist Charles Russell once hung out as a youth in its original location, Fort Benton. The small log building beyond is an original to Nevada City: its jail. *Philip Varney*

that Virginia City received in 1899 when dredging operations began had no effect upon Nevada City: by that time, the latter town was mostly a memory.

Enter Charles and Sue Bovey and the renaissance of Nevada City.

Several "pioneer towns"—places where historic buildings have been brought together to be preserved and enjoyed—exist in the West. South Park City, Colorado, mentioned later in this book (page 287), is one of the best, and Nevada City is in the same class. Of the sixty-nine buildings I counted on the site, only nine are original to Nevada City. But virtually all others are documented, historic structures that were carefully disassembled, transported, and reassembled with expert care from sites all over Montana. Virtually all of them would no longer exist if it were not for the Boveys. The overall effect is a charming, interesting town worthy of being in the movies—and

Nevada City's Applebound and Crabb Store, which was featured in the film *Little Big Man* (Dustin Hoffman played Jack Crabb), was originally an outbuilding on a ranch near Ennis, east of Virginia City. Beyond the store is a building now used to display assay equipment. *Philip Varney*

it has been, including *Little Big Man* and *Missouri Breaks*, along with several television programs.

You will be given a walking guide and map upon paying an appropriate admission fee (which covers two days, if you wish to return).

On the north end of Nevada City's California Street stand, from left to right, the Parmeter House, once the home of Sheridan's mayor, O. F. Parmeter; a residence from the vanished town of Iron Rod; and the former Twin Bridges Schoolhouse. *Philip Varney*

The guide begins with the town's depot, one of Nevada City's few inauthentic structures. It is a replica of a depot in Minnesota.

Many of Nevada City's buildings contain portions of the huge collections of memorabilia that the Boveys accumulated, so visitors really can have a nineteenth-century experience. Some of the better examples are found in the Dry Goods Store, the Cheap Cash Store, the Applebound and Crabb Store (used in *Little Big Man*—Dustin Hoffman's character was Jack Crabb), Sullivan's Saddlery, the Sedman House, the schoolhouse, and, especially, the Music Hall, where you will find an astonishing assortment of mechanical musical devices.

To visit the Nevada City Cemetery, drive 0.2 of a mile west of town, turn north, and proceed another 0.2 of a mile to the cemetery entrance, where you will see wrought-iron and wooden fences and several headstones. On your way to the cemetery, you'll pass the elaborate 1895 Guinan House, which was moved from nearby Laurin and was not, at this writing, open to visitors.

WHEN YOU GO

From Bannack, drive 25 miles east to Dillon. From Dillon, head 29 miles northeast to Twin Bridges on Montana Highway 41. From there, take Montana Highway 287 for 30 miles to Virginia City. You will pass through Nevada City 1.5 miles before reaching Virginia City.

COMET

Comet is a wonderful, genuine ghost town, the third best in Montana, after Bannack and Garnet. It features more than three dozen wooden buildings, including a huge mill, a two-story mill workers' and miners' dormitory, and numerous wood or log cabins.

Comet came to life in 1883, nine years after silver ore was located in the area but not substantially developed. The town of Wickes, 4 miles north, smelted the Comet Mine's ore by way of a tramway. Its most prosperous days were during the 1880s, when the town could boast of a population of three hundred, but the Silver Crash hit hard in 1893 and it was deserted by the end of World War I.

It was not deserted for long. A second mining operation began in the 1920s; a new mill, the one still standing at Comet, was built in 1926, and the population returned to its pre-1893 level. That prosperity ended with the beginning of World War II. Many mines in the American West, such as Comet, never reopened after World War II because an industrial surge for consumer goods offered jobs in manufacturing that paid better wages and were far less dangerous than mining. Eventually, more restrictive mine safety standards made reopening old mines prohibitively expensive.

Comet's boarding house is one of the few two-story structures in residential Comet. As you can see, it badly needs restoration or at least propping up. *Philip Varney*

Your first glimpse of Comet will be of two ore chutes on your left as you approach the site. You then round a corner, and Comet stands in a panorama before you. Across the draw to the east is the Comet Mine's last mill and its two-story dormitory, both clad in tin sheets. The mill's tailings were removed in 2000 as an environmental hazard, so the mill stands there in an eerie parklike setting.

To your immediate left are the general store, several residences, a two-story boarding house, and many mine-related structures. Up on the hill behind these

Here is an excellent example of ghost town safety: Do not attempt to climb the stairs of the Comet boarding house, or you might be the last person who does. *Philip Varney*

A nearby forest fire gave Comet's mill, dormitory, and stack an eerie glow in this early morning photograph. *Philip Varney*

buildings are at least a dozen miners' shacks, standing in various states of decay. Amid them is an occupied residence, and I, for one, am very glad they are there. I was watched each time I have been to Comet; with that vigilance, Comet should last much longer than if it were abandoned. But what Comet really needs is to be purchased and protected by the State of Montana.

This Chevrolet in Comet is well past restoration. Behind stand miners' cabins in various states of decay. *Philip Varney*

WHEN YOU GO

From Nevada City, head west on Montana Highway 287 for 28 miles to Twin Bridges. Take Montana Highway 41 and then Montana Highway 55 for 28 miles north to Whitehall, where you join Interstate 90. From there, it's 22 miles west to Butte, which features a remarkable, decaying, historic downtown. From Butte, take Interstate 15 northeast for 30.2 miles to Exit 160, High Ore Road. Follow High Ore Road over the Boulder River, cross a cattle guard, and head north for 4.5 miles to Comet.

ELKHORN

Photographs of Elkhorn taken in the 1970s show an extensive townsite with dozens of deserted wooden buildings. Unfortunately, time, weather, fire, and capitalism have reduced it to what it is today: an amalgam of ruins, modern occupied structures, a certain amount of junk—and two of the best buildings in the ghost town West.

Gravity and Montana's harsh winters helped some deserted structures collapse. Fire destroyed one of the town's premier residences. But several of the better buildings, including the two-story Grand Hotel, were dismantled and sold for the valuable siding or for reassembly elsewhere. If it weren't for Gillian Hall and Fraternity Hall, which constitute the smallest state park in Montana, Elkhorn wouldn't be included in this book. But every ghost town enthusiast simply must see these two buildings.

The rush to Elkhorn began when Swiss prospector Peter Wys found rich silver ore in 1870. He died only two years later, however, and it was Anton M. Holter, a miner from another of Montana's booming camps, Virginia City, who made the fortune from Wys's claim beginning in 1875. His Elkhorn Mine became a solid silver producer, which, when sold in 1888 to a British corporation for $500,000, was bringing in $30,000 monthly. That corporation improved the mining and milling processes and recouped their investment within two years.

But they only had three more years of prosperity, because the Silver Crash of 1893 was the beginning of the end for Elkhorn. The once-vibrant town of twenty-five hundred people lost more than three-quarters of its population in two months. Limited mining, along with a reworking of old tailings, occurred sporadically until 1951, but the post office only held on until 1924.

Except for the two halls, Elkhorn is all on private property, but you can see almost everything from the road. I'd recommend leaving your car in the parking area just south of town. Walk into town and notice the posted signs that either tell what purpose a structure served in the community or what used to occupy a now-vacant site.

The buildings that brought you to Elkhorn are hard to miss: the 1880s Gillian Hall and the 1893 Fraternity Hall dominate the town. At this writing, you can walk into each building (but be sure to secure the doors when you leave). The older Gillian Hall featured one commercial enterprise after another on the main floor, while the upstairs had a saloon and dance hall. Its neighbor, Fraternity Hall, was built through donations to be a community center, complete

Two of the most photogenic and famous ghost town buildings of the Mountain West are Elkhorn's Gillian Hall (left) and Fraternity Hall. *Philip Varney*

with a first-story auditorium, featuring a proscenium arch stage for theatrical productions and dance bands. On the second floor was a meeting place for various lodge groups. The building was officially opened, with the Cornish Glee Club and the Elkhorn Brass Band leading the celebration, on July 4, 1893. The euphoria was short-lived: in November of that year came the calamitous drop in silver prices and the emptying of Elkhorn.

Directly across the street from the halls stands a white clapboard structure that served as the town's general store well after the peak years of Elkhorn's prosperity.

Beyond the halls are several vacant lots and small cabins. At the north end of town, closed to the public, are the considerable remains of the Elkhorn Mine's milling remnants.

Elkhorn's cemetery is 0.9 of a mile away from town, so you might want to return to your car. Follow the main road north from town as it winds around to the east and then to the south (a sign points the way). For part of your journey, you'll be on an old railroad bed.

One of the first headstones at the cemetery is for Peter Wys, the original discoverer of Elkhorn's riches. His monument was placed in 1912 as a commemoration, forty years after his death, of his importance to the community. The graveyard, which is still in use, features several dozen markers of various materials: wood, marble, and at least one of pot metal. (These metal markers, which were usually purchased from mail-order catalogues, look like dark marble, but if you tap them with a coin, you will hear that they are metal.) You will also find several markers of young children who died in 1889 during a diphtheria outbreak.

On your way back to the townsite, stop for a moment to survey the town and, especially, the huge workings of the Elkhorn Mine's mill. What you could not see from street level spreads out before you.

WHEN YOU GO

From Comet, return to Interstate 15 and drive 4.3 miles northeast to Exit 164. Follow Montana Highway 69 through Boulder (make a one-block detour west on Third Avenue to see the handsome 1888 Jefferson County Courthouse) for 7.2 miles to Forest Road 517, which is marked for Elkhorn. In 3.1 miles, turn left onto Forest Road 258, which in 8.2 miles will take you to Elkhorn. As you near the townsite, you'll see a stone powderhouse on your right, followed immediately on your left by a huge tailings pile with a rusting boiler at its base.

GARNET

arnet's prosperity came late in the Montana mining game. Although placer gold deposits were discovered in the 1870s in the Garnet Range, the country was so remote that prospectors looked elsewhere for easier strikes. The discovery of plentiful silver in western Montana and northern Idaho caused miners to abandon questionable gold claims and rush to get in on those bonanzas. But with the Silver Crash of 1893, miners looked again at older gold claims that had been staked but abandoned.

Many of those miners returned to the Garnet Range, where a small settlement was built around a stamp mill erected in 1895 by Armistead L. Mitchell. The community was originally called Mitchell in his honor, but by 1897, the year the town received its post office, it was known as Garnet, named for the semiprecious, rubylike mineral. The town's population swelled to about a thousand by the end of the nineteenth century.

Garnet was unusual in that it was a peaceful community, more of a family place rather than a rowdy town of ne'er-do-wells. Although it had the usual saloons and brothels, it also featured refinements such as a doctor's office, a candy store, family residences instead of miners' shacks, and a miners' union hall. That union hall was pivotal to the orderly atmosphere in Garnet: every miner in Garnet was a member of the union, and the union resolved disputes. Miscreants either changed their ways or left town. There was a jail, but it served principally as a drunk tank.

Garnet's boom was short. By 1905, the population had shrunk to less than two hundred, and a fire in 1912 caused many holdouts to leave. Only a few people remained after the United States entered World War I because war-related jobs were steadier and paid better than haphazard gold mining work.

During the Great Depression, Garnet saw a modest rebirth. Because employment opportunities were scarce, and because the price of gold had more than doubled to thirty-five dollars per ounce, about 250 people returned to rework old mines and waste dumps with improved technology that retrieved gold that earlier, cruder processing had missed. Then came World War II and the enactment of Law 208, closing mines that were not directly assisting the war effort. In 1942, the year the post office closed, the sole resident was Frank Davey, owner of the town's last store. Sent a document by the Internal Revenue Service requiring him to sign in front of a witness, he gazed into his mirror, signed in both places, and noted to the IRS that he was the only resident of Garnet, Montana.

The dusty dining room of the J. K. Wells Hotel in Garnet is exactly what ghost town seekers hope to find instead of empty, vandalized buildings. In its heyday around the turn of the twentieth century, the Wells was considered quite luxurious.
Stephen Saks Photography/Alamy

This is your first view as you walk from the parking lot to Garnet. Prominent in the lower center is Kelly's Saloon. Next door stands Frank Davey's store. The large, three-story building in the right background is the J. K. Wells Hotel. *Philip Varney*

Davey died in 1947, and the auction of his effects served as the beginning of Garnet as a true ghost town.

You will park your car in a lot that is about a six-minute walk from Garnet (a separate handicapped lot is closer to the townsite). You will be stepping back in time, and when you come to an overlook of Garnet, you might even gasp: you'll be looking at more than a dozen log and wood-frame buildings under roof—and you won't be seeing them all.

Immediately prior to entering the townsite are toilets, drinking water, and a stand with an excellent tour brochure. A few buildings in town are private, but most others are open for your inspection. Be sure to walk into Kelly's Saloon, the first building on your left; Frank Davey's Store and annex, next door to the saloon; and, across the street, Ole Dahl's Saloon, a 1938 building from Garnet's last hurrah that now serves as a visitors' center. The biggest treat comes from exploring the 1897 J. K. Wells Hotel. You can enter almost every room, all the way to the third floor.

Residences, the original post office, a blacksmith's shop, and the town jail fan out across the meadow behind the center of town. The privately owned schoolhouse stands west of the jail.

A separate walking tour goes north from the parking lot to the Sierra Mine workings. A brochure for that interpretive trail is available at the trailhead.

The last resident of Garnet, Frank Davey, lived in the kitchen of the Wells Hotel. When he died in 1947, everything in the hotel was sold. Items on display are representative of what was once in a typical hotel kitchen. *Philip Varney*

WHEN YOU GO

The second route is for back roads–loving ghost town enthusiasts. Get off Interstate 90 at either the Drummond exit, Exit 153 (from the east), or the Bearmouth exit, Exit 138 (from the west), and follow the frontage road to Bear Gulch Road (10 miles from Drummond or 5.5 miles from Bearmouth). This road, better with a high-clearance vehicle, proceeds through placer detritus on a road that, despite the narrow canyons and steep grades, is excellent in good weather. You'll pass historic mine workings and old cabins, because this is the route the Garnet pioneers took. At 6.6 miles, the route splits. A longer, easier one goes right, while the original goes up First Chance Gulch, the more narrow, steep, and historic choice—and the only way I've gone in. You'll be at the Garnet parking area in 3.1 miles from the beginning of First Chance Gulch.

In the Frisco Cemetery, Charles K. Odell's epitaph reads: "Farewell my wife and my children all / From thee a father Christ doth call / Mourn not for me it is in vain / To call me to your side again." *Philip Varney*

UTAH

CHAPTER **7**

tah's history is far different from that of the other states in this book. In the others, settlers were encouraged, often even enticed, by the United States government to explore and tame the Western wilderness of the United States. When Brigham Young brought his Latter-day Saints to the Great Salt Lake in 1847, he was intentionally leaving the United States—a country that had repeatedly persecuted the Mormons—for Mexico, whose land it was. His mission was to create a utopian society, called Zion, away from outside interference, and Mexican influence there was minimal. In fact, when the Mormons came to Utah, that was the very beginning of non-Indian settlements in the Great Basin of North America, which had previously been called the Great Desert, a fundamentally uninhabitable area.

In Zion, the settlers created a provisional state in 1849 called Deseret, a word meaning "honeybee" in the Book of Mormon. Deseret was never recognized by the United States, which created the Utah Territory in 1850. In February 1851, Brigham Young was chosen as the first governor of the territory, which included all of Utah, most of Nevada, and small portions of Wyoming and Colorado. Two months later, the State of Deseret dissolved itself and Utah became the operant name. (The word "Deseret" remains, however, as the name of a Mormon church–affiliated newspaper, and it is symbolized by the hive of the honeybee on the Utah state emblem.)

In 1849, at the beginning of the California gold rush, Brigham Young told his followers that California was no place for Mormons, but he did encourage the mining of that which could be of practical use, such as iron and coal. As a result, silver towns such as Frisco had little Mormon influence, but the lovely farming town of Grafton did. They are the two best ghost towns in the state and are featured here.

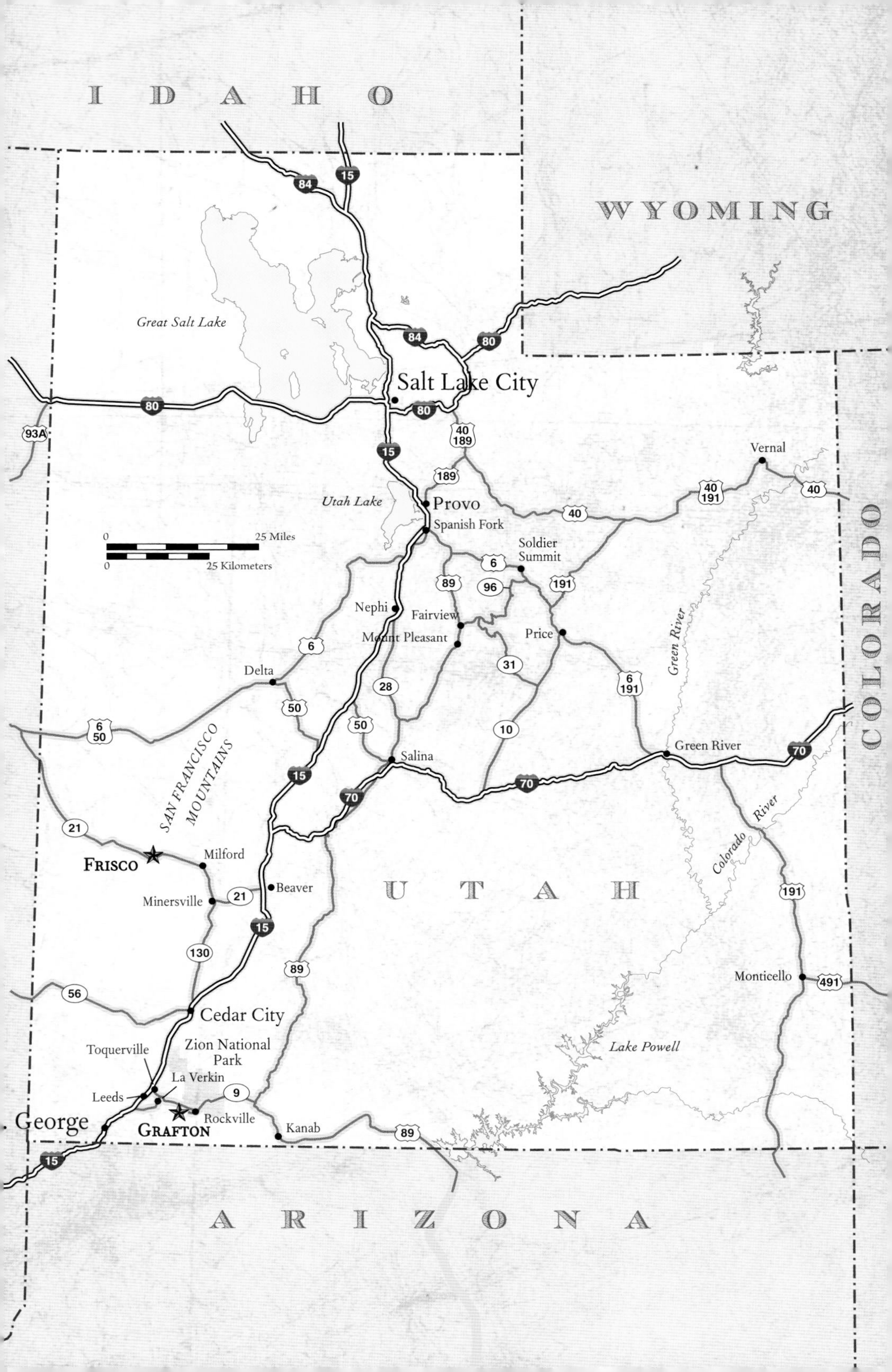
IDAHO
WYOMING
COLORADO
ARIZONA
UTAH
Great Salt Lake
Salt Lake City
Utah Lake
Provo
Spanish Fork
0
25 Miles
0
25 Kilometers
Soldier Summit
Vernal
Nephi
Fairview
Mount Pleasant
Price
Delta
Green River
Green River
SAN FRANCISCO MOUNTAINS
Salina
Colorado River
FRISCO
Milford
Beaver
Minersville
Monticello
Cedar City
Zion National Park
Toquerville
La Verkin
Leeds
Rockville
George
GRAFTON
Kanab
Lake Powell
15
84
80
93A
40 189
189
40
40 191
6
96
191
89
31
28
6 191
10
50
6 50
70
21
130
56
9
491

GRAFTON

Mormon Church President Brigham Young sent out pioneers in all directions from Salt Lake City to claim territory by settling in desirable locations for agriculture.

One crop he believed would help the Mormons achieve self-sufficiency was cotton. He sent settlers to what would become Santa Clara, a community west of present-day St. George, to plant cotton in 1854.

The experiment was a success, which caused Young to send out more settlers to do the same. The cotton-producing area of southern Utah became

Hollywood has used Grafton at least a half-dozen times because of its lovely buildings and remarkable backdrop of Zion National Park. On the left is the town's combination chapel and school; on the right is the home of Alonzo and Nancy Russell. *Philip Varney*

known as Dixie as a nod to the American South. One of Dixie's cotton settlements, begun in 1859, was Grafton, a community established on the south side of the Virgin River and reportedly named after Grafton, Massachusetts.

Two years later, the Civil War made cotton a more precious commodity outside of the Confederacy, and Young's foresight made him look like the prophet the Mormons believe he was.

But you can't eat cotton, and originally the Grafton farmers overplanted the crop in lieu of others and had trouble feeding their families. From then on, cotton production was secondary to corn and other staples, including fruit orchards.

A Virgin River flood in 1862 that destroyed their townsite caused Grafton residents to relocate a mile upstream, on higher ground, the present location of Grafton today. Despite frequent battles with the unpredictable river (irrigation ditches were constantly being destroyed, filled with sand, and rerouted), the small community of fewer than two hundred prospered.

The town was abandoned temporarily between 1866 and 1868 when hostilities with Ute Indians caused Brigham Young to order a consolidation of villages for mutual protection. During that time, Grafton residents tended their crops by day and retreated at night. At least three graves in the Grafton Cemetery attest to the dangers of that time. When hostilities ceased, Grafton returned to its for-

Grafton's John and Ellen Wood Residence is on private property. It and a neighboring barn have been stabilized by the owners. *Philip Varney*

mer life. In 1906, many Grafton farmers assisted in the digging of the Hurricane Canal, which promised a more reliable and predictable source of irrigation water for agriculture. They also were digging the grave of Grafton, because most families moved to the new area, about 20 miles downstream from the townsite. Grafton slowly became a ghost town. The last residents to leave were the son and daughter-in-law of Alonzo Russell, who lived in his father's house from 1917 until they moved to St. George in 1944.

But Grafton was not a completely forgotten ghost town. Hollywood has featured the picturesque spot several times, most notably in the 1969 film classic *Butch Cassidy and the Sundance Kid.*

The headstones of the Grafton Cemetery blend in seamlessly with their surroundings. Three of the dead in the graveyard died from a Navajo raid. *Philip Varney*

You will pass the Grafton Cemetery as you approach the townsite. I suggest that you first go to the townsite and, when you have explored it, return to the cemetery, because you will then be able to attach more importance to at least two graves.

As you enter Grafton, listed on the National Register of Historic Places, you'll pass a wooden barn and the 1877 brick home of John and Ellen Wood. Beyond that house is a parking area in front of one of the most picturesque ghost town sights in the American West: Grafton's 1886 adobe schoolhouse and the 1862 home of Alonzo and Nancy Russell, a two-story residence also made of adobe, both constructed with bricks crafted on the site. Behind the buildings rise the stunning red cliffs of Mount Kinesava in Zion National Park. Across an open area from the Russell home stands the 1879 hand-hewn wood cabin of Louisa Maria Foster Russell, who was Alonzo Russell's fourth wife and Nancy's sister. She and her nine children lived in the home directly across from Alonzo and his second wife, Nancy, who also bore nine children, but the last four died in infancy. (Alonzo's first wife had died in childbirth, and his third marriage ended in divorce after the birth of three children.)

The schoolhouse, which also served as a church meetinghouse and community center, has a foundation of lava rocks quarried nearby and features beams that were brought more than 75 miles to this site from Mount Trumbull in northern Arizona. The building last had students in 1919. The schoolhouse has been saved from deterioration and vandalism by a complete restoration, finished in 2000.

The Grafton Cemetery contains, according to a sign at the site, between seventy-four and eighty-four graves. In addition to the original settlers, that includes some Southern Paiutes, who assisted the early residents.

The cemetery features the graves of Alonzo Russell (1821–1910) and his second wife, Nancy (1825–1903), who is remembered on her epitaph as "a kind and affectionate wife, fond mother, and a friend to all." His fourth wife, Louisa, who was thirteen years younger than Nancy and who outlived Alonzo by seven years, is buried on the other side of Alonzo.

Other markers attest to the violence of frontier life. According to their headstones, Robert M. Berry, his wife Mary Isabelle, and his brother Joseph were killed on the same day in 1866 by Navajo raiders. They were not Grafton residents, nor were they killed there, but their bodies were brought to this cemetery because Grafton was the county seat at that time. They were attempting to reach their home in Glendale, a now-vanished town near present-day Colorado City, Arizona.

The year 1866 was particularly difficult for settlers: In less than four months, eleven people died in the small community because of diphtheria, scarlet fever, or murder by Indians. In addition, two young girls, Loretta Russell (age fourteen) and Elizabeth Woodbury (age thirteen), died in a "swing accident." This last seems unnecessarily tragic and makes one wonder about the circumstances; playing on a swing shouldn't, after all, be fatal.

WHEN YOU GO

From St. George, Utah, drive northeast on Interstate 15 for 9 miles to Exit 16, the turnoff to Highway 9 and to the town of Hurricane. Continue on Highway 9 for 27 miles to Rockville. In Rockville, a sign on the east side of town directs you to Grafton, 3.4 miles away. That sign is on Bridge Road, the only street in Rockville that crosses the Virgin River. Not long after traversing the 1924 steel-truss bridge, you'll turn west as Bridge Road becomes Grafton Road. The route turns to dirt in 2.2 miles from Rockville, which in dry weather should be fine for a passenger car. The left turnoff to the cemetery is 0.9 of a mile from the road's turning to dirt, and the townsite is 0.3 of a mile to the right, toward the river, beyond that turnoff.

FRISCO

Frisco is what the devoted ghost-towner seeks. It sits in the middle of nowhere, its population is zero, and it features several ruins, a forlorn cemetery, and five beehive charcoal kilns.

When rich horn silver was found at the foot of San Francisco Mountain in 1876, the mining camp of Frisco came into being adjacent to the aptly named Horn Silver Mine. Frisco, which had a peak population of about four thousand, was entirely dependent upon shipping for its existence. Everything, even water, had to be hauled to the remote desert town, originally by mule trains and later by the Utah Southern Railroad, which was extended to Frisco in 1880.

The scarcity of water apparently required alternative means to slake thirst, as more than twenty saloons operated in what became known as one of the wildest towns in the West. One wag described it as "Dodge City, Tombstone, Sodom, and Gomorrah all rolled into one." A tough-minded marshal hired from Pioche, Nevada, was brought in. He reportedly killed six outlaws on his first day on the job. That seemed to encourage other members of the criminal element to depart, and Frisco calmed down.

When day-shift workers reported for duty at the Horn Silver Mine in February 1885, they were told to stay outside because of tremors in the ground. The night shift came to the surface, and within minutes, a huge cave-in occurred with such a jolt that it was felt in Milford, almost 15 miles away. The timing

Frisco is an abandoned site, one that should be on every ghost town enthusiast's "must see" list. The town's ruins stand beyond these charcoal kilns. *Philip Varney*

was amazing: no one was even injured. The mine returned to production within the year but never at the level it had formerly achieved. Prior to the collapse, more than $60 million in silver, gold, copper, lead, and zinc had been extracted from the mines in less than ten years. In the next thirty years, it produced only $20 million more.

Frisco declined steadily after the cave-in, and, by the turn of the twentieth century, the town had a mere handful of businesses and a population of a few hundred. It was a complete ghost by the 1920s.

As you head west from Milford, you'll come to the Frisco Summit. It's easy to miss the ruins of Frisco 0.4 of a mile beyond the summit to your right, because they're back over your shoulder as the highway turns (see "When You Go," below). When you enter the townsite, at this writing you'll find large iron vats, a wooden building still under roof, numerous rock walls and foundations, mining debris such as an old boiler, and a water tank fallen on its side. That would suffice for most ghost town purists, but the best remnants are standing on a western hill: five stone beehive charcoal kilns, used to turn wood into charcoal to feed smelters (for a more detailed explanation, see the Bayhorse, Idaho, entry, page 143). Of the five kilns, three are virtually intact.

The cemetery, southwest of the townsite, features some excellent headstones. One, for Boswell W. Hopkins (1852–1879), has the Latin inscription from Horace, *Non Omnis Moriar* ("Not All of Me Shall Die"). Another, for Tommy James, who died at ten months in 1883, bears the epitaph "Whose all of life's a rosy ray / Blushed into dawn and passed away."

WHEN YOU GO

From Grafton, retrace your route to Exit 27 on Interstate 15. Drive northeast for 39 miles, just north of Cedar City, to Exit 62. Proceed north on Utah Highway 130 for 37 miles to Minersville. From there, take Utah Highway 21 for 13 miles to Milford. From the intersection of West Center Street and Main Street (where Highways 21 and 257 split) in Milford, go west on Highway 21 for 14.2 miles. There a turnoff heads north into the Frisco townsite. If you miss that turnoff, do not go beyond the historical marker on the right side of the highway, which is 0.2 of a mile past the turnoff. From there, you can backtrack to the turnoff and head in to the townsite, which will then be clearly visible. Or, heading west from that marker, you can take the southern of two roads (the northern is an old railroad bed that takes you to the locked gate of the Horn Silver Mine) for 0.5 of a mile to the fenced Frisco Cemetery.

The Gold Dust Saloon was built in 1908, when the metal of choice in Gold Point's mines was horn silver, not gold. *Philip Varney*

NEVADA

CHAPTER 8

When gold and then silver were found in the Utah Territory in the late 1850s, many California argonauts rushed to the area, especially when word of the Comstock Lode's enormous quantities of silver reached their state. The newcomers, however, did not want to be part of a territory that was governed by Mormon leader Brigham Young. People in the Carson Valley formed their own territorial government, which they had no right to do, because the recognized government resided in Salt Lake City.

Two years later, however, the US Congress effectively legitimized the Carson Valley dissidents, creating the Nevada Territory by essentially cutting the Utah Territory in half. (Nevada, incidentally, means "snow-covered" or "snow-capped," as in the Sierra Nevada mountain range.) The territory was then rushed into statehood in 1864, just before that year's national election, because Abraham Lincoln needed more votes for the Thirteenth Amendment (abolishing slavery) and because the Union needed another state to support Lincoln to demonstrate to the Confederacy that the Union was strong. Lincoln signed the statehood proclamation even though Nevada did not have the sixty thousand citizens required for statehood. Patriotism was running high in the new state, and citizens wanted to do what they could to support the United States. Hence their state motto: "All For Our Country."

The best ghost towns in Nevada demonstrate the wide variety of sites in the Mountain West. Belmont is a true ghost, off the power grid and with no gas station, no restaurants, and only one place for lodging. It also has some of the loveliest and most picturesque remnants in this book.

Goldfield is an excellent example of the boom-and-bust cycle of ghost towns. It features an enormous but vacant hotel, an elaborate but crumbling high school, and an imposing fortresslike courthouse. But Goldfield is barely hanging on, its railroad long gone and its future not promising.

Gold Point is the best surviving mining camp in the West that is not protected as a state park. It has about three dozen wood-frame structures, including false-front commercial buildings and miners' shacks. Most towns like it have long since disappeared because of neglect, weather, and vandalism. Gold Point is a rare treasure.

Rhyolite is a reminder that permanence is relative. Except for its glorious depot and its unusual bottle house, Rhyolite shows only photogenic skeletons of its glory days.

BELMONT

Silver discovered in late 1865 caused a rush to the Toquima Range, with eager prospectors abandoning their workings in Austin, Ione, and other Nevada camps. The town that formed near the diggings was called Belmont, apparently for another town elsewhere in the United States. This Belmont first appeared in print in Austin's newspaper, the *Reese River Reveille* in June 1866, and in February of the following year, the same newspaper crowed, "the excitement . . . appears to be unabated, and the influx of strangers continues, and many a traveler is lucky if he finds a place to lay his head under shelter."

Later that same year, Belmont's own *Silver Bend Reporter* featured advertisements for an array of enterprises, including mercantile stores, saloons, a drugstore, restaurants, hotels, a brewery, a bank, a dentist's office, and the Austin & Belmont Stage Company. A ten-stamp mill processed silver ore, and five sawmills provided lumber from the native pine and cedar.

Belmont took the seat of Nye County from Ione in 1867 when its population grew to two thousand citizens. It became the hub of commerce for a radius of almost 100 miles, but it remained isolated, with goods coming by rail from San Francisco and Sacramento to Austin, where they were then shipped

Belmont's former Nye County Courthouse was completed in 1876, at about the same time that the area's silver deposits depleted. Belmont lost the county seat in 1905 to Tonopah. *Philip Varney*

The second Monitor-Belmont Mill, often mistakenly called the Highbridge Mill, was built in 1915 using Combination Highbridge Mill bricks. Its stark walls are a favorite subject of photographers. *Philip Varney*

by pack train 90 miles to Belmont. East of town, the open flats and numerous springs brought farmers and ranchers to Monitor Valley.

The bonanza years, as was often the case in mining towns, were short. Only ten years after the discovery of silver, the mines began to play out, even as an elegant, brick, two-story courthouse was completed. Minor discoveries kept Belmont in business into the 1880s, but the population declined to less than two hundred, with many of those employed by Nye County for governing duties.

When Tonopah became a rising mining star beginning in 1900, Belmont's days were numbered. The county seat was moved to Tonopah in 1905, and Belmont lost its post office six years later. Sporadic mining and reworking of old mill tailings kept a few people in town, but by the end of World War I, Belmont was a ghost.

As you enter downtown Belmont from the south, you'll see a series of ruins on either side of the street. The brick remnant on your left was the First National Bank, followed by a series of slate walls of other businesses. On the opposite side once stood a restaurant, the two-story Cosmopolitan Saloon, a market, two hardware stores, a saloon, and a mercantile store. At the end of the street stands the former Combination Mining Company building, now a delightful bed-and-breakfast inn.

The Combination Highbridge Mill east of Belmont was dismantled in 1914 to erect the second Monitor-Belmont Mill. *Philip Varney*

The two-story brick courthouse, one of the more photographed historic buildings in Nevada, stands on a knoll west of town. Tours are offered occasionally. The interior, at this writing, is largely vacant, but the building is structurally sound, due to recent foundation, roof, and exterior refurbishment. Carved into one of the first-floor doorframes is the name of Charles Manson, who, with his "family," camped in nearby Monitor Valley in 1969, the same year as their ghastly Tate and LaBianca murders in Los Angeles. Ironically, along with his name and date, Manson also carved the peace symbol made famous in the 1960s.

On a hill east of downtown Belmont is a replica, dedicated in 2001, of the 1874 Catholic church that was moved in 1906 to the nearby pioneer town of Manhattan, where it still stands.

Belmont's most photogenic ruins lie east of town. From the town's flagpole, head east, where in 0.9 of a mile, you'll see the ruins and 90-foot brick stack of the 1867 Combination Highbridge Mill, a forty-stamp mill that was dismantled in 1914. Beyond those ruins 0.2 of a mile is a dirt road heading south. In 0.6 of a mile, you'll come to the dramatic brick skeleton of the second Monitor-Belmont Mill, which was constructed in 1915 using the brick from the Combination Highbridge Mill. This flotation mill, which failed after only two years of operation, is often incorrectly referred to as the Highbridge Mill; it even appears as such on the 1971 Belmont East USGS Topographic Map.

You passed the turnoff to the cemetery as you entered Belmont. Drive 0.9 of a mile south from Belmont's flagpole and turn east on Cemetery Road. Proceed south along the cemetery's western fence and turn east to the main gate.

The Belmont Cemetery is a well-kept, attractive graveyard, with pines and junipers nicely trimmed by volunteers. Several wooden picket fences surround headstones. As a reminder that some mistakes are indeed "carved in stone," there's an attractive I.O.O.F. marker for Andrew Anderson, who died in 1886 at age sixty-five. He was a native of "Sweeden."

WHEN YOU GO

From Tonopah, drive 5 miles east on US Highway 6 to the junction of Nevada Highway 376. Proceed north for 12.8 miles, where Nevada Secondary Route 882, the clearly marked road to Belmont, heads northeast. Belmont is 26.3 miles from that turnoff. The road is paved all the way to Belmont, but not beyond.

wo turn-of-the-twentieth-century towns, Goldfield and Tonopah, came to the rescue of Nevada. The boom-and-bust cycle of gold and silver mining had caused a severe depression in Nevada in the 1880s that lasted for almost twenty years and emptied the state of a third of its population. That bleak period ended when enormous gold strikes were found in 1900 in Tonopah. Two years later, a Shoshone prospector named Tom Fisherman showed Tonopah prospectors Billy Marsh and Harry Stimler gold-laden samples from hills more than 30 miles south of the booming town.

The Goldfield Hotel is an appropriate symbol of the boom-and-bust nature of mining towns. The massive 1908 brick structure at one time served lobster to wealthy patrons. Later it became a near-flophouse as Goldfield dried up. It is vacant at this writing. *Philip Varney*

In blowing alkali dust, Marsh and Stimler went to Fisherman's find and discovered gold on what would become known as Columbia Mountain. In honor of the weather, they called their initial claim the Sandstorm. They felt sure they had a true bonanza and made camp, calling the place Grandpa, because they felt this would be what all prospectors would seek: "the granddaddy of all gold fields."

Prospectors flocked to the area the following fall. By the end of 1903, Grandpa had been renamed Goldfield because early citizens felt the latter name would be much easier to promote to attract new investors. They were correct; the stampede was on, because the rumors were true and the deposits were deep. By August 1904, mines were producing a stunning $10,000 per day in gold.

With such a promising future, Goldfield rapidly became a city of permanence. Stone and brick edifices were erected. Residences had electricity and running water. The Tonopah & Goldfield Railroad was completed in 1905, assuring a reliable way to get the gold to market. On the return trip, it brought necessities—and luxuries—to a city that was approaching twenty thousand citizens. Eventually, Goldfield was served by four railroads.

By 1907, Goldfield was the largest city in Nevada, with four schools, many four- and five-story buildings, and two exchanges where mining stocks were madly bought and sold with every new rumor.

The Goldfield Hotel, completed in 1908, was the final jewel that exemplified the town's exalted status. It cost almost a $500,000 to build—a four-story brick beauty that featured 154 rooms, a lobby adorned in mahogany, and a dining room where patrons feasted on oysters and lobster.

The Nixon and Wingfield Bank, with its graceful diagonal northwest corner, was constructed in 1907 by two powerful Goldfield entrepreneurs, Senator George Nixon and George Wingfield. *Philip Varney*

And the gold just kept on coming. The output in 1909 was $9 million, double that of the previous year, and in 1910, the mines produced almost $11 million in gold, bettering the impressive showing of the previous year.

The very nature of mining towns, however, is that they are created only eventually to fail. In 1913, a flood from a desert monsoon damaged many structures in Goldfield, which were never rebuilt. Gold deposits faltered, and production never again approached the peak year of 1910. In 1918, when the one-hundred-stamp Consolidated Mill stopped production, Goldfield began to fade. A huge fire in 1923 destroyed fifty-three square blocks of the town, but Goldfield was moribund long before that. But what a glorious run it had been: In fifteen years of production, the Goldfield Mining District had yielded more than $80 million of the precious metal and was, for that period, the most important gold-producing district in the state. And Goldfield mining was not completely dead—a more modest output of about $400,000 per year lasted from 1927 until 1940.

If you are coming from Tonopah, you will notice, before you enter Goldfield, the huge step-up-the-hill foundations of the Goldfield Consolidated Mines Company mill on the side of Columbia Mountain.

As the highway takes a bend to the east entering downtown Goldfield, you can see, on your right, the 1908 West Crook Avenue School, which now serves as the town's library.

Goldfield High School, built in 1907, badly needs preserving and restoring, but the costs to the private owners are daunting. *Philip Varney*

The highway into town becomes Crook Avenue, and at the northeast corner of Crook and Columbia Street is the town's landmark building: the Goldfield Hotel. It operated into the 1940s, going from the most elegant hotel found between Chicago and San Francisco in Goldfield's heyday to almost a flophouse during the lean times. Several people with grandiose plans have sunk thousands upon thousands of dollars into the hotel, but at this writing it is closed to the public.

Two blocks east of the hotel, on the northeast corner of Crook and Euclid Avenues, stands the Esmeralda County Courthouse. The stone block fortresslike building opened in 1908, and its main attraction is the second floor's district courtroom, which is elegantly appointed with dark wood and gold trim. Despite its decline in population, Goldfield has remained the county seat almost by default, because no other town in the county rivals even its reduced size. (Esmeralda County is one of the least-populated counties in the contiguous United States.)

A kitchen sink in a Goldfield miner's cabin has dusty utilitarian dishes ready for a washing that never came. *Philip Varney*

The Firehouse Museum, on the southeast corner of Crook and Euclid, features a fire truck, an ambulance, antique fire equipment, and other memorabilia in the former Goldfield Fire Station No. 1.

On the southeast corner of Columbia and Ramsey Avenues is the handsome, three-story, cut-stone Nixon and Wingfield Block, built in 1907. It served as the headquarters of the Goldfield Consolidated Mines Company and features a graceful, curving northwest corner where its entrance stands on the diagonal.

The dining area of the same cabin shows the mean circumstances in which many Goldfield miners lived.
Philip Varney

On the northwest corner of Ramsey and Euclid Avenues is the photogenic Goldfield High School, erected in 1907. During Goldfield's short bonanza years, it served four hundred students annually. It was condemned in the 1940s. Esmeralda County currently has no high school. Students are bused to Tonopah, the seat of Nye County.

The cemetery is west of town. Take US Highway 95 toward Tonopah, where a sign will direct you to the graveyard, which will be visible to the west, not long after the highway turns from west to north.

The Goldfield Cemetery is made up of many sections, including Sacred Heart (Catholic), Knights of Pythias, Elks Rest, Odd Fellows, and Masons. To the southwest of the main cemetery is a section for the Goldfield Pioneers. These were graves disinterred and moved from downtown to this location in 1908, when the Las Vegas & Tonopah Railroad needed the land for its depot. A sign at the Pioneer Cemetery mentions that those who had the grim job of relocating the graves were known as "official ghouls."

WHEN YOU GO

oldfield is 36 miles south of Tonopah on US Highway 95.

GOLD POINT

The town now known as Gold Point had its name changed several times depending upon what was being mined there. Originally, when lime deposits were found in 1868, the small community that grew near the deposits was called Lime Point. Silver was discovered in the 1880s, but the silver was thoroughly embedded in surrounding rock, making it unprofitable to mine. Discoveries in Tonopah and Goldfield at the turn of the twentieth century, however, brought renewed interest in the surrounding hills.

As a result of this more intense examination, significant amounts of silver were found at Lime Point in 1905, followed by a bonanza of high-grade horn silver in 1908. As miners descended upon the site, the camp became known as Hornsilver. Eventually, it became a town featuring more than two hundred wood-frame buildings with the usual stores, thirteen saloons, and a post office. The town's growth was hampered somewhat by never having a railroad; the nearest station was at Ralston, 15 miles east.

Gold Point's false-front buildings are the kind that, if not protected, will disappear into the desert. These have survived in part because of the present owner, Coleen Garland. *Philip Varney*

Gold was discovered in 1927 within the Great Western silver mine, and by the 1930s, when more gold was being mined than silver, Hornsilver became Gold Point. But when World War II began, the federal government closed mines of nonstrategic metals. Gold Point became a ghost, but not before more than $1 million in gold and silver had been extricated from its mines.

As mentioned in this chapter's introduction, Gold Point is this book's finest example of an early mining camp that is not part of a state park. Most camps like it have long since disappeared. But Gold Point contains more than three dozen buildings, most of them tiny miners' quarters, along with some rudimentary commercial structures. For this preservation, we can thank many former residents and volunteers, but special gratitude goes to two people: Ora Mae Wiley, who moved to Gold Point in 1930 and watched over the town until her death, at age eighty-three, in 1980; and Herb Robbins, who started buying Gold Point buildings in 1980 and is still there at this writing, carefully shoring up and restoring his properties.

On the west side of town are photogenic false-front, wood-frame buildings, including Mitchell's Mercantile, the Expiration Mercantile, and the Turf Saloon and Grill, all dating from about 1908. A block south of those buildings is the picturesque 1908 Gold Dust Saloon and a series of miners' residences. One block east is the post office—which closed in 1967—along with some carefully restored miners' cabins (occasionally available for lodging) and the attractive Hornsilver Townsite and Telephone Building, now a saloon. Many mining artifacts and an eclectic array of fire engines placed throughout the town add to the charm of Gold Point.

WHEN YOU GO

From Goldfield, head south on US Highway 95 for 13.5 miles to Lida Junction. Turn southwest on Nevada Highway 266 and drive 7 miles to Nevada Highway 774, the road to Gold Point, which is just beyond a state historical marker. Gold Point is 7.2 miles southwest of that marker.

RHYOLITE

Frank "Shorty" Harris (1856–1934) was one of Death Valley's most color-ful characters. He was a charmer, a braggart, a drunk, and a man with a knack for finding mineral wealth in one of Earth's most desolate places. He also, unfortunately, had a knack for boasting endlessly about his strikes, ensuring that the riches ended up in the hands of others who rushed to his dis-coveries while Shorty drank to his newfound wealth. His memory is etched in Death Valley at Harrisburg, named for him; at Ballarat, where he was the sole resident before his death; and at a spot just north of the Eagle Borax Works, where Shorty is buried, at his request, next to his friend Jimmy Dayton, who had been buried there for more than thirty years before Harris's death.

Shorty's most dramatic discovery was made in 1904, when he and fellow prospector Ernest "Ed" Cross found gold at what they would call the Bullfrog claim because the first piece of rock had a greenish tint and was about the size of a bullfrog. Shorty crowed to his buddies that the find was a "crackerjack" and added, "The district is going to be the banner camp of Nevada!" The two went to have their ore assayed in Goldfield. Harris, in a drunken celebration of their find, apparently sold his half for a mere $1,000, which he immediately squandered. Cross held on and did much better, eventually selling his claim for a reported $125,000. He used the money to buy a large ranch in Escondido, near San Diego. Harris was out of the picture and continued prospecting in Death Valley for his next big strike, which never came.

The real jackpot was located a couple of miles north of the Bullfrog claim, and the strike at the Montgomery Shoshone Mine made E. A. "Bob" Mont-gomery Death Valley's first mining millionaire. The town that formed nearby was called Rhyolite in honor of the silica-laden volcanic rock found in the area.

By 1908, the Bullfrog Mining District was a true bonanza. In addition to Rhyolite were the satellite communities of Bullfrog, Gold Center, and Beatty. Population estimates of Rhyolite vary widely, from four thousand to double that number. The town could boast of all the modern conveniences, including elec-tricity, telephones, and abundant running water, which was piped from springs at the source of the Amargosa River, one of the world's longest underground rivers. Rhyolite featured a stock exchange, a board of trade, the Miners' Union Hospital, an ice plant, stores and hotels, the First Presbyterian and St. Mary's Catholic churches, the Arcade Opera House, the highly popular Alaska Glacier Ice Cream Parlor, and three public swimming pools.

Three railroads eventually served Rhyolite: the Las Vegas & Tonopah, the

This mercantile in Rhyolite was built in 1906 of rudimentary materials. It is east of Golden Street, where the town's more elaborate places of business stood. *Philip Varney*

Tonopah & Tidewater, and the Bullfrog & Goldfield. Even as all these refinements were blossoming in Rhyolite, most of the mines in the Bullfrog District were quickly tapping out. The big exception was the Montgomery Shoshone, which was the mainstay of Rhyolite, producing more than $1 million in bullion in just three years. Virtually none of the stockholders, however, received a penny in dividends because of stock speculation and questionable financial dealings. Stock in the Montgomery Shoshone went from twenty-three dollars per share to a mere three dollars even as the mine was making money. By 1911, with the ore playing out, the stock value plummeted to four cents per share.

The financial demise of the Montgomery Shoshone and its subsequent closing was the final blow for the once-booming Bullfrog District. The last train left Rhyolite in 1913, the same year the post office closed. The Nevada–California Power Company took down its power lines in 1916.

As you drive up the wide dirt road from Nevada Highway 374, you will pass a turnoff 0.7 of a mile from the highway. That will take you to the townsite of Bullfrog, where there is one modern building and one ruin. It is also the route to the Bullfrog-Rhyolite Cemetery. More on that later.

The remnants of Rhyolite begin 0.7 of a mile north of the turnoff to Bullfrog.

The Bureau of Land Management manages the site, and occasionally volunteer caretakers oversee the site. If volunteers are there, they will likely be near the 1906 Tom T. Kelly Bottle House, which was erected in less than six months principally using Adolphus Busch beer bottles—about thirty thousand of them. A walking tour handout may be available at the restored bottle house, which is surrounded by elaborate fencing worthy of a high-security prison. Next door is a former general store.

The main drag through town is Golden Street, where Rhyolite's most dramatic ruins reside, including the roofless, concrete, two-story schoolhouse, built in 1909 and the last major building to be erected in Rhyolite. When it was finished, the town was already beginning to empty, and the school was never at capacity.

North of the schoolhouse are the foundations and walls of once-three-story Overbury Block. Across the street is the lonely façade of the 1906 Porter Brothers

The John S. Cook Bank remains one of Nevada's most photographed ruins. It has appeared in everything from music videos to Hollywood movies. *Philip Varney*

Store. H. D. and L. D. Porter brought merchandise across Death Valley from their store in Randsburg, California, and purchased a lot in Rhyolite for the then-outrageous sum of $1,200. Their store became the favorite of Rhyolite's citizens, a place where, according to the Porter brothers, "We handle all good things except whiskey."

Up the street stands the 1908 John S. Cook Bank, one of the most photographed ghost town structures in the American West. The jagged ruins have appeared in calendars, television shows, and movies. In its prime, the three-story building featured Italian marble floors, Honduran mahogany woodwork, and stained-glass windows. The bank occupied the first floor, brokerage offices filled the upper floors, and the Rhyolite post office was in the basement.

Farther up Golden Street is the most imposing—and, at $130,000, the most expensive—edifice in town, the 1909 Las Vegas & Tonopah Railroad Depot. At this writing, a chainlink fence unceremoniously surrounds it, but there are hopes of eventually restoring it and opening it to the public.

If you follow a dirt road southeast from the depot, you will come around to two substantial buildings, a 1907 rock residence that perhaps was a brothel and, nearby, the 1907 concrete jail. As you walk or drive the back streets of town, you'll see many signs pointing out what once stood at various locations.

As mentioned earlier, you passed the turnoff to the cemetery on your way into town. Return to that junction, turn west, and head 0.3 of a mile to the old railroad grade heading south. Down that grade 0.6 of a mile is the turnoff east to the Bullfrog-Rhyolite Cemetery, where you will find about two dozen graves marked by a fence, a headstone, or both. The most unusual marker is a carefully carved cylindrical stone for James C. Clayton (1866–1905), who died just as Rhyolite began to boom.

WHEN YOU GO

R hyolite is 3.9 miles southwest of Beatty on Nevada Highway 374. Beatty is 68 miles southeast of the Lida Junction turnoff to Gold Point, 83 miles southeast of Goldfield and 116 miles northwest of Las Vegas.

Claim markers stand as silent sentinels to the scarce remnants and faint traces of the White Hills that remain on the rock-strewn desert plain. *Kerrick James*

ARIZONA

CHAPTER 9

Arizona harbors amazing geographic and geologic diversity. Stark, sterile desert plains; towering snowcapped mountains; deep red rock canyons where thundering waterfalls spill into turquoise blue pools; and alpine meadows bordered by forests of towering pines are contained within Arizona's man-made borders.

For centuries, Arizona's gorgeous landscapes have served as the backdrop for a cavalcade of human history. Almost a thousand years before Columbus, ancestral Puebloans (Anasazi) built cities that were engineering marvels among the towering canyon walls. The Hohokam built villages in the fertile soils of the desert river valleys and transformed the surrounding arid lands into a paradise with the masterful development of an irrigation system that lasted long after their settlements had disappeared from the horizon.

The Spanish Conquistadors came in search of gold and souls, and built villages of their own, often on the ruins of those who came before. With the passing of years, time reclaimed many of these.

American traders, explorers, and adventurers seeking a faster route to the gold fields of California rolled west and discovered unexpected treasures along the way. Fueled by fortunes of pelts and gold, silver and empires of cattle, timber, and the railroad, a new wave of towns and cities sprang from the rugged lands.

Isolated desert valleys became modern, bustling metropolises in mere weeks and became as empty as the ancestral Puebloan canyon homes just as quickly. More than a few of these towns are immortalized as legends forever associated with larger-than-life figures: Tombstone and Wyatt Earp, Fairbank and Jeff Milton.

Over time, the dusty desert winds reclaimed the valleys, and time swept the names of once prosperous communities from the map, as well as memory. Soon only picturesque ruins and legends remained.

A few villages that survived as shadows of their former glory found new life in new booms. Others clung to life as an outpost in a harsh land for a new breed of adventurers: motorists. In time, many of these villages succumbed to the changing times, and another sea of ghost towns dotted the desert plains.

Today the ruins framed by majestic scenery and breathtaking landscapes stand in silent testimony to the power of hopes and dreams. The towns that cling to life with dust swirling along once busy thoroughfares and those that remain as faint traces in the desert sands lure visitors with scenic wonder, tangible links to a colorful history, or the prospect of lost treasure.

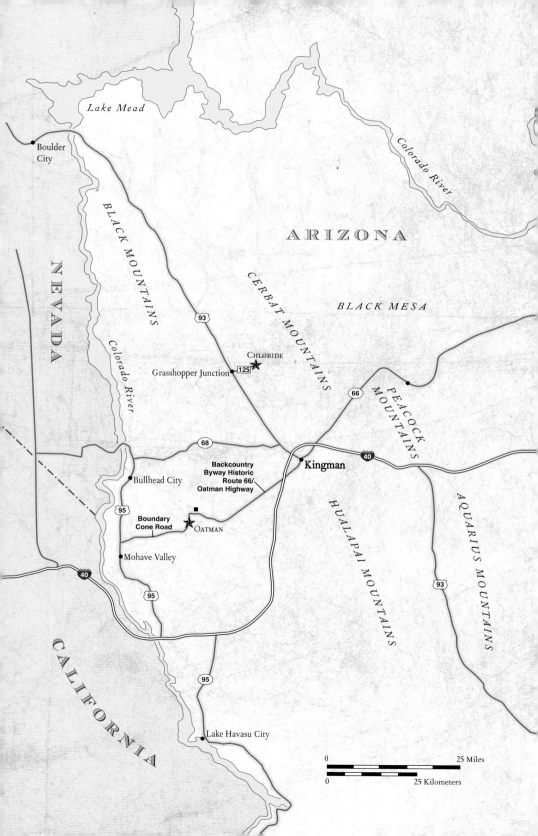

Lake Mead

Boulder
City

Colorado River

NEVADA

BLACK MOUNTAINS

Colorado River

ARIZONA

CERBAT MOUNTAINS

BLACK MESA

93

CHLORIDE
125

Grasshopper Junction

66

PEACOCK MOUNTAINS

68

Kingman

40

Bullhead City

Backcountry
Byway Historic
Route 66/
Oatman Highway

95

Boundary
Cone Road

OATMAN

HUALAPAI MOUNTAINS

AQUARIUS MOUNTAINS

Mohave Valley

40

95

93

95

CALIFORNIA

95

Lake Havasu City

0   25 Miles

0   25 Kilometers

Beautiful blooms are in the foreground of the hills of Oatman.
Kerrick James

atman, located on the western flanks of the rocky Black Mountains above the Colorado River, is a relative newcomer in northwest Arizona. The town dates to 1902, when Ben Taddock made a significant gold discovery in the shadow of the looming Elephant's Tooth, a distinctive rock formation. With the sale of the property to the Vivian Mining Company in 1903, development of the mines and the mining camp began to proceed at a rapid clip.

Within two years, the community, then called Vivian, consisted of a very active chamber of commerce, two banks, several stores, and a population of more than one hundred. The community was renamed Oatman in 1909, a year after the next big gold deposit discovery and the subsequent formation of the Tom Reed Mining Company.

The speculation is that the name change was in honor of Olive Oatman, a young girl who was kidnapped near Gila Bend in 1851, traded to Mojave Indians, and was subsequently rescued near the townsite. A secondary story added the element of a son; it stemmed from a man who prospected in the area and claimed to be the son of Olive.

The town began to boom thanks to the opening of the United Eastern Mine in 1913 and the National Old Trails Highway in 1914, predecessor to Route 66. Estimates place the population at several thousand during its peak in the early 1930s.

The Oatman Hotel is the largest adobe structure in Mohave County. It is also where Clark Gable and Carole Lombard spent their first night as husband and wife. *Kerrick James*

Over the years, the town has had several brushes with fame. In 1914 Barney Oldfield and Louis Chevrolet, as well as a half dozen other drivers, roared through town in the last of the Desert Classic Cactus Derby races. In the late 1930s, Clark Gable and Carole Lombard, after marrying in Kingman, spent an evening at the Oatman Hotel, the largest adobe structure still standing in Mohave County.

Elephant's Tooth is the name of the unique rock formation that towers over Oatman. *Kerrick James*

The distinctive rock formations and the picturesque Black Mountains that loom above the town, as well as its scattering of weathered buildings, present the illusion that Oatman is a movie set, which is exactly what it was on several occasions. The most notable movies filmed here were *Foxfire* in 1955, *Edge of Eternity* in 1959, *How the West Was Won* in 1962, and *Roadhouse* 66 in 1984.

Oatman's population dwindled to less than fifty in the 1950s as a result of mine closures in 1942 and the realignment of Route 66 in 1953, but the old town has experienced a new boom with resurging interest in Route 66. Although only a handful of original buildings remain, the recreated storefronts, narrow main street (Route 66) crowded with traffic, free-roaming burros, and throngs of tourists provide a fair picture of what it was like in its heyday.

WHEN YOU GO

Oatman is located 32 miles southwest of Kingman on the original Route 66 alignment. The last 9 miles are the steepest grades and sharpest curves found anywhere on Route 66. For vehicles such as trucks with trailers and motor homes, access is via Boundary Cone Road that connects Oatman with Arizona Highway 95.

CHLORIDE

hloride dates to the discovery of a deposit of silver chloride in the early 1860s and is the oldest surviving mining camp in the Cerbat Mountains. Tucked into the foothills of those towering mountains, it is also one of the most scenic mining camps.

The remote location initially required ore to be shipped overland to Hardyville, where it then traveled down the Colorado River by steamboat to the Gulf of Mexico and Pacific Ocean, and then to England by ship for milling. This extended travel route, as well as persistent problems with the native Hualapai, limited the development of the mines until a mill was built in Mineral Park in the 1870s and the railroad line to nearby Kingman was completed in 1883.

For the next fifteen years, Chloride enjoyed a steady growth of both residents and businesses. In 1898, this prosperity led the Arizona & Utah Railroad to build a spur line across the Sacramento Valley to connect with the Santa Fe Railway main line at McConnico, which is south of Kingman.

A gas station ringed by train tracks survives on the main street of Chloride. *Kerrick James*

Great fanfare and celebration commemorated the arrival of the railroad in Chloride. Incorporation followed this stellar event, which made Chloride the first community in Mohave County to do so.

Throughout the first decades of the new century, Chloride entered a period of stability, even though the railroad proved to be a short-lived venture. The town's population was near two thousand at its peak.

The mine closures that started in the 1930s escalated into the 1940s and culminated with the closure of the Tennessee-Schuylkill, one of the deepest mines in Arizona, in 1947. The highway was rerouted around the town during the same time period. The town quickly settled into a quiet, sleepy existence.

Today, Chloride is a delightful village of more than one hundred retirees, crusty desert rats, and eccentric artists. Two pleasant cafés, several gift shops, a combination market/museum/gift shop, a post office, and a bar constitute the business district. The best way to enjoy Chloride is on foot. Stroll the dusty streets and give your imagination free rein.

There are vestiges from the glory days on almost every street. Among the most picturesque are the railroad depot, a 1930s service station, a motel complex that now houses a café and art gallery, the jail, the post office, and the Tennessee Saloon. A quiet cemetery is located south of town and offers wonderful views of the valley.

WHEN YOU GO

From Kingman, drive 18 miles north on US Highway 93. Turn northeast on County Road 125 and drive 4 miles. The first four-way stop will be the central business district of Chloride.

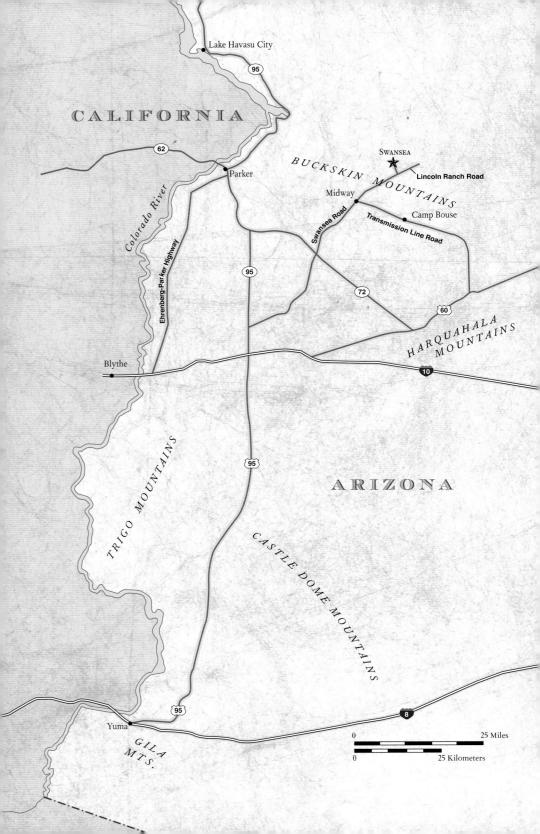

The history of the Southwest's frontier era is confusing—with many twists, turns, and contradictory documentation. The story of Swansea is a perfect example.

Sketchy information indicates prospectors were working rich deposits of silver in the area of the Buckskin Mountains as early as 1862. Only the purest and most profitable ores were extracted because of the elaborate shipping procedures necessary: The ore had to be transported 30 miles west to the Colorado River. It was then shipped downriver to the Gulf of California below Yuma, and then all the way across the Pacific Ocean and around Cape Horn to Wales.

Although the community in Wales was the inspiration for this desert community's name, it was not the result of this association. George Mitchell, a metallurgist for the Consolidated Gold and Copper Mining Company who hailed from Swansea, bestowed the name.

Prospecting and mining continued sporadically until 1886 when the profitable silver bodies were exhausted. The prospectors moved on to new finds and left behind vast deposits of copper, a mineral not profitable enough to work in such a remote location. In 1904, the Signal Group purchased a large number of the old mining claims and planned to develop them for the copper reserves. There were even plans for a small community, Signal, to be built on site.

Preservation efforts in Swansea include keeping roofs on the remaining structures to ensure future generations can experience the haunting beauty of a desert ghost town. **Kerrick James**

As was so often the case, the company lacked adequate capital for such an endeavor and began to search for investors in 1906. Enter George Mitchell who made the 21-mile trip from Bouse, the closest town with a railroad, with T. J. Carrigan of Consolidated Gold and Copper Mining Company.

The arduous journey was a failure for the Signal Group because the new investors decided to purchase the claims outright rather than partner for development. However, the trip was a resounding success for Mitchell, who was awarded a lucrative position with the new company.

Vestiges from a time when the streets of Swansea teemed with activity (the town even supported an automobile dealership) are scattered among the desert brush. *Kerrick James*

By the early spring of 1909, the new mining camp had a large enough population to warrant a post office. Through the following decade, the fortunes of the mines fluctuated with the price of copper, but the town continued to grow.

Swansea's era of isolation ended with completion of a spur line from Bouse. Its residents enjoyed a wide array of amenities, including a theater, a

The substantial ruins of the smelter in Swansea produce unusual blends of shadows and color in the desert sun. *Kerrick James*

realty company, several general merchandise stores, a barber, a physician, saloons, restaurants, an automobile dealership, and a newspaper, *Swansea Times.*

After the Consolidated Gold and Copper Mining Company went bankrupt in 1912, various other companies worked the mine and operated the mill until 1922. The town began a rapid slide into abandonment with the closure of the mines.

Today Swansea is a true ghost town with a population of zero. However, unlike most ghost towns in the Southwest, the Bureau of Land Management maintains the remnants of the community in an arrested state of decay.

WHEN YOU GO

From Parker, drive south 12 miles on US Highway 95. At the junction of US Highway 95 and Arizona Highway 72, continue on Highway 72 for 14 miles to Bouse. In Bouse, follow Main Street to Rayder Avenue, which will turn into Swansea Road, and turn left. Bear left at the first fork in the road shortly after leaving Bouse. Three landmarks ensure you are on the right road: the crossing of the Central Arizona Project Canal; the interpretive kiosk at Midway, a former water stop for the railroad spur from Bouse to Swansea; and a four-way stop where you will turn left. The road is sandy and rocky. Four-wheel drive is not a necessity, but ground clearance is a definite must. Fall, winter, and early spring are the best months to visit.

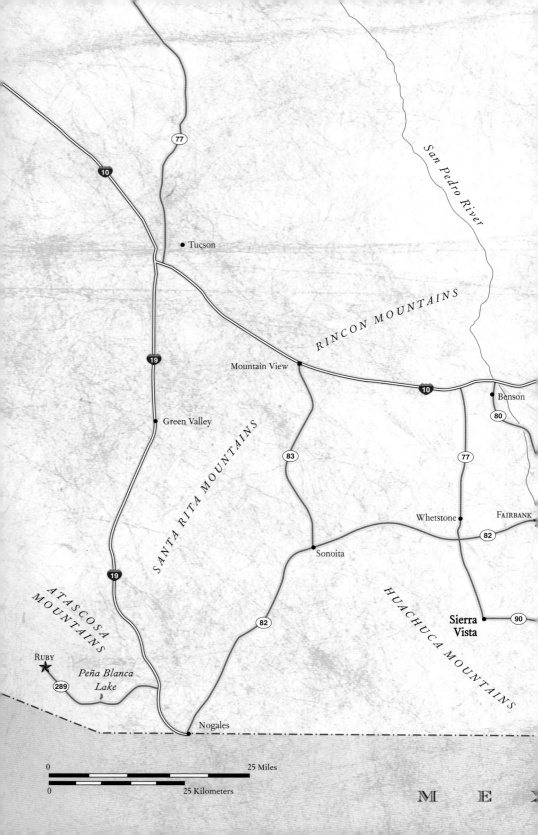

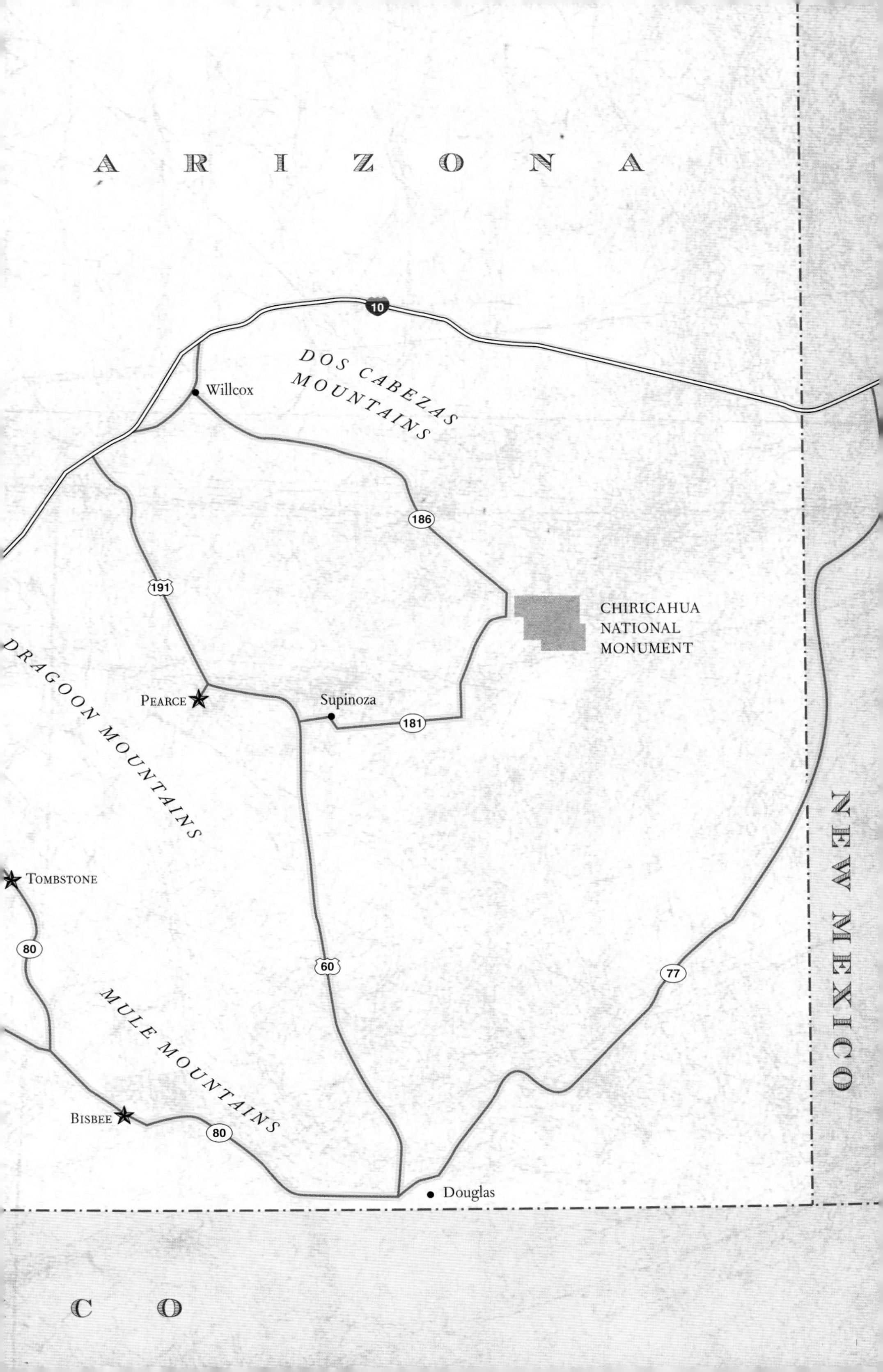

A R I Z O N A

DOS CABEZAS
MOUNTAINS

10

Willcox

186

191

CHIRICAHUA
NATIONAL
MONUMENT

DRAGOON MOUNTAINS

PEARCE

Supinoza

181

TOMBSTONE

80

60

77

MULE MOUNTAINS

BISBEE

80

Douglas

NEW MEXICO

C O

RUBY

Extracting the deposits of silver ore found in the shadow of Montana Peak dates to the mid-eighteenth century. However, a full century passed before work began in earnest after Herman Ehrenberg and Charles Poston discovered a rich ore body in 1854.

For more than thirty years, miners and prospectors worked their claims and were continuously lured on by new discoveries that always seemed to be one step away from the mother lode. The little community established to meet the miners' needs reflected the hardscrabble life of the men and was little more than a ragged collection of shacks and tents known as Montana Camp.

The mercantile was established in 1888, and the big strike finally came three years later, and the boom was on. As a testimony of the camp's promising future, Julius Andrews, the owner of the mercantile, made an application for a post office and named the community Ruby in homage to his wife, Lillie B. Ruby, in 1909.

The town prospered with the expansion of the mines. At its peak, the primary mine employed three hundred men. The school's enrollment was almost 150 students during the same time period. In 1941, the Eagle Pitcher Company, operator of the mine, suspended operations. The town was a true ghost with a population of zero within five years.

Tragically, a series of brutal murders gave Ruby notoriety rather than silver or gold. The camp's remote location and proximity to the Mexican border, less than 20 miles away, made the area a haven for bandits and parties of renegade Apaches.

An abundance of water made Ruby unique among Arizona mining camps. Today it is an oasis for Arizona ghost town hunters. *Kerrick James*

The scattered remnants of everyday life in Ruby have a haunting, surreal air that suggests the town is suspended between abandonment and collapse. *Kerrick James*

In February 1920, a Mexican ranch hand stopped at the store and found Alex and John Frazier, two brothers who were the storekeeper and postmaster, shot dead. The safe was open and empty, and the town's only phone was ripped from the wall. Months of investigation failed to identify the murderer or murderers.

In August 1921, the store was robbed again and its new owners, Frank and Myrtle Pearson, were killed, and

A vintage truck silently guards the ghostly secrets and colorful history of Ruby. *Kerrick James*

Elizabeth Purcell, a sister-in-law, was wounded. The local area was stirred to vigilante levels because the robbers used their gun to remove Myrtle's five gold teeth as she lay dying.

A posse set out to look for the outlaws, and for the first time in Arizona history, an airplane aided in the search to track the bandits. The trail was lost at the Mexican border, but in April 1922, a bartender in Sonora notified authorities about a man trying to sell gold teeth. Manuel Martinez and Placido Silvas were arrested and quickly extradited to Arizona.

After a short trial, Martinez received the death penalty and Silvas was sentenced to life in prison, but during transport to the state prison at Florence, they overpowered two deputies and caused the car to overturn. One outlaw's freedom lasted six days, and on August 10, 1923, the execution of Martinez proceeded on schedule.

Today, Ruby is preserved thanks to the Arizona State Parks. A heritage grant allows for a caretaker and limited maintenance of structures. This state of preservation, as well as the beautiful mountain scenery, makes a trip to Ruby one not quickly forgotten.

WHEN YOU GO

From Nogales, drive 8.5 miles north on I-19 to Exit 12. Continue west for 24.2 miles, passing by Peña Blanca Lake along the way. Four-wheel drive is not needed, but ground clearance is important.

PEARCE

Jimmie Pearce and his wife were hardworking, frugal folks who dreamed of owning a ranch. After working at mines in a number of camps, they arrived in Tombstone during its boom. Jimmie worked in the mines, and his wife worked in a boarding house. Both ventures proved lucrative, and soon they had saved enough for their ranch.

With their sons, who longed to be cowboys, the Pearces purchased a spread in the wide Sulphur Springs Valley in the shadow of the Dragoon Mountains. Legend has it that in 1894,

The looming clouds of a summer storm and deep blue desert skies serve as a backdrop for the haunting emptiness of downtown Pearce, Arizona. *Kerrick James*

Jimmie was resting on a hilltop, surveying his corner of paradise, when a piece of quartz caught his miner-trained eye. Jimmie was literally sitting on a gold mine. He named his new find the Commonwealth and staked out five claims, one for each member of the family.

For a while, the mine was a family affair, although the enterprise attracted numerous offers from eager buyers. John Brockman, a banker from Silver City,

As seen from the front porch of the Pearce general store/museum to the distant horizon, little indicates that this was once a prosperous and bustling town. *Kerrick James*

The Pearce post office opened its doors in March 1896, but a diminishing population since the 1930s makes its continuous existence tenuous at best. *Kerrick James*

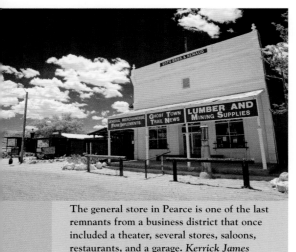

The general store in Pearce is one of the last remnants from a business district that once included a theater, several stores, saloons, restaurants, and a garage. *Kerrick James*

New Mexico, finally persuaded Jimmie to sell the mine for the sum of $250,000 and agreed that Jimmie's wife would have exclusive rights to operate the only boarding house at the mine.

The town of Pearce appeared on the valley floor below the mine almost overnight. Because Tombstone was in decline, a few businessmen there dismantled their businesses and shipped them over the Dragoon Mountains to take advantage of the new opportunities. Another Pearce legend is that the first rooming house was built of lumber from the Tombstone jail.

By 1919, a rail line from Wilcox linked Pearce to the outside world, and the business district boasted a theater and several restaurants, saloons, hotels, and garages. The community also supported a school, mill, and several churches.

The hard times of the Great Depression and the decline of profitable and accessible ores led to the mine's closure in the early 1930s. Pearce was a ghost town within weeks of the mine's closure.

Today the town's business district consists of a combination general store and museum that is randomly open, and a post office. The remainder of the town consists of a wide array of ruins and scattered relics.

WHEN YOU GO

From Wilcox, drive 28 miles south on US Highway 191. Pearce is about 0.5 of a mile off the highway on a well-marked road.

ombstone is a larger-than-life legend built on one shootout near the O.K. Corral in the fall of 1881. A fascinating and colorful history is lost in the shadow of this event.

Ed Schieffelin had been a prospector since his teenage years, when he searched for riches in Oregon with his father. By the time he arrived in the Arizona Territory during the mid-1870s, he was well seasoned and quite capable of reading formations.

Legend is that when he informed his traveling companions, a cavalry troop riding for Fort Huachuca from California, that he planned to explore the San Pedro Valley, which was the very heart of the Apache defenses, they told him that all he would find was his tombstone. When Schieffelin staked two claims near the San Pedro River on the richest silver deposits found in the territory at the time, he named them Tombstone and Graveyard.

Watervale became the moniker for the mining camp built around Graveyard, but the mine proved to be a pocket rather than a vein. Schieffelin was not concerned about the setback, as he had discovered an even richer deposit nearby. The camp residents soon relocated to the new find that became the legendary Toughnut Mine.

Tombstone's historic district blends authentic historic re-creation and movie-set romanticism built on the legend of the O.K. Corral. The Bird Cage Theatre dates to 1881 and initially served as a saloon, burlesque theater, brothel, and dance hall. *Kerrick James*

The historic Boot Hill cemetery in Tombstone is famous for its headstones with quirky epitaphs set against cinematic western backgrounds. *Kerrick James*

Small crosses planted among piles of stones that reflect the frontier era in countless mining camps are scattered among the fanciful headstones in the Tombstone cemetery. *Kerrick James*

The first cabin in Tombstone was built in April 1879. The town was incorporated by 1881. By the end of 1882, the town boasted five churches, a school with 250 students, two banks, a newspaper, and 150 establishments licensed to dispense alcohol.

Fire swept through the town in June 1881 and in May 1882 and left little more than smoking ruins. The community rebuilt and continued to grow and prosper until the population neared ten thousand.

Wyatt Earp, Doc Holliday, and Johnny Ringo are the names most often associated with Tombstone. Few realize the community was home to a surprising number of individuals who carved a niche in history but lived lives of relative obscurity.

Dr. George Goodfellow became world famous as "the gunshot doctor," an indication of Tombstone's wildness. His work and published papers on the topic contributed greatly to advances in trauma treatment. He was also the first doctor to arrive in Sonora, Mexico, after the great earthquake of 1887. Mexican President Porfirio Diaz awarded him a special medal for his efforts.

Tombstone's glory days were surprisingly quite short in number. In 1886, fires destroyed the pumps at the Contention and Grand Central mines and caused them to flood. The Panic of 1893, a tumultuous economic event that included the collapse of silver prices, was another blow.

In spite of what the signage that welcomes visitors to Tombstone may indicate, the town was relatively peaceful, at least in comparison to other frontier-era mining towns. *Kerrick James*

Efforts to reopen the flooded mines began in 1901, but the pumps failed in 1909. In 1914, Phelps Dodge purchased most of the mining equipment at a receiver's sale. By 1929, Tombstone was well on its way to being a ghost town when Bisbee became the county seat.

Today, Tombstone consists of numerous historic buildings with an overlay of modern, tourist-oriented reconstruction, including wooden-board sidewalks in the historic district.

WHEN YOU GO

Drive south 14 miles on the dirt road leaving Pearce through the minor ghost town of Courtland to Gleeson, another minor ghost. From Gleeson, drive 16 miles west to Tombstone.

FAIRBANK

airbank—named for N. K. Fairbank, a Chicago merchant and primary investor in the Grand Central Mining Company in Tombstone—is one of those special places where the mists of time have obscured a rich and colorful past. Spanish explorers discovered a Santa Cruz village on the banks of the San Pedro River in 1692. Almost two hundred years later, its location near a dependable supply of fresh water and lush grass made it an important stop for stages running between Tucson and Tombstone. The arrival of the railroad in 1881 added to the community's importance because it was a primary stop on the rail line connecting Guaymas, Mexico, with Benson, which made it a key staging area for passenger and freight companies that served the area.

By 1900, almost twenty years after its initial settlement, the town had a population of nearly one hundred, a Wells Fargo office, a meat market, a general store, several saloons, and a steam-powered mill. With the exception of occasional floods, life in Fairbank was relatively quiet until February of that year.

Bill Stiles and Bert Alvord were Cochise County deputies but also leaders of an outlaw band that frustrated many citizens because they seemed immune from capture. Jeff Milton was an ex–Texas Ranger with a well-deserved reputation for integrity and proficiency with a gun. He was employed as a guard for the railroad and would ride the routes and protect the strongbox. The other players in the drama that cold winter evening were Three Fingered Jack Dunlop, a

The ruins of Fairbank are the centerpiece of the San Pedro Riparian National Conservation Area and thus are spared further degradation by vandals. *Kerrick James*

cruel, vicious outlaw; Bravo Juan Yaos, another outlaw wanted on both sides of the border; and two brothers whose names have been lost to history.

As an officer of the law, Bill Stiles discovered Jeff Milton would not be guarding the strongbox on the targeted train. What he could not know was that at the last minute, a sick employee prompted the company to substitute Milton on the run north from Mexico.

When the train arrived in Fairbank, the outlaw band posed as drunken cowboys and mingled with the crowd. Milton stood in the open door of the baggage car as freight was loaded and unloaded. The outlaws recognized Milton and opened fire. The former Texas lawman was struck twice in the arm. Unable to return fire for fear of hitting innocent bystanders, Milton stumbled back in to the baggage car and retrieved a shotgun with his good arm.

The bandits charged the train car after they saw Milton fall. The return fire from Milton was deadly; Three Fingered Jack was struck in the chest and Yaos was shot in the back as the outlaws turned to flee.

As the outlaws riddled the car with gunfire, Milton tossed the keys for the strongbox into the night and made a tourniquet from his shirt. The frustrated outlaws had no choice but to flee with armed men from Fairbank on their heels.

Three Fingered Jack was abandoned by his comrades and discovered in the brush 9 miles from Fairbank. He lived long enough to make a confession and name his accomplices, who later received lengthy prison terms. Milton recovered, although he never regained full use of his arm. He was hired by the US Immigration Service and patrolled the border. Milton died in 1947 at the age of eighty-five.

Fairbank slipped into obscurity with the closing of the mines in Tombstone and the mills at Contention City along with the subsequent abandonment of the railroad. An Arizona guide from 1940 noted a population of fifty. The school closed in 1944, and the post office that originally opened in 1883 closed in 1973.

In 1987, the town received a last-minute reprieve from total abandonment when the Bureau of Land Management incorporated it into the San Pedro Riparian National Conservation Area. Efforts to retain what remained of the adobe commercial building that housed the post office were successful. The schoolhouse that was built in 1920 to replace the original destroyed by fire is now a visitors' center and museum.

WHEN YOU GO

From Tombstone, drive north for 3 miles on Arizona Highway 80. Turn west on Arizona Highway 82 and drive 7 miles.

BISBEE

The Mule Mountains, located 15 miles south of Tombstone, are a relatively small but rugged range running about 30 miles in length from north to south and 15 miles wide. The craggy canyons and numerous springs made them a veritable fortress for the Apaches who launched raids into the Sulphur Springs Valley and the San Pedro Valley.

A steep-sided canyon pass filled with numerous springs and seeps is located at the southern end of the mountains. Mexican traders named the canyon Puerto de las Mulas, which translates to Mule Pass. In 1877, Jack Dunn, a government tracker, was trailing an Apache war party through this canyon with the Sixth Cavalry, Company C, when he stumbled upon a rocky ledge with a wide quartz vein laced with gold. Developing the claim was not a priority or feasible for Dunn because the area was essentially a war zone at the time.

By 1880, opportunists from throughout the world had come to the area due to word of mouth, the company mining Dunn's find had expanded at an astounding rate, and a town quickly had spread into the surrounding canyons.

By 1881, the Copper Queen Mine was running twenty-four hours a day and was one of the most productive mines in the country. Enter Dr. James Douglas, a world-famous geologist and metallurgist who was commissioned by a group of eastern speculators to evaluate properties at Jerome and throughout Arizona. He was so impressed with what he found in the Mule Mountains that he convinced the speculators, owners of Phelps Dodge, an import/export business, to expand into mining.

Bisbee was named after Judge DeWitt Bisbee, a principal financial backer of the mine. The town that sprang up around the Copper Queen was a typical

Long afternoon shadows cloak Bisbee, a venerable mining camp that bridges the past and present with seamless beauty. *Kerrick James*

rowdy mining camp. The town's namesake never visited the canyon-bound community.

By the late 1880s, Bisbee was well on the way to becoming a modern city with two distinct districts. Tombstone Canyon became the main thoroughfare, and Brewery Gulch was in an intersecting canyon and known as the shady side of town. Al Sieber, legendary scout for General George Crook during the Apache campaigns, opened

From near the mouth of the Mule Pass Tunnel, Bisbee appears suspended in time, with only traffic to break the illusion. *Kerrick James*

the first business in the gulch when he dug a hole in the side of the canyon and established a brewery; hence, the canyon's name.

By the turn of the century, Bisbee was a substantial community built of cut stone and brick with a reputation for being a cultured, modern city with the latest amenities and marvels. Residents enjoyed the luxury of electricity, phone service, a streetcar line, and even a stock exchange.

With the closure of the mines in 1974, the queen of the mining camps became a frontier-era time capsule as a quiet village nestled in gorgeous scenery. The narrow canyons squeezed Bisbee into a series of terraces cut into the canyon walls, which made it a treasure box of unique historic architecture and a photographer's paradise.

The prosperity derived from being the county seat and one of the world's richest mineral sites is still evident throughout Bisbee—from the stately Copper Queen Hotel, built in 1902, and the old stock exchange, which is now a bar, to the museum in the Copper Queen Mining offices built in 1897 and the Victorian-styled houses and miner's cabins that appear to march up the steep canyon sides.

Bisbee is not a true ghost town in the sense that more than five thousand people still call it home, but its current population is a far cry from its peak of twenty thousand residents. But for the ghost town hunter or fan of western history, Bisbee should be on the top-ten list of must-see places in Arizona.

WHEN YOU GO

isbee is located 19 miles southeast of Tombstone on Arizona Highway 80.

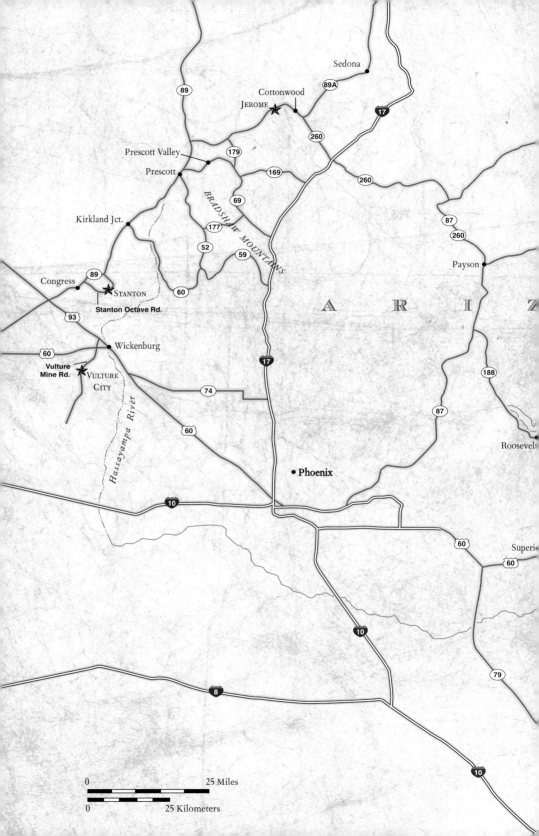

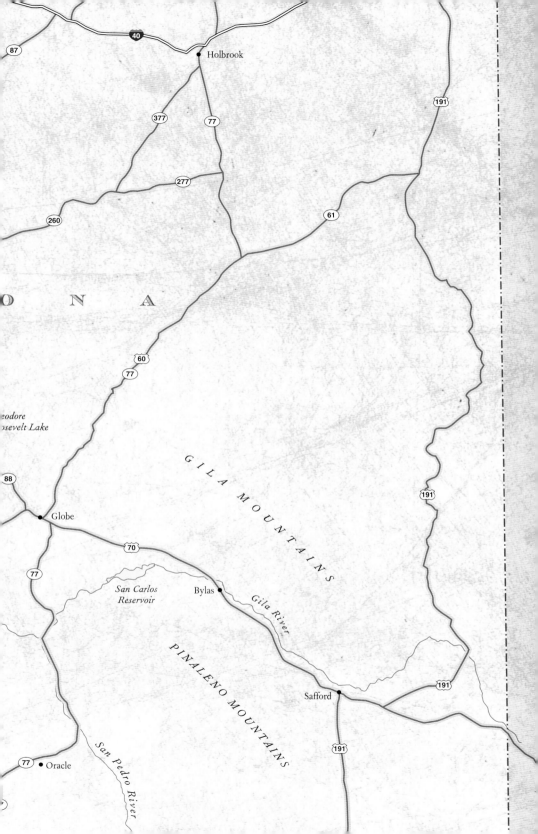

By the early 1860s, a number of American prospecting parties had followed the Hassayampa River into the Bradshaw Mountains to find the next big mining vein and had various degrees of success. However, none of these discoveries came close to the one made by Henry Wickenburg in 1863.

Rather than incur the astronomical cost of shipping and milling raw ore, Wickenburg wisely chose to sell it from his Vulture Mine for fifteen dollars per ton and let the buyer worry about those formalities. Because water was a scarce commodity at the Vulture Mine, a town named for

An effort to present Vulture City, a privately owned ghost town, in a state of preservation gives an eerie impression. *Kerrick James*

the Austrian-born discoverer of the mine mushroomed along the banks of the Hassayampa River about 11 miles to the north. Wickenburg had a supportive infrastructure, including a mill, to alleviate the water problem at the mine.

After the Central Arizona Mining Company acquired controlling interest in the property, a six-inch pipeline that ran for 12 miles from the Hassayampa to the Vulture Mine was constructed. A state-of-the-art eighty-stamp mill was also constructed on site to eliminate the expense of hauling raw ore.

Before the new mill was built, the tailings of waste and low-grade ores were deemed too cost-prohibitive to process. After the mill was completed, the tailings became an asset. The original assay office was built from local stone and waste from the mine, but it, along with most of the other original buildings at the site, were later processed for their gold content.

In the fall of 1880, the small camp of hardworking miners and their families who were living in the shadow of the mine's head frame and mill received official recognition as Vulture City with the opening of a post office. The population had risen to almost five hundred by 1889, and the Vulture Mine was the largest gold producer in the territory.

Many original buildings in Vulture City were recycled after the discovery that the stones with which they were constructed were valuable ore. *Kerrick James*

Vulture City's downward turn began in 1891. The vein in the main shaft abruptly ended at a fault. Failure to relocate the vein prompted the mine's sale, but the new owners had better luck. Shortly after the vein was reconnected, another fault resulted in costly exploratory work. This process continued for a short period until the frustrated and broke owners sold the mine. The new owners fared even worse. They literally brought the roof down when they tried to expand operations.

Legend is that the "jail tree" did double duty, with outlaws chained to its stout trunk and as a lynching post for miscreants in Wickenburg and Vulture City. *Kerrick James*

The post office closed in April 1897 and served as the postmortem for the once-prosperous enterprise. There were numerous attempts to reopen the mine over the years that included sinking a new shaft in 1931 and aborted efforts to rework the tailings in late 1941.

Vulture City has survived into the modern era relatively intact as the result of private ownership. Sadly, the man who discovered the mine did not fare as well.

In 1865, Henry Wickenburg sold four-fifths interest in the mine for $85,000. Wickenburg received $25,000 before a question pertaining to his title to the property led to lawsuits and a lengthy court battle. When the dust cleared, the initial $25,000 was all Wickenburg received, and he spent most of the money on attorneys in a vain effort to recover the rest.

The hapless prospector spent the next forty years in a similar pattern. In 1905, after a flood devastated his small farm near Wickenburg, he committed suicide in the shade of a mesquite tree on the banks of the Hassayampa River.

WHEN YOU GO

Drive 2.5 miles west of Wickenburg on US Highway 60. Turn south on Vulture Mine Road, and continue for 12 miles. The current owners allow self-guided tours, but there are no set hours and there is an admission charge to visit the property.

Pauline Weaver was a renowned trapper and guide in the Arizona Territory during the early 1860s. When he announced he would be leading a party up the Hassayampa River into the Bradshaw Mountains in 1862, a long list of men wanted to accompany Weaver on his trek. At the top of a granite knoll, a landmark later listed as Rich Hill, Weaver and his party discovered the richest placer discovery in Arizona history. According to legend, the Weaver party, with little more than knives and the toes of their boots, had gathered almost $100,000 in loose nuggets and flakes within a few weeks. This discovery sparked a gold rush into the Arizona Territory.

Several years after the discovery, Charles Stanton established a store and station on the stage line that ran through the valley in the shadow of Rich Hill. The two businesses, in conjunction with a half interest in the nearby Leviathan Mine (an investment acquired through questionable means while he was working in the assay office at the Vulture Mine), provided a comfortable living. Stanton, however, suffered from an extreme case of greed.

As the collection of tents and shacks gave way to houses and stores, the area became a real community known as Antelope Station. As the community grew, Stanton's holdings increased proportionally to the number of competitors who disappeared or who sold their properties to Stanton for a bargain price. Many people in the area suspected that his ostentatious lifestyle was funded

A surprising number of vestiges from Stanton's past have survived into the modern era, presenting the illusion that this town is a forlorn time capsule. *Kerrick James*

The old mining camp at Stanton has been given a new lease on life as an RV park bearing modern amenities for the prospectors of the twenty-first century. *Kerrick James*

Weathered boots on a weathered wall in Stanton reflect the tough qualities of the pioneers who first wrestled gold from the surrounding mountains. *Kerrick James*

with more than his many business interests provided.

By 1875, the camp dwarfed its neighbors, Octave and Weaver, and Stanton had the town renamed after him with the approval of a post office application. The town of Stanton was at its peak fifteen years later with several hundred residents, a five-stamp mill, and a thriving business district. However, one resident who was conspicuously absent from town in 1890 was Charles Stanton.

Frontier justice was often swift in Arizona's territorial years, and few bad men lived long enough to enjoy their ill-gotten gains. On November 13, 1886, Pedro Lucero, a member of a gang used by Stanton for nefarious activities, corrected an insult to his sister in Stanton's store with two well-placed shots.

Today, visitors to Stanton, Octave, and Weaver will find little more than ruins, mine tailings, and scenery. A prospectors' club has transformed much of the mining camp into an RV park for those who seek desert solitude or wish to try their hand at prospecting. Many of the surviving structures are being refurbished to provide services for campers, including a library and game room.

WHEN YOU GO

From Wickenburg, drive 6 miles north on US Highway 93 and follow US Highway 89 north. Three miles north of Congress turn right (east) onto the Stanton–Octave Road and continue approximately 7 miles. Road conditions depend on the time between the most recent rain and grading. The best time for visiting or exploring is in late fall, early spring, or winter.

JEROME

Nevada had the Comstock Lode, Colorado had Cripple Creek, and Arizona had Jerome. After the mines permanently closed in 1953, Jerome remained perched precariously on the slopes of Cleopatra Hill and featured million-dollar views of the Verde Valley, which became known as the "billion-dollar copper camp."

The amazing story of this ghost city begins in 1583 with the explorations of Antonio de Espejo, the discovery of silver in the hills above the valley, and evidence of previous mining. Explorations followed in 1598 and 1604, but the remote location and rugged terrain prevented development of the finds for more than two centuries.

In the early 1870s, Al Sieber, a scout for the US Army, began working claims on Cleopatra Hill in an area that bore evidence of the older exploratory work. By 1882, mining on the cone-shaped treasure trove that was Cleopatra Hill was in full swing, and a roughshod mining camp was quickly spreading along the flanks of the hill.

John and Ed O'Dougherty and John Boyd, with financial backing by Territorial Governor Fred Tritle and Bill Murray, all worked the claim. The partners needed money to further develop the property and turned to Eugene Jerome, a wealthy New York financier whose cousin was Jennie Jerome, mother to Winston Churchill.

The new venture, the United Verde Mine, extracted $80,000 in silver in 1883, also the year the mining camp officially became known as Jerome thanks to the establishment of a post office. The cost of transporting ore to the rail line

Jerome, spread along the slopes of Cleopatra Hill in the Mingus Mountains, is Arizona's "ghost city" with a population in the hundreds. *Kerrick James*

at Ashfork was twenty dollars per ton and prohibitive to all but the richest deposits. This fact, along with the exhaustion of the primary ore body in 1884, led to an almost complete abandonment of the fledgling mining camp.

In 1888, William Clark, a Montana mining magnate, purchased the United Verde Mine and several other properties. In 1892, Clark financed the construction of a narrow-gauge rail line from Jerome Junction, now Chino Valley, to Jerome, and the boom was on.

Fires swept through Jerome in 1897, 1898, and 1899, but after every fire, the community was rebuilt on a larger and grander scale with hotels such as the Montana, a plush two hundred–room palace that offered amenities equal to any hotel in New York or San Francisco; a state-of-the-art hospital; blocks of offices and stores; and mansions. In 1920, a highway carved from the slopes of Mingus Mountain linked Prescott

Years of underground blasting shook many buildings in Jerome, including the jail, from their foundations, which resulted in their slide down the steep mountain slopes. *Kerrick James*

and Jerome to further fuel the town's growth and led to the development of businesses that provided modern services to travelers.

When the stock market crashed in 1929, the population had reached its pinnacle of fifteen thousand. The collapse of copper prices led to the closure of the United Verde Mine. It reopened in 1935, but the town's downturn had begun.

The mines closed again in 1950, and abandonment of the city began in earnest. By the mid-1960s, the population had dwindled to a few hundred citizens residing among the ruins that framed spectacular views. However, the ghost city of Jerome began to experience a rebirth of sorts as eclectic artists and tourists discovered these stunning vistas, picturesque ruins, and the delightful territorial-style architecture of the remaining buildings.

Like most frontier-era mining camps, Jerome had its share of colorful characters, but what makes this one of the most fascinating ghost towns in the

The rising sun's golden glow gives the towering Jerome ruins a sense of timelessness. *Kerrick James*

Southwest today is the unique character of the town. First, Jerome offers panoramic views of the Verde River Valley and the red rock country of Sedona to the north. Also, large portions of the town have become a slide zone for remaining buildings, the result of extensive underground blasting in the 1920s that loosened buildings from their foundations. As an example, the jail has slid more than 200 feet down the steep slope of Cleopatra Hill.

Adding to the allure is Jerome's wide array of attractions. The beautiful Douglas Mansion is the centerpiece of the Jerome State Historic Park. The home of the chief surgeon for the Little Daisy Mine is a delightful bed and breakfast. Dining options run the gamut from simple fare in original cafés— including the English Kitchen that dates to 1899 and is the oldest continuously operated restaurant in Arizona—to five-star meals in a former speakeasy.

The rendering of iron into artistic fencing painted with the patina of age adds a classical feeling to Jerome's ruins and cemetery. *Kerrick James*

WHEN YOU GO

From Prescott, go north on Arizona Highway 89 for 5 miles and take a right onto Arizona Highway 89A. Follow Highway 89A for 29 miles to Jerome.

Since 1887, the towering Hoyle House, built at a reputed cost of forty thousand dollars, has been a landmark in White Oaks. *Kerrick James*

NEW MEXICO

10

The ghosts of northern New Mexico are a diverse lot. They run the gamut from remnants of lost civilizations to once prosperous gold mining towns nestled against snow-covered peaks and Spanish colonial outposts in desert sands, with numerous quaint, centuries-old villages; pueblos that are even older; and colonial settlements that are now cities in between. Add some of the most beautiful and breathtaking scenery in the country and hunting for ghost towns easily becomes a series of unforgettable vacations. It is also an excellent introduction to discover why New Mexico is known as the Land of Enchantment.

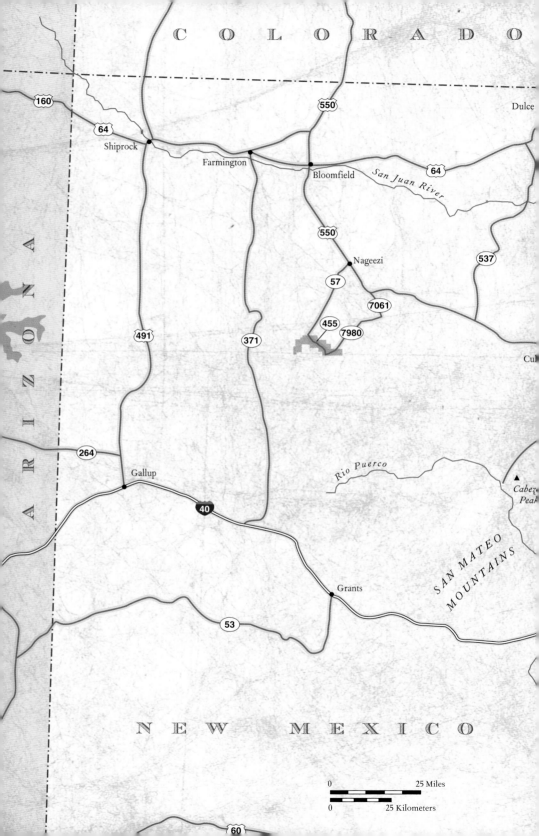

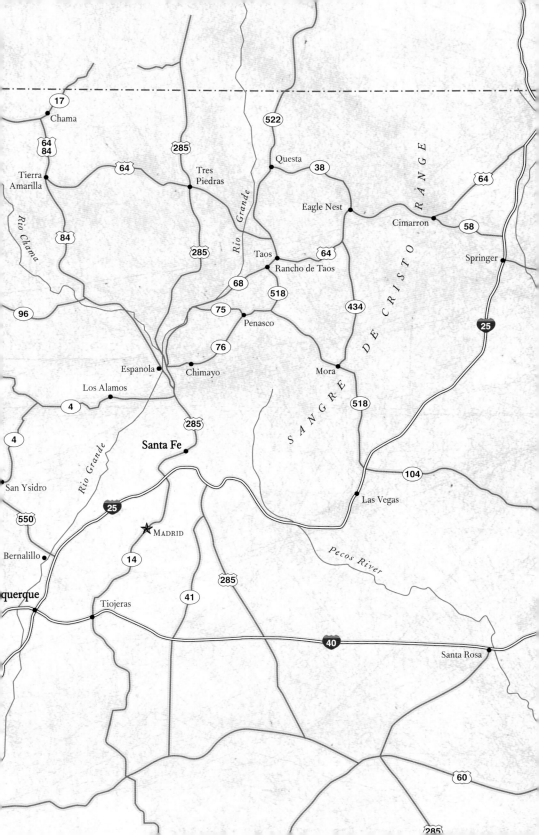

MADRID

adrid, as with many frontier-era communities in the Southwest, is rooted in the discovery of gold and silver. However, Madrid, which locals pronounce with the emphasis on the first syllable, is unusual because the mines that kept it alive through 1954 never produced one ounce of the precious yellow metal or silver.

Native Americans mined turquoise about 5 miles north of Madrid for centuries before the Spanish began mining silver and lead with the help of Native American slave labor at Los Cerrillos. After the Pueblo Revolt of 1680, the mining of silver and lead from these hills was sporadic until the mid-1850s, when mining began in earnest.

Several large discoveries sparked a boom in the 1870s, and the camp, renamed Cerrillos, soon became an orderly settlement of laid-out streets and established districts. Ample amounts of coal used for heat during the cold winter months were among the many luxuries enjoyed by Cerrillos residents.

The construction of a southern transcontinental rail line reached Cerrillos in 1880, and the coalfields to the south became a commodity almost as valuable as gold or silver. A rare geologic anomaly resulted in anthracite, and the presence of bituminous coal in the area added to the field's importance.

In addition to developing the coal mines, the railroad also established Madrid by importing company houses from Kansas and reassembling them on site, and it built a spur line from Cerrillos. By 1900, the mines were running three shifts, and the town boasted a population of twenty-five hundred.

In 1906, the railroad leased the entire Madrid operation to the Colorado Fuel & Iron Company. This enterprise didn't last long after a major fire in one of the tunnels forced mining to stop completely. In an instant, the residents of Madrid faced community abandonment and no source of income.

The crisis passed quickly when the Hahn Coal Company in Albuquerque acquired the mines and town and initiated operations with the most modern

Madrid, New Mexico, stretches the definition of ghost town, as it is home to dozens of residents, a vital artist community, and numerous surviving structures. *Kerrick James*

The Old Boarding House Mercantile in Madrid exemplifies the historic coal-mining town's rebirth as an artist colony in recent years. *Kerrick James*

equipment and methods. Under the leadership of Superintendent Oscar Huber, the town blossomed from a sooty, dreary company town into a showplace. Flower boxes added color to bland row houses, the water supply became consistent, pavement alleviated the dust on the main street, miners and their families had access to the hospital for three dollars per month, and electricity provided to employees at no charge eliminated the danger of fire that had plagued the community for years. Organization of an employees' club provided a wide array of recreational opportunities, and the company paid for transportation when the town's baseball team was on the road.

All of these transformations paled in comparison to Huber's efforts to bring the community together during Christmas. The first holiday after the town was wired for electricity, Huber commissioned the construction of huge, lighted nativity figures as an illuminated Bethlehem on the hill above town.

The display grew larger every year until colorful biblical scenes covered both sides of the canyon and colorful lights shone brightly on most houses and businesses. Choral groups strategically placed throughout the town performed every evening during the week before Christmas. Visitors from as far away as Albuquerque made the pilgrimage to see the spectacle.

As natural gas replaced coal to heat homes and locomotives switched from steam to diesel, the demand for coal declined, and the mines curtailed production. In mid-1954, the mines closed. Within weeks, Madrid became a ghost town and home to four families.

In the mid-1970s, Oscar's son, Joe, decided to revive the town by offering the old houses for pennies on the dollar. The efforts were successful in the sense that today Madrid is a small art community with a café, museum, and colorful history.

WHEN YOU GO

Madrid is located 30 miles south of Santa Fe on New Mexico Highway 14.

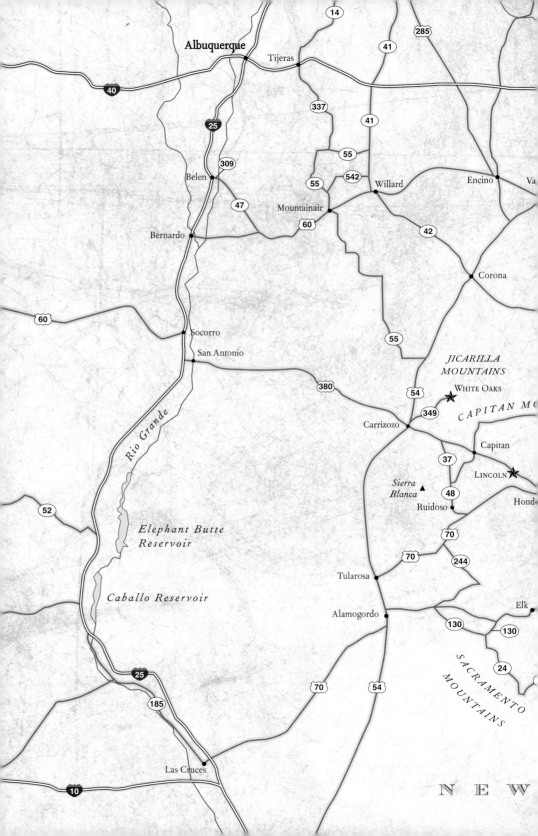

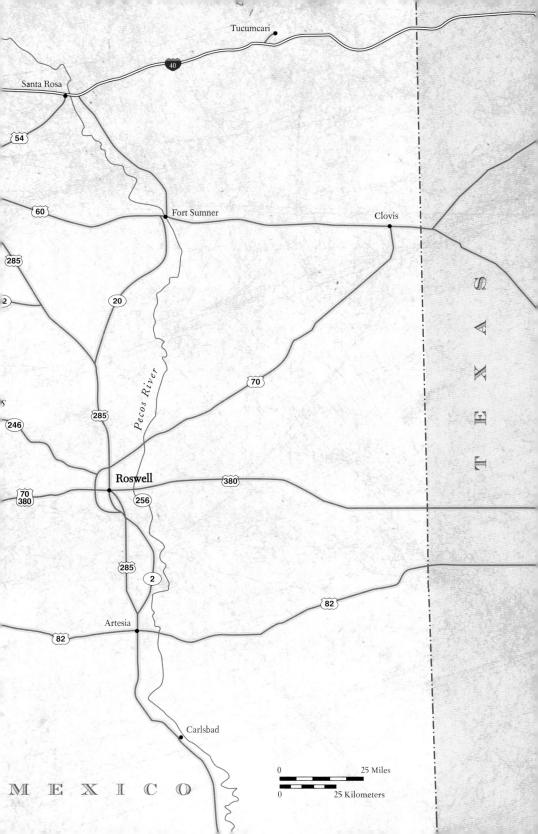

WHITE OAKS

The founding of White Oaks is the quintessential western mining camp story, at least according to legend. Four prospectors working their way through the Jicarilla Mountains in 1879 discovered a fabulously rich outcropping of gold ore in a quartz vein along the eastern slope of Baxter Mountain. One of the prospectors, a wanted fugitive, sold his share in the claim for a pony, a bottle of whiskey, and forty dollars when it appeared the vein was merely an anomaly. The others stuck it out, and the North Homestake Mine soon became one of the largest producers in the territory.

The 1893 Brown Store that once served as the jail in White Oaks gets a new lease on life thanks to an extensive renovation. *Kerrick James*

The school in White Oaks served its original purpose from 1895 to 1947. It was a community center in the years that followed the school's closure. *Kerrick James*

Whatever the origin of White Oaks may be, within three years a town had mushroomed in the shadow of Baxter Mountain, and miners pulled astounding loads of profitable ores from mines such as the Lady Godiva, Rip Van Winkle, and Boston Boy. As a historical footnote, the town's Old Abe Mine was reputedly the deepest dry shaft in the world at 1,375 feet.

Watson Hoyle, operations supervisor at the Old Abe, built an intricate Victorian-style residence that is still a source of pride for the old mining town. A beautiful brick schoolhouse on a hill above town, an opera house, a church, a bank, saloons, and a newspaper contributed to the establishment of the largest community in Lincoln County.

The number of stars on the flag in front of the old law offices in White Oaks provide a clue this photo was not taken in 1890. *Kerrick James*

A doorless safe in White Oaks fuels the imagination as to what role it played in the history of this colorful mining camp. *Kerrick James*

Celebrities associated with White Oaks include Billy the Kid; Susan McSween-Barber, the "Cattle Queen of New Mexico"; and Madame Varnish, proprietor of the local casino that dispensed other forms of entertainment. Perhaps the most notable was William McDonald, a local attorney who later served as the first governor of New Mexico.

Two blows struck the community in 1897: the depletion of primary gold deposits and the rerouting of a planned railroad. By the turn of the twentieth century, the town had settled into a state of slumber that persists to this day. A surprising number of original buildings are still here, and no visit to White Oaks is complete without a stop at the Cedarvale Cemetery.

WHEN YOU GO

From Carrizozo, drive north on US Highway 54 for 4 miles to New Mexico Highway 349. Continue on Highway 349 for 5 miles to White Oaks.

LINCOLN

Only Tombstone enjoys more notoriety in western history and lore than the ghost town of Lincoln, which is situated in the lovely Rio Bonito Valley. Lincoln, unlike Tombstone, is preserved in its entirety as a national historic landmark.

The origins of this charming community date to the mid-1850s, shortly after the Mexican-American War, when displaced Mexicans began farming in this valley and established the village of La Placita del Rio Bonito, which translates to "Little Village by the Pretty River." The centerpiece of the new village was a round, brick fortification to provide protection from Apache raiders.

With the establishment of Fort Stanton a few miles to the west in 1855, the valley entered an era of tranquility and prosperity. The next transitional milestone for the community was in 1869 when the territorial legislature approved

Lincoln, New Mexico, has been preserved in such an original state that Billy the Kid could still find his way around town if he were to return today. *Kerrick James*

Lincoln is a bona fide time capsule of frontier life in the New Mexico Territory. *Kerrick James*

The Torreon Tower dates to the 1850s and was built for defense against Apache warriors. It is one of the oldest structures in Lincoln. *Kerrick James*

the creation of Lincoln County and the town was renamed Lincoln and appointed as the county seat.

The feeling of utopia ended in 1878 after a five-day gun battle marked the culmination of the Lincoln County War, which established the town's violent reputation. Vestiges from that bloody period abound in Lincoln.

Juan Patron built Casa de Patron in the

The Tunstall-McSween Store in Lincoln is a true Old West throwback because much of the inventory dates to the time when Billy the Kid stood in this store. *Kerrick James*

mid-1860s. It served as his home and a store. Billy the Kid was held under house arrest at the Casa de Patron after he was convicted in Mesilla for killing Sheriff Bill Brady. The Montano Store next door has an extensive display on the town's history.

The Ellis Store also survives as a bed and breakfast. The store served as the headquarters for the Regulators, an armed gang formed to avenge the murder of John Tunstall. Billy the Kid was among the gang's members. More than a thousand items of original inventory at the Tunstall Store are still on display, and this also is the headquarters for the Lincoln State Monument.

Additional time capsules include the Lincoln County Courthouse, originally the Murphy-Dolan Store, from which Billy the Kid escaped in the spring of 1881; the 1921 adobe school, now an art gallery; and the Wortley Hotel, built in 1881.

There are no souvenir shops here, only a package of historic buildings that leave the town looking as it did during the tumultuous days of the Lincoln County War. A walking tour that begins at the Anderson-Freeman Visitors Center and Museum is the best way to experience this rare gem.

WHEN YOU GO

From Roswell, drive east for 47 miles on US Highway 70. At the junction of US 70 and US Highway 380, turn onto US 380 and continue 6 miles.

MONTICELLO, PLACITA, CHLORIDE, AND WINSTON

he towns of Winston and Chloride, and to a lesser degree Placita and Monticello, are among the rare survivors of the Black Range boom. These beautiful, forested, well-watered mountains and canyons were the home of the Apache who fought to maintain their hold until the early 1880s. Initially farming and ranching lured intrepid pioneers to attempt to gain control of the area. The promise of mineral riches was the motivation in later years.

The initial settlement of Placita began in the 1840s. It was situated along Alamosa Creek at the southern end of Monticello Canyon. The little village developed into a quiet little farming community in spite of sporadic raids by the Apache. American influences increased with each passing year and took root farther up the canyon with the establishment of Canada Alamosa in 1856 (renamed Monticello in 1881).

Monticello was in actuality a small square fortification for protection against raids. However, as with its neighbor to the south, the town settled into peaceful stability over time. Placita and Monticello maintain small populations and have active churches (the one in Monticello dates to 1908), but pictur-

Rusting relics of the modern era blend seamlessly with traces of the frontier era under cinematic western skies in Monticello. *Kerrick James*

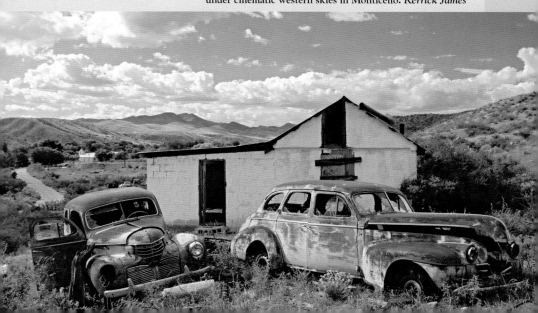

The ruins of the Works Projects Administration–built school in Monticello hint of better times in this forgotten mining town. *Kerrick James*

esque ruins, such as the 1930s-era, WPA-built school in Monticello, attest to better times. Both towns are located along the Geronimo Trail Scenic Byway.

Chloride and Winston are a few miles to the west and located on the west side of the Sierra Cuchillo Mountains. These towns were the antithesis of their neighbors in that they were rowdy mining camps. Their needs fueled the prosperity of Monticello and Placita.

Harry Pye, a muleskinner by trade who had dreams of being a successful prospector, founded the settlement that eventually became Chloride. He discovered a rich deposit of silver along Mineral Creek while hauling supplies from the town of Hillsboro to the army encamped at Ojo Caliente during the spring of 1879.

Pye patiently fulfilled his military contract and returned in 1881 to file a claim.

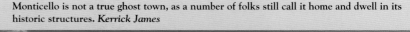

Monticello is not a true ghost town, as a number of folks still call it home and dwell in its historic structures. *Kerrick James*

As word of the discovery spread, miners, prospectors, and those who prospered from their success flooded the area in spite of the infringement on Apache lands and subsequent reprisals.

The settlement originally known as Pyetown officially became Chloride with the establishment of a post office. The town's name indicated what the ore found there was composed of. By the late 1880s, the town consisted of more than one hundred homes; numerous stores, including a butcher shop and candy store; an attorney's office; a doctor's office; a Chinese laundry; a hotel; a boarding house; a stage line that connected the mountain community with towns to the south; and a newspaper.

In the modern vernacular, Winston would be called a suburb of Chloride, although Winston's population dwarfed its neighbor for a brief time in the late nineteenth century. Winston was originally called Fairview, but its name was changed to honor Frank Winston, a successful prospector turned businessman who was also a philanthropist in the remote mountain mining camps.

The financial Panic of 1893 fueled a collapse of silver prices and would have destroyed both communities if it had not been for the fortuitous discovery of rich copper, lead, and zinc deposits. This find kept both frontier-era mining camps alive into the modern era.

Winston's downward slump was slow and began with closure of Chloride's mines in the early 1930s. By 1940, the population was several hundred, down

The Pioneer Store in Chloride, New Mexico, still has an original inventory that dates to the 1920s. *Kerrick James*

Chloride's main street has fewer hints indicating this isolated community was once the gem of the Black Range. *Kerrick James*

from a peak of several thousand. Today the population is near the single digits, yet the town consists of more than thirty buildings.

Chloride's decline largely mirrored Winston's. The log-constructed Pioneer Store that was built in 1880 was "temporarily" closed in 1923. Don Edmund, whose family has saved numerous structures in Chloride, purchased the store in 1989 and was surprised to find a large percentage of the inventory remained.

All four of these towns are well worth the effort to seek them out. The communities are easily accessed, except after snowstorms in the winter.

WHEN YOU GO

From Truth or Consequences, drive north on Interstate 25 to Exit 83. Then drive north on New Mexico Highway 181 for 5 miles, and turn west on New Mexico Highway 52. The drive to Winston is 27 miles, and Chloride is 2.5 miles farther to the west. Placita is located 24 miles from Truth or Consequences. Follow the directions to Winston/Chloride, but after driving 5 miles on Highway 52, turn north on New Mexico Highway 142. Monticello is just over 2 miles northwest of Placita on Highway 142.

SHAKESPEARE

The foundation of the old adobe town of Shakespeare was a commodity more precious than gold in the desert: water. Yet when silver, gold, diamonds, and rubies were found in the area, Shakespeare became a boomtown.

In 1868, Jack Frost and John Everson, employees of the National Mail & Transportation Company, established a station at the north end of the Pyramid Mountains at one of the few dependable, year-round water holes in the desert. The Mexican Springs station was a desolate and lonely place for a short time.

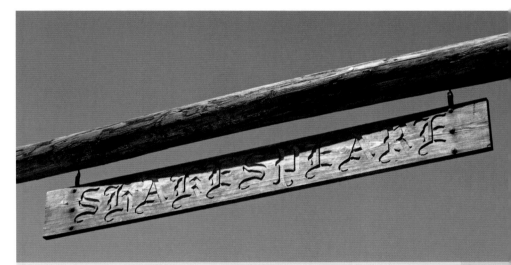

Diamond hoaxes, a mysterious California suicide, a Shakespearean remake, and connections with Lew Wallace, author of *Ben Hur*, make Shakespeare one of the unique ghost towns of the Southwest. *Kerrick James*

The following year, prospectors discovered extensive silver deposits in the Burro Mountains to the north and small deposits near Mexican Springs. Neither discovery would have been enough to launch a boom or transform Mexican Springs into a town if William C. Ralston, founder of the Bank of California, hadn't intervened.

Ralston saw great profit potential in the silver discovery. He began exaggerating the results of assay reports, leaking well-placed rumors, and funding his ventures with money from outside investors. He then acquired the property around Mexican Springs, which was occasionally referred to as Grant, laid out streets, sold lots, and renamed the settlement after himself.

The owners of Shakespeare have gone to great lengths to ensure its visitors experience an immersion into life in the frontier era of the desert Southwest. *Kerrick James*

The boom had busted by 1871 as the result of sparse returns from the mines and improperly filed claims. In the fall of 1872, two prospectors, Philip Arnold and John Slack, saved the town from complete abandonment with an amazing discovery of a vast field of diamonds and rubies.

The prospectors needed financial backing to develop the diamond mines and ventured to California to meet with the town's namesake. Ralston, excited by the discovery, was quite suspicious of the find. First, he had a sampling of the stones appraised. Then he hired a trusted mining engineer to evaluate the site. Then and only then did he offer to purchase the entire claim for a reputed $600,000. The scammer had been scammed.

Ralston replayed his highly profitable gambit from the silver mines, and the town of Ralston boomed larger than before. The population was estimated at three thousand by the following spring.

The diamond rush, as with the silver rush before it, was short-lived. The town was almost a complete ghost by 1875. The Bank of California collapsed that same year, and soon after the collapse, William Ralston drowned in San Francisco Bay, a rumored suicide.

A new era dawned in Ralston in April 1879 when English-born Colonel William G. Boyle, a mining engineer, and his brother, General John Boyle, purchased the townsite and the primary silver mines discovered in 1870. The brothers created the Shakespeare Gold & Silver Mining Company, which led to changing Ralston's name to Shakespeare. Main Street continued with the Shakespeare theme and was renamed Avon Avenue. The refurbished hotel became the Stratford on Avon.

Within a few years, the town was firmly rooted in real mine development and had grown to one hundred residents who supported several saloons, an assay office, and a general store. Among the luminaries to invest in and visit the small mining town was Lew Wallace, governor of the New Mexico Territory from 1878 to 1881 and author of the novel *Ben Hur*.

The mines at Shakespeare were in decline when the Panic of 1893 brought silver mining to a complete stop (there had been no discovery of gold in profitable quantities). The final blow was in 1894 with the establishment of Lordsburg 4 miles to the north along the new Southern Pacific Railroad tracks.

Most of the businesses and residents of Shakespeare relocated to Lordsburg. A few others moved a few miles southwest to a new camp named Valedon, built around the 85 Mine, a new and promising discovery.

Shakespeare waned so much that construction of a spur line run connecting Lordsburg to the 85 Mine ran right down the center of Avon Avenue in 1914.

The next chapter for Shakespeare began in 1935 when Frank and Rita Hill purchased a large section of acreage that included the ruins and townsite

The Grant House is one of the oldest structures in Shakespeare and has served a number of functions, including as a stage station. *Kerrick James*

for use as a ranch. They refurbished one of the original buildings as their home, other buildings received similar treatment as time allowed, and the town opened as a tourist attraction.

Rita published an interesting booklet for visitors that chronicled the town's history. To promote the ghost town as an attraction, Frank and his daughter, Janaloo, with extensive press coverage and numerous interviews given en route, rode horseback all the way to San Diego, California.

Today, Shakespeare is somewhere between recreated, resurrected, and pure ghost. The town is open on select weekends and by appointment.

WHEN YOU GO

From Lordsburg, drive south for 4 miles on Highway 494.

MOGOLLON

Mogollon, nestled within the narrow confines of Silver Creek Canyon, is a scenic wonder. The ruins have a rich patina of age and sit amidst a stunning setting of natural beauty, making this one of the most photogenic ghost towns in the Southwest.

Other prospectors may have discovered the silver-bearing ores in a canyon along Mineral Creek in the Mogollon Mountains, but Quartermaster Sergeant James C. Cooney of the Eighth Cavalry of Fort Bayard made them public knowledge. Despite the near constant threat of Apache attacks in the rugged, isolated mountains, Cooney declined an army commission in 1876 and returned to develop his find as a civilian.

Mogollon is squeezed into a narrow and scenic canyon of the Mogollon Mountains and is a photographer's delight. *Kerrick James*

The J. P. Holland General Store is an example of why Mogollon ranks at the top of any favorite ghost town list. *Kerrick James*

As his claim developed and other prospectors arrived in the area, the small mining camp of Cooney, located a few miles north of present-day Mogollon, blossomed. Cooney enjoyed the profits of his find, but only for a short time. He died during an Apache raid in Alma during the spring of 1880.

Cooney's brother, Michael, assumed control of the mine and shepherded it through expansion and development. Meanwhile, larger deposits of silver and gold found south of Cooney and within the confines of Silver Creek Canyon sparked a parallel rush and the development of Mogollon.

By the late 1880s, Mogollon rapidly eclipsed Cooney, which was in a steep fall. A variety of stores, several hotels and churches, a theater, an ice plant, and numerous saloons and homes crowded the narrow canyon floor and cascaded up the canyon walls in Mogollon.

Floods and fires struck Mogollon several times, but the mountain mining town was rebuilt after each incident, each time more grand than the previous incarnation. After a period of unusually heavy rains in 1914, the tailings of the Little Fanny Mine on Fannie Hill slid to the canyon floor, dammed the creek, and created a lake that threatened to flood the center of the town. With heroic efforts, miners cleared the channel and saved Mogollon from complete annihilation.

Transportation was, and is, the primary problem in Mogollon. Today a paved, 9-mile road with grades in excess of 25 percent, hairpin curves, precipitous drops, and single-lane spots in many places provides access. As late as 1915—the year the mines reached their zenith and the town consisted of more than two thousand residents—the 90-mile trip to Silver City, the primary shipping point and supply center for the area, required ten days in severe weather. Teams of eighteen or twenty-four mules were the primary choice for freight haulers until 1917. The switch to trucks did not translate into faster service, due to the area's rugged terrain.

Mogollon has many ruins, with Silver Creek flowing along the main street and many buildings that require wooden bridges for access. Some of the highlights are a bed and breakfast housed in a renovated two-story adobe store built in 1885 and a delightful museum in another store across the street and creek. A few of the buildings were refaced or modified for the movie *My Name Is Nobody*, which was filmed in the early 1970s and starred Henry Fonda.

WHEN YOU GO

From Silver City, drive 58 miles west on US Highway 180. Turn east on New Mexico Highway 159, and continue for 9 miles. The drive on Highway 159 is not for the timid, those pulling trailers, or oversized vehicles. The road is steep, contains hairpin curves, and is one lane in many places. During the winter months, it can be snowy and icy.

Baby Doe Tabor was told by her dying husband, Horace, to hold on to Leadville's Matchless Mine at all costs. She became a pauper, freezing to death in the building at the left rear, still heeding her husband's advice. *Philip Varney*

COLORADO

Gold fever! The Colorado gold rush began west of Denver, the "Pikes Peak or Bust" frenzy that brought a hundred thousand people to Colorado in 1859 alone. In January of that year, placer gold discoveries along Clear Creek gave rise to Idaho Springs, a delightful former mining town now located right along Interstate 70. Five months after the Clear Creek discovery, lode gold was found where Central City now stands.

As prospectors poured into the area, late arrivals expanded the boundaries of the excitement, searching for the next big strike. Not long after the Central City bonanza, Clear Creek gold seekers found pay dirt upriver from Idaho Springs, and Georgetown and its sister community of Silver Plume were born.

From those early beginnings, prospectors spread out to virtually every corner of Colorado, with some areas being complete busts. But there were many booms as well, and the best of the ghost towns are contained in this chapter.

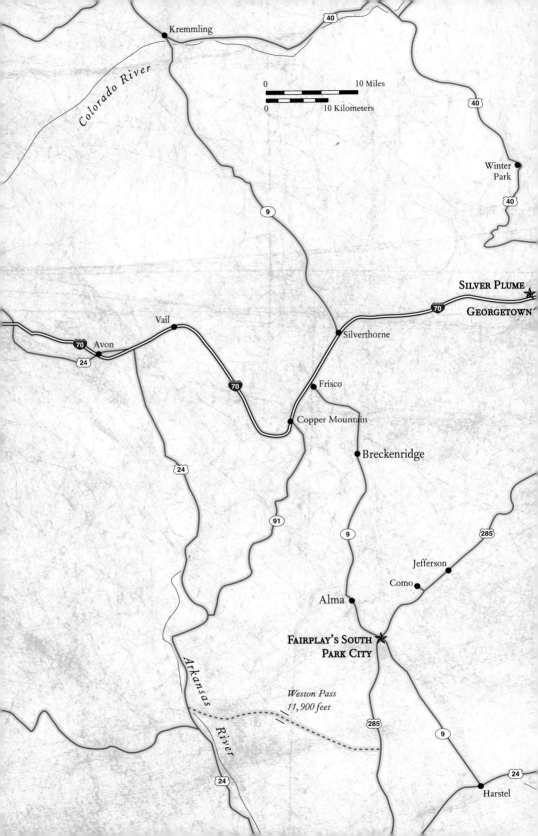

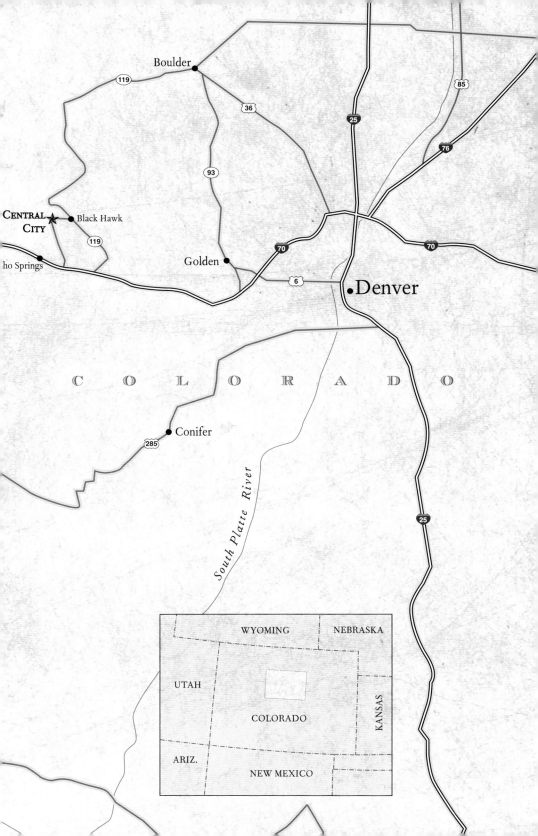

CENTRAL CITY

Central City and its next-door neighbor, Black Hawk, have been rivals since 1859. Their history and geography are so interconnected that it is impossible to write about one without including the other.

The rivalry has intensified in the last few years. When limited-stakes gambling came to the two towns in 1991, Black Hawk received a disproportionate amount of the revenue, partially because Denverites arrived at Black Hawk first. Central City responded with an enormously expensive parkway designed to ignore Black Hawk's existence (no mention of the town is made on any of the billboards along the way) and bring gamblers into Central City first. Has the gamble paid off? For every dollar gambled in Central City in 2008, seven dollars were spent in Black Hawk. At this writing, many buildings in Central City are vacant. Perhaps it will return to the near–ghost town status it experienced in the mid-twentieth century.

Black Hawk, for those interested in historic buildings, has paid a steep price for its gambling success. It still has some good buildings of antiquity, but they are harder and harder to find. Central City has kept its soul, but Black Hawk has not.

In January 1859, placer gold discoveries were made along Clear Creek near what is now Idaho Springs, and on May 6 of that year, Georgian John H. Gregory staked a claim that established the first gold lode in Colorado. The excitement along Clear Creek turned into a mad rush in Gregory Gulch. Several thousand prospectors were at work in less than a month. Within two months, thirty thousand people were fueling the gold frenzy in what was called the "Richest Square Mile on Earth."

Casinos occupy several of the historic buildings, many dating from 1874, of Central City's Main Street. This photo was taken before the casinos opened and the shuttle buses arrived, bringing hopeful gamblers. *Philip Varney*

The camp that formed was Gregory Diggings, later called Mountain City. A Gregory Diggings post office was established in January 1860, but the town was simply absorbed by Central City, its neighbor to the west. Central City was likely named because it was central among area mining camps. Black Hawk was a secondary part of the gold rush. Located down the gulch from Gregory Diggings, it was probably named because a mill erected there came from the Black Hawk Company of Rock Island, Illinois. While water was scarce to its upper-gulch neighbors, Black Hawk had an abundant supply, as it was located along the north branch of Clear Creek. Because it had the enormous quantities of water necessary to power several mills, Black Hawk became known as the City of Mills.

In 1867 Nathaniel Hill, a Brown University professor, put his theories of extracting gold from sulfide ore into practice by erecting in Black Hawk the first successful smelter in the territory, the Boston and Colorado Smelting Works. This solidified Black Hawk's importance in a rebounding mining industry. Ore could now be shipped in concentrate, significantly lowering transportation costs.

This marker was erected in the City of Central Cemetery for siblings who died in 1872 and 1875, respectively. Their stone reads: "Sleep on, sweet babes and take thy rest / For such as thee the Savior blessed." *Philip Varney*

The best ore bodies near Central City were depleted by the 1880s; from then until the early 1900s, area mines were steady producers, but the bonanza times were over. Mining continued as shafts went deeper, but inflation and the unchanging price of gold made mining less profitable. Before and after World War I, buildings in both towns were dismantled and moved to other communities. Although mining continued on a lesser scale, Central City and Black Hawk seemed headed toward obscurity.

Tourism brought the area somewhat back to life beginning in the 1950s, when I first gaped at the towns as a wide-eyed eleven-year-old. They were then dying, but not dead, as curious visitors glimpsed a past that was colorful but, for the townspeople, not particularly profitable.

When casino gambling came to Central City and Black Hawk, the stakes literally changed, for better or worse. Today the Richest Square Mile on Earth doesn't try to remove pockets of gold from the hills; it tries to remove the gold from your pockets. Central City is the star for the ghost town enthusiast, where you can find, well, a jackpot of history.

A good place to begin your tour of Central City is the Schoolhouse Museum (open daily during the summer), which is located on High Street, one block north of the highway. Downtown Central City features many buildings from the gold rush days. Two structures of particular interest are the Teller House and the Central City Opera House, both located on Eureka Street. The Teller House, built in 1872, was considered one of the West's finest hotels. When President Ulysses S. Grant visited in 1873, silver bricks worth $16,000 were placed so he would have a path appropriate for a president as he walked from his carriage to the Teller House. Because gold made Central City famous, he is supposed to have inquired why they had chosen silver. The answer? Gold was too common.

The 750-seat opera house was constructed in 1878 by Cornish stonemasons and features a central chandelier, hickory chairs, and decorative murals. Known for its excellent acoustics, it is still in use.

Eureka Street continues northwest for 1 mile from Central City to six of its seven cemeteries. The cemeteries fan out around a triangle intersection of roads. Starting across from the Boodle Mill, the graveyard farthest to the northwest is the International Order of Odd Fellows (I.O.O.F.) cemetery.

East of the I.O.O.F. graveyard is a small cemetery for the Red Man Lodge. Behind it is the large Catholic cemetery, where many natives of Italy, Ireland, and Germany are buried. The most interesting feature here is a double-thick brick beehive ovenlike structure. According to local author-historian Alan Granruth, its purpose is a mystery. He thinks perhaps it served as a temporary burial location during winter months when digging a grave in the frozen ground would have been difficult. It is also conceivable that it simply predates the cemetery and was a kiln used to convert wood to charcoal.

The Knights of Pythias cemetery is across the road to the east. Adjacent to it is the City of Central Cemetery. Most of the older graves are found in the southeast corner. Beyond that cemetery is a small graveyard for the Ancient Order of the Foresters.

Central City's Masonic cemetery is on the other side of town. At the beginning of the Central City Parkway is a turnoff to the small ghost town of Nevadaville. Just before you reach a curious stone structure on your left (which may have been a Buddhist temple), you will see a road to your right, which leads to the cemetery.

WHEN YOU GO

From Denver, take Interstate 70 west for about 30 miles to Exit 243 and follow the Central City Parkway for 8.1 miles to Central City.

GEORGETOWN

Georgetown displays Colorado's best china and finest crystal. Hardly a mere "mining camp," it has an elegance and refinement that few other towns can match. Up the hill from Georgetown is Silver Plume, whose architecture may lack the finesse of its sister to the east, but its main street looks like what people expect from the frontier American West.

The Fish Block, built in 1899 by banker Charles Fish, stands at the corner of Sixth and Rose Streets. Behind it stands the 1891 Masonic Hall. *Philip Varney*

Brothers George and David Griffith, farmers from Bourbon County, Kentucky, headed to the newly discovered gold fields of Colorado in 1859 only to find that the best claims around Central City and Idaho Springs were already taken. So they prospected farther west up Clear Creek where, in June of the same year, they found placer gold. They staked a claim and established the Griffith Mining District. Their gold discovery, however, was to be the only important one in the district.

A delicate fountain and a solarium demonstrate the stately elegance of the Hamill House, an 1867 home that was extensively remodeled in 1878 and 1879 to become Georgetown's most elaborate residence. The stone building in the rear is the carriage house and stable. *Philip Varney*

As others joined them, a camp grew, known as George's Town (named after the older brother). A second community, called Elizabethtown (probably named for the Griffiths' sister), came to life south of the first camp when silver was discovered there in 1864. These were the first mines in Colorado in which silver was mined as the principal ore, not as a lesser byproduct to gold.

In 1868, Georgetown and Elizabethtown consolidated as one community. That same year, Georgetown displaced Idaho Springs as the seat of Clear Creek County in a bitter election. By 1870, the population had climbed to eight hundred, and Georgetown settled in as "Queen of the Silver Camps." In that year, Georgetown citizens presented a silver spike to commemorate the rail

The Gothic Revival–style six-hole outhouse at the Hamill House features a cantilevered overhang above its two entrances and a ventilating cupola. *Philip Varney*

link between Denver and Cheyenne that joined Colorado to the Union Pacific Railroad and therefore to the rest of the nation.

By 1880, the population of Georgetown had soared to more than three thousand. The town had schools, churches, and hotels, as well as one saloon for every 150 citizens. Four independent fire companies helped the community avoid a major conflagration.

In 1893, however, disaster of another variety hit Georgetown. A steady decline in silver prices, due to increased supply and decreased coinage, culminated in the repeal of the Sherman Silver Purchase Act. This act had guaranteed acquisition of almost nine million ounces of silver per month by the federal government. Its repeal meant that the coin of the realm was gold—and only gold. This was a major blow, not just to Georgetown but also to the entire state; at the time, Colorado had been producing an astonishing 58 percent of the nation's silver. Mines and mills closed, and miners departed to gold fields in Cripple Creek and Victor (see page 292). Georgetown went into a precipitous decline.

Not until the middle of the twentieth century did Georgetown bloom once again, this time as a mountain retreat and tourist attraction. It and Silver Plume were declared a National Historic Landmark District, and both civic groups and private individuals began in earnest to restore their lovely towns.

Start your walking tour of present-day Georgetown at the Community Center, formerly the 1868 courthouse, at Sixth and Argentine Streets. There you can pick up brochures and a free walking tour map. (However, a more helpful tour guide on Georgetown and Silver Plume is for sale.) Historic photos are on display in the first-floor courtroom, where district court was held. The county courtroom, jury deliberation rooms, and public restrooms are upstairs.

Sixth Street contains too many fine commercial structures to enumerate here. If you go inside only one, visit the marvelous Hotel de Paris. Frenchman Adolphe Francois Gerard, who immigrated

The dining room of Georgetown's Hamill House. The 1879 original wallpaper had to be hand-painted after a 1974 fire caused smoke and water damage. The Renaissance Revival sideboard (left, rear) and the dining table are Hamill family originals. *Philip Varney*

to New York in 1868 at age twenty-two and headed west with the US Cavalry, brought the grand hotel into being. He deserted in Cheyenne, came to Denver in 1869, and changed his name to Louis Dupuy.

In 1873, Dupuy was working as a miner in Georgetown when he was injured in a dynamite explosion. He retired from mining and bought a small bakery, which over the years evolved into one of the finest hotels in the West.

The First United Presbyterian Church was dedicated upon its completion in 1874 after two years of construction. It was completely restored in 1974 to celebrate its centennial. *Philip Varney*

The Colonial Dames of America purchased the hotel in 1954 and began a thorough restoration. Touring the Hotel de Paris is a delight, from its guest rooms to wine cellar to kitchen to dining room to Dupuy's own quarters.

One residence open to the public and well worth touring is the opulent Hamill House, located at 305 Argentine Street, two blocks west of the Maxwell House.

A fairly modest home when it was constructed in 1867, the house became a showplace when it was remodeled and expanded in 1879 by its new owner, William A. Hamill, a prominent mine owner and silver speculator. The elegant Gothic mansion features a solarium, a schoolroom, and such refinements as central heating, a zinc-lined bathtub, and gold-plated doorknobs.

The Hamill House also has Colorado's most elaborate outhouse, a Gothic-styled six-seater with a cantilevered overhang above the entrance and a ventilating cupola. Later preservationists found pieces of expensive china, apparently broken by maids or scullions and dropped into the privy to conceal their clumsiness.

Georgetown also features many other exquisite private homes, firehouses, churches, and a delightful public school. Since you should have a tour guidebook or brochures, I'll leave the exploration to you.

Another excellent attraction in Georgetown is the Georgetown Loop Railroad and Lebanon Silver Mine Tour. I highly recommend both. Information for both is widely available in town.

If you wish to visit Georgetown's cemetery, drive toward the interstate on-ramp, but instead of going onto I-70, proceed 3.2 miles north on Alvarado Road, which loosely parallels the highway.

The Alvarado Cemetery will be on your right with a conspicuous main gate. On the other side of the road is the old Georgetown Cemetery, which was relocated to this site in 1972 from the shore of Georgetown Lake.

The Alvarado Cemetery, like many large graveyards, is divided into sections for religious and fraternal groups. Hundreds of graves cover many acres, with considerable space between various sections. One of the first graves you will see, near a flagpole, is for David Griffith, the cofounder of Georgetown, who died in 1882.

WHEN YOU GO

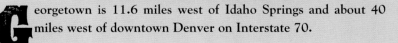

Georgetown is 11.6 miles west of Idaho Springs and about 40 miles west of downtown Denver on Interstate 70.

SILVER PLUME

s the silver claims around Georgetown flourished, late-arriving prospectors naturally tried their luck in nearby areas. The most obvious place was farther up Clear Creek, whose placer deposits had begun the strikes at both Idaho Springs and Georgetown.

In the mid-1860s, another mining camp grew in a location beyond Georgetown as the result of that continued prospecting, and in 1870, major silver discoveries fueled a genuine bonanza. The most colorful account of the naming of the new town involves Commodore Stephen Decatur, editor of Georgetown's *Colorado Miner*. He had been shown ore samples featuring feathery streaks of silver in a plume shape. When asked what to call the new but unnamed camp, Decatur proclaimed, "The name? You've already got the name! It was written on the ore you brought me!" He rhapsodized:

> The knights today are miners bold,
> Who toil in deep mines' gloom!
> To honor men who dig for gold,
> For ladies whom their arms enfold,
> We'll name the camp Silver Plume!

Many of Main Street's false-front buildings were erected immediately after Silver Plume's disastrous fire of 1884. *Philip Varney*

The rich mines were in the steep canyon walls above the new camp. They were reached by trails, many of which are still visible today, zigzagging up from town.

Silver Plume was incorporated in 1880 and within a couple of years could claim saloons, boarding houses, butcher shops, mercantile stores, fraternal lodges, a theater, a school, and Catholic and Methodist churches. With its modest frame buildings packed into narrow streets along the canyon floor, Silver Plume lacked the splendor of Georgetown. It was proudly proclaimed a "miners' town," whereas its more cosmopolitan neighbor was the home of mine owners and managers.

Many of those modest buildings disappeared on the night of November 4, 1884, when a fire started in Patrick Barrett's saloon. The flames spread down Main Street,

The Silver Plume School was erected in 1894, a year after the great Silver Crash of 1893. The townspeople built the school to demonstrate their confidence in the long-term vitality of their community. It is now a museum. *Philip Varney*

consuming most of downtown. Devout women and children knelt in front of St. Patrick's Catholic Church and prayed for divine intervention. Although the fire seriously damaged the east wall, the church was spared. The next morning, Barrett's body was found in the ashes of his saloon.

Rebuilding began the next day. Citizens floated a bond issue for a waterworks and increased fire protection, including purchase of the town's first pumper, shipped from St. Louis. The business district was completely rebuilt by 1886, with saloons prevailing on the south side of Main Street while other businesses, such as the post office, barbershop, print shop, and mortuary, stood on the north side.

The prosperity of Silver Plume was short-lived. Like neighboring Georgetown, the community reeled from the blow of the Silver Crash of 1893.

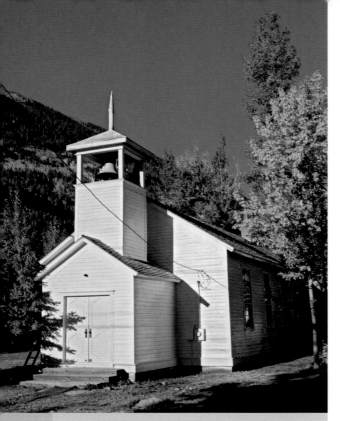

This Methodist church was originally equidistant between Brownsville and Silver Plume. When the former town declined as the latter boomed, the church was moved a half mile closer to Silver Plume in 1891. *Philip Varney*

Silver Plume today features several homes and the lovely two-story 1880s New Windsor Hotel, now a private residence.

Turn left on Main Street, where you'll pass the 1875 two-cell stone jail, in service until 1915. Farther west on Main is the rebuilt pump house at Brewery Springs, so named because Otto Boche's Silver Plume Brewery and Bowling Alley once stood across the street.

At Main and Hancock is the attractive Methodist church, built in the 1880s and moved to this site in 1890. Still farther west is the two-story, four-classroom, 1894 brick schoolhouse, where classes were last held in 1959. Today the building is the George Rowe Museum, named for an eighty-seven-year resident of Silver Plume who donated much of the memorabilia inside.

Silver Plume's business district has more than a dozen historic buildings, including the 1886 Hose Company No. 1 and Town Hall, the 1904 bandstand, the 1874 St. Patrick's Catholic Church (enlarged after the 1884 fire), and the Knights of Pythias Castle Hall. The hall was moved from Brownsville, a now-vanished community west of Silver Plume, in 1895.

WHEN YOU GO

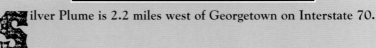

Silver Plume is 2.2 miles west of Georgetown on Interstate 70.

FAIRPLAY'S SOUTH PARK CITY

When prospectors came to the early South Park diggings at Tarryall, a now-vanished mining camp, they found miners there in no mood to share and so nicknamed the place "Grab-all." When they moved on and found placer gold in the South Platte River, the men wanted a counter to the name Grab-all for their new diggings and decided upon Fair Play in rebuke. The post office opened in that name in the summer of 1861.

On the southwest end of South Park City stand (from left to right) the office of the *South Park Sentinel*, Simkins General Store, the Bank of Alma, and J. A. Merriam Drug Store. All were brought from other towns to this location. *Philip Varney*

In 1869, Fair Play became South Park City, but the name lasted only five years, when it reverted to its earlier name. Fair Play became a supply and social center for area mines after placer diggings gave out, and in the 1890s, dredging of the South Platte led to a resurgence of activity that lasted well into the twentieth century. The US Post Office shortened the town's name to one word in 1924. When noted ghost town author Muriel Sibell Wolle visited Fairplay in 1942, a dredge was busy 2 miles away. She remarked that, despite its distance from town, she could hear it "shrieking and clanging." Those dredging operations left behind extensive gravel piles along the river. They are particularly visible from the north end of town.

Fairplay's earlier name of South Park City was resurrected when a pioneer museum of that name was opened to the public in 1959, the centennial of the Pikes Peak gold rush. One of the West's best outdoor, living-history pioneer villages, South Park City features a remarkable collection of thirty-four buildings, seven at their original locations and the remainder moved from nearby communities. The price of admission is very reasonable.

This schoolhouse, built in 1879, stood at Garo, now mostly a place name southeast of Fairplay on the road to Hartsel. *Philip Varney*

Built in 1862, the log Park County Courthouse was originally located in the now-vanished town of Buckskin Joe. It was moved to Fairplay in 1867 when that town was granted the county seat, an honor it still holds. *Philip Varney*

Moved from Alma, Rache's Place has authentic saloon furnishings and gambling equipment from the late 1800s. Note the conveniently located potbellied stove. *Philip Varney*

South Park City's street scene is attractive enough, but the adventure really begins when you enter the wonderful buildings. Ghost town enthusiasts dream of finding an empty town filled with artifacts that long-ago citizens left behind. South Park City is the incarnation of that dream. Some sixty thousand items pertinent to the buildings are on display. An 1879 one-room schoolhouse, with its belfry-capped vestibule, features a complete classroom. The 1880 Bank of Alma retains its teller cages and safe. J. A. Merriam Drug Store has an astonishing array of patent remedies still in their wrappers. Rache's Place displays gambling equipment similar to what was used when it operated in nearby Alma. The 1914 Baldwin locomotive is reminiscent of the type used on the narrow gauge Denver, South Park & Pacific Railroad that once served Fairplay.

WHEN YOU GO

From Silver Plume, drive west 23 miles on Interstate 70 to Frisco. Head south on Colorado Highway 9 for 10 miles to the attractive former mining town of Breckenridge. Fairplay's South Park City is 24 miles south of Breckenridge on Colorado Highway 9.

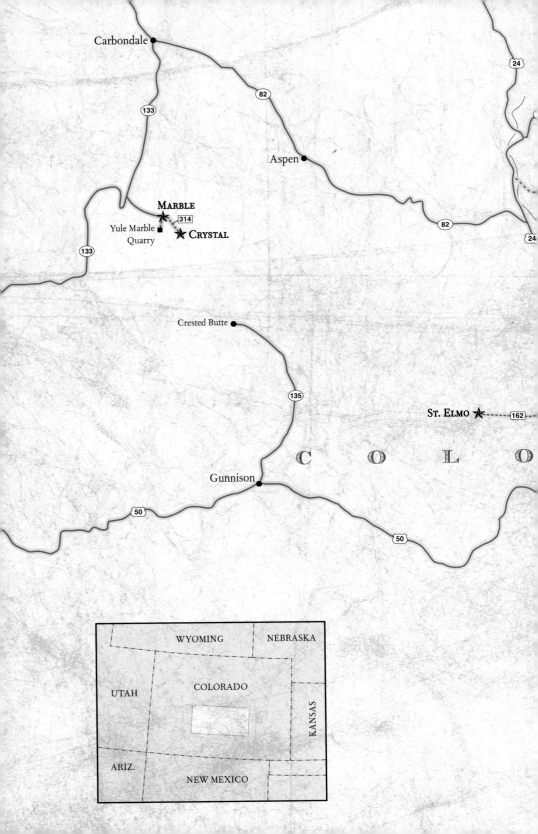

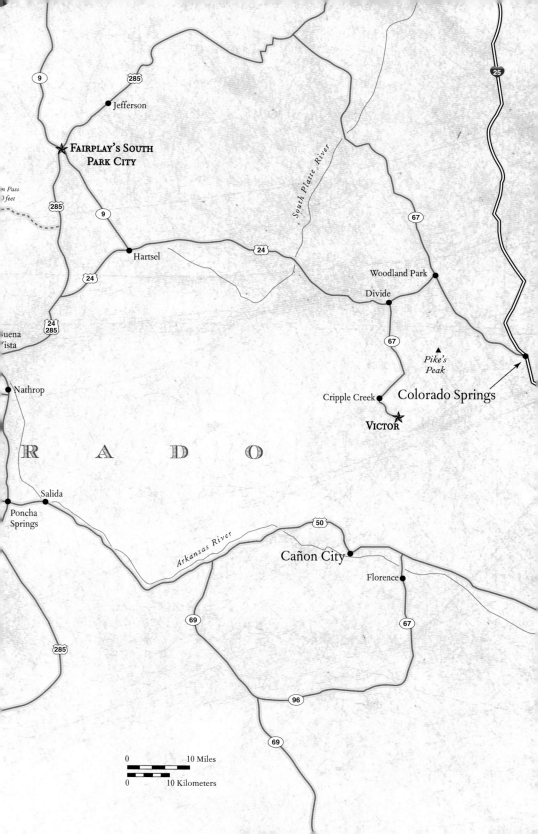

VICTOR

Victor and its more glamorous sister, Cripple Creek, practically saved Colorado. When the state was reeling from the Silver Crash of 1893, Cripple Creek and Victor were alive and thriving because gold, not silver, surrounded the towns.

Victor and Cripple Creek share much in common with Central City and Black Hawk (see page 276). Both sets of towns were rivals and shared much of their history. All four were ghosts in the 1950s, until limited-stakes gambling beginning in 1991 rejuvenated three of the four. Only Victor was unaffected, and for that ghost town enthusiasts can rejoice. Cripple Creek hasn't been altered as much as Black Hawk, but it nevertheless has huge, modern casinos. Because Victor was overlooked in the gambling rush, it has a somnolent, decaying beauty that the other three lack. It is, for me, one of the West's best ghost towns.

Cripple Creek's colorful name supposedly came from a mishap involving a cowboy on horseback chasing a cow into a creek, resulting in a broken leg to the horse and the cow and a broken arm to the cowboy. On hearing the account, a wag was supposed to have remarked, "That is a Cripple Creek."

Victor's name had more prosaic beginnings. It was either named for the nearby Victor Mine or for homesteader Victor Adams.

Prospectors began to explore the Cripple Creek–Victor area in 1874, but little was found. This wasn't a place where gold should appear. The geology seemed wrong, and the deposits were hard to extract. The place confounded prospectors, confused miners, and bankrupted speculators. In 1884, a local scam brought investors to salted claims. As a result, the hills around Mount Pisgah had a tainted reputation.

The *Victor Daily Record* newspaper was printed in the single-story brick building on the right. Next door is the triple-corniced Masonic Hall. Both buildings stand on Victor's Fourth Street. *Philip Varney*

A sometime Cripple Creek prospector, Colorado Springs carpenter Winfield Scott Stratton, persisted in his search for the major lode. He found it southeast of Cripple Creek on Battle Mountain, near where Victor now stands, where he made the Independence claim on July 4, 1891. He became a multimillionaire from the gold.

Victor's Gold Coin Club still has residents. In its heyday it could boast a library, a bowling alley, and a swimming pool.
Philip Varney

Cripple Creek and Victor boomed as silver towns floundered. Fortunately for laid-off silver miners, they could be gold miners as well, and they were Cripple Creek–bound.

Victor and Cripple Creek became natural rivals. Cripple Creek was home to investors and mine owners, while Victor was a miners' town. Victor, therefore, enjoyed any chance for one-upmanship. For instance, in 1897, Victor entered a float in a Salt Lake City festival with the queen of Victor aboard. She generously invited the Cripple Creek queen to ride as well. The *Victor Daily Record* wryly noted, "We might say that Cripple Creek took a ride on Victor's band wagon, but Cripple has often done that commercially and the habit is growing."

Victor even surpassed its rival in size for a short time but only because of a fire in Cripple Creek in 1896. When Cripple Creek rebuilt, however, it was again larger and even grander. When a fire decimated Victor in 1899, it also rebuilt, but its best times were already over.

In 1900, the mining district hit its peak in gold production at $18 million, when Cripple Creek was Colorado's fourth-largest city. The Cripple Creek and Victor bonanza became the second-largest gold district in US history, with about twenty-one million ounces of gold extricated, worth over $10 billion in today's dollars. And it is not finished, at least at this writing. An open pit operation that began in 1995 on Battle Mountain is chewing into many legendary mines, which will add to the gold-production total. Unfortunately, it is also chewing into some old mining camps.

Even though its more genteel neighbor always outshined Victor, the town was something special in its prime. The Portland Mine was "Queen of the District,"

The Caffery Building has an attractive cut-stone front, built on a slight diagonal, with bricks making up the other three walls. *Philip Varney*

producing half of Battle Mountain's gold. One of its muckers was a kid named William Dempsey, later famous as a heavyweight boxer under his brother's name, Jack.

Ore was found all around Victor and even within the city itself. The workings were so rich that supposedly worthless tailings were used to pave Victor's streets. When Harry Woods and his brother Frank were excavating a foundation for the Victor Hotel, they discovered a rich ore body. The hotel plan was shelved, and the Gold Coin Mine opened, eventually yielding $6 million in gold. After the Gold Coin's buildings were destroyed in the 1899 fire, the Woods brothers rebuilt the shaft house with ornate touches such as stained-glass windows. Their showy gesture demonstrated their confidence in the district. That confidence was ill-founded, however; within a few years, they were bankrupt.

Victor's city hall features pressed-tin ornamentation and a handsome two-tiered tower.
Philip Varney

Aspens signal the fall season at Sunnyside Cemetery, located southwest of Victor. *Philip Varney*

Deteriorating ore bodies and labor troubles initiated Victor's decline. As a miners' town, it became the center for labor unrest when the Western Federation of Miners attempted to standardize wages and shorten the working day. Strikes and violence slowed production of nearly pinched-out mines. When miners left practically en masse to join World War I, Battle Mountain mines never recovered. The only other "mining" effort Victor saw was during the Depression, when the low-grade ore that had been used to pave the streets was scraped up and milled.

Although Cripple Creek has succumbed to the glitter of casino gambling, Victor remains authentic—a bit dowdy, even dilapidated, but completely delightful.

Attractions for the ghost town enthusiast abound, including the Lowell Thomas Museum. There you will find interesting memorabilia and items about Lowell Thomas, a Victor High School graduate whose radio voice became familiar to millions of Americans. That same intersection features the Fortune Club on the southwest corner, with an elaborate painted advertisement on its wall. South of Third from the Fortune Club is the Isis Theater, a turn-of-the-twentieth-century building that went from live theater to silent movies to talkies. Its sloping floor still has several rows of theater seats.

Farther down Victor Avenue at Fourth stands the completely renovated Victor Hotel, originally a bank. It has a huge vault in the lobby and a wonderful elevator.

Drive the back streets south of the main business district to see countless boomtown-era homes, businesses, a church, and a Masonic Hall that range from the abandoned to the neglected to the carefully restored.

North of the business district is Pikes Peak Power Company Substation No. 1, and the once-elegant Gold Coin Club. Built for the workers of the Gold Coin Mine, the club featured a library, bowling alley, and swimming pool. The mine itself, the one that was discovered while the Woods brothers were building the foundation for a hotel, is across the street.

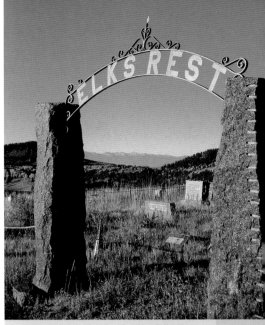

The stone and wrought-iron Elks Rest entrance leads to that fraternal organization's section of Victor's Sunnyside Cemetery. *Philip Varney*

Another fine building on Victor Avenue is the 1900 Victor City Hall with its ornate tower. West of city hall 0.1 of a mile is South Seventh Street, the turnoff south to the cemetery, which is 0.8 of a mile away from town.

The Victor Sunnyside Cemetery has several fraternal sections: Moose, Odd Fellows, Masons, Eagles, and Elks. It also features a large number of wooden markers surrounded by wrought-iron fences.

WHEN YOU GO

To reach Cripple Creek from Colorado Springs, take Colorado Highway 24 west for 25 miles to Divide. Go south 18 miles on Colorado Highway 67. Victor is 6 miles southeast of Cripple Creek on Highway 67. Incidentally, there once was another way to get from Cripple Creek to Victor: Battle Mountain is so extensively tunneled that one could actually walk between the two cities completely underground.

ST. ELMO

t. Elmo is what many people picture when someone says "ghost town." With its gorgéous scenery and attractive buildings, it's one of Colorado's premier ghost destinations.

Originally, the townsite that grew along Chalk Creek in 1879 was aptly called Forest City for the numerous spruce and pine trees in the area. But the US Postal Service refused the name since a Forest City already existed in California. A committee of three chose St. Elmo (the patron saint of sailors) because of a popular 1866 novel of that name.

Silver and gold strikes in the Chalk Creek Mining District early in 1880 brought hundreds of people to St. Elmo. The town became a supply center for nearby mines and a jumping-off point for prospectors heading over passes to boomtowns such as Tincup and Aspen.

When the Denver, South Park & Pacific Railroad was completed to St. Elmo, the town's future seemed assured. It became a favorite place for miners, freighters, and railroad workers to spend their Saturday nights, as they enjoyed St. Elmo's many saloons.

Because of the travel trade, the town had five hotels. One guest, upon arriving at a hotel that was still getting its finishing touches, asked for a private room. The hotelier drew a chalk line around one of many beds and told him that he had given him a suite.

St. Elmo, with its dirt streets and wooden boardwalks, has the true look of a ghost town.
Philip Varney

The failure of one mine after another and the closing of the railroad's Alpine Tunnel in 1910 began the decline of St. Elmo. The Stark family, who owned the first house in town, remained after all others left. Muriel Sibell Wolle fondly recalls Mr. Stark in her classic book *Stampede to Timberline: The Ghost Towns and Mining Camps of Colorado*. She said he was very gracious, insisting upon bringing her an armchair while she sketched. When she left his store in the otherwise-empty town, he warned, "Watch out for the streetcars!" She does not identify him except as Mr. Stark, but it was brothers Roy and Tony, along with their sister Annabelle, who ran the store until the late 1950s. After Wolle's book came out in 1949, the Starks criticized her for daring to call St. Elmo a ghost town and blamed her for their lack of business.

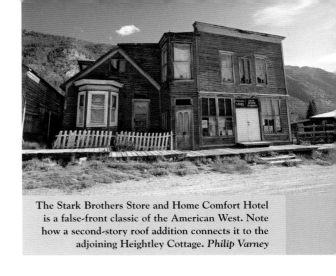

The Stark Brothers Store and Home Comfort Hotel is a false-front classic of the American West. Note how a second-story roof addition connects it to the adjoining Heightley Cottage. *Philip Varney*

St. Elmo today has more than forty antique structures. As you enter town, you'll pass two restored buildings, the Pawnee Mill's livery stable and its blacksmith shop. A house across the street is the information center for the Colorado Historical Society.

The current center of activity is the Miners Exchange, a log building with a frame false front, where you can purchase all manner of Colorado and ghost town merchandise. Perhaps the most enjoyable item to buy is food for the insatiable chipmunks that cadge snacks from visitors.

Down the street is an authentic reconstruction of the town hall and jail, which burned in 2002 along with two other buildings. Across the street is the Stark Brothers Store and sixteen-bedroom Home Comfort Hotel, built around 1885 and closed to the public at this writing. The store also housed the post office, telephone exchange, and telegraph. Attached to the Stark store (in an architecturally creative fashion) is the 1881 Heightley Cottage.

The road to Tincup Pass heads north from town. Take that road to see the completely restored 1882 one-room schoolhouse; then follow the road as it turns west to view two stores and several residences. Beyond St. Elmo, the road to Tincup Pass is for four-wheel-drive, high-clearance vehicles only.

WHEN YOU GO

St. Elmo is 24 miles southwest of Buena Vista, which is 90 miles northwest of Victor. From Buena Vista, drive south about 8.5 miles to Nathrop on US Highway 285. South of Nathrop only 0.3 of a mile is County Road 162. Take that road west for 15.4 miles to St. Elmo. The road is an old railroad grade and is suitable for passenger vehicles in good weather.

MARBLE

"T"he Marble Capital of the United States" was initially settled by prospectors who formed a camp known as Yule Creek, named for pioneer George Yule. Gold, silver, and lead were mined there from 1880 into the 1890s.

Even before the prospectors found their deposits, geologist Sylvester Richardson had noted in 1873 the beds of marble in Whitehouse Mountain. The marble was merely a curiosity then, because it was on the Ute Indian Reservation.

After the Utes were moved west to allow prospectors in, attempts to quarry the stone in the 1880s resulted in limited profitability because of the area's remoteness from a railhead. That changed when the standard gauge Crystal River & San Juan Railroad was completed from Carbondale to Marble in 1906, connecting Marble's finishing mill with the Denver & Rio Grande branch line to Aspen. That rail link, combined with a 4-mile-long electric railway that transported marble from the quarry to the huge finishing mill, made production much more lucrative. The first large order, for a Cleveland, Ohio, courthouse, invigorated the community.

The best years followed, peaking from 1912 to 1917. The town was, literally, made by and of marble. Entire buildings were constructed of it, as were foundations and even sidewalks.

The town of Marble had its share of setbacks. A fire in 1916 destroyed much of downtown. Avalanches buried the finishing mill and the railroad tracks. Financial problems forced the closure of the quarry in 1941, as consumers began to order veneers instead of blocks or to choose cheaper marble substitutes. Mudslides in that year destroyed large portions of the town's business section. Machinery, rails, and even metal window frames were salvaged for scrap during World War II. Its glory days apparently over, Marble became a town of pleasant summer cabins.

The quarry reopened in 1990, when the first new block of marble in almost fifty years was brought down to Marble itself, causing a "Block Party."

When you come to a stop sign in Marble, you're in central downtown at Park and Third Streets. A right turn takes you to the town's major attraction, the ruins of the Yule Quarry Finishing Mill, where blocks were cut, polished, and carved into everything from monuments to building blocks to tombstones. Exploring this enchanting place, for which a donation is requested, is like wandering through an Indiana Jones adventure—an ancient city with its marble pillars, brushy overgrowth, and occasional quarry blocks. One finished slab is

The octagon, according to the mill site tour brochure, was to be turned into a column cap, but the work was never completed. *Philip Varney*

The Marble Community Church stands invitingly open on a lovely summer day. Inside is an operating pump organ. *Philip Varney*

a huge octagon about 6.5 feet high that looks like a sacrificial stone from some primitive civilization.

Downtown Marble is quietly alive with a bed-and-breakfast inn, a general store, several residences, galleries featuring marble sculptures, and a museum housed inside the old high school—a wooden building with a marble foundation and marble columns on its porch. The museum is located on Main west of Third Street. There you will find a pamphlet of a self-guided walking tour that directs you to the town's attractions.

Farther east is the Marble Community Church, moved from Aspen in 1908 on a railroad flat car. The graceful bell tower was added in 1912. The Marble City State Bank Building is on Main near First Street, and beyond it are some attractive residences. Farther east is the Beaver Lake Lodge, which features accommodations including old quarry workers' cabins. East of the lodge is Thompson Park, where Marble's two-cage jail sits. Beyond the park are Beaver Lake and the four-wheel-drive-only road to Crystal.

You pass the Marble Cemetery on your way into town. It is on the north side of the road 2.2 miles west of the intersection of Park and Third. As you would expect, most markers are indeed made of marble.

The Yule Marble Quarry is on private property and trespassing is forbidden.

WHEN YOU GO

From Aspen, a former mining town and now a ski resort mecca, drive northwest on Colorado Highway 82 for 30 miles to Carbondale. Turn south on Colorado Highway 133 and proceed south for 21.9 miles. Turn east on Gunnison County Road 3 and go 5.9 miles to downtown Marble.

CRYSTAL

The sign east of Marble indicates four-wheel-drive vehicles only to Crystal. Heed that warning. When I first saw Crystal in 1987, I was on a mountain bike, so I wasn't too concerned about the road. In 2008, I took a Jeep tour with a driver who makes the journey all summer long (inquire in Marble). The road was noticeably worse than when I rode my bike in, and I was glad to have an expert at the wheel.

If you are a collector of books on Colorado, you will immediately recognize the first sign of Crystal: the remains of what is called the Crystal Mill, perched dramatically on a rocky crag.

Everyone says this structure is the Crystal Mill, but it really isn't. When Muriel Sibell Wolle made a drawing of the 1892 Sheep Mountain Tunnel Mill in 1947, her sketch shows a dilapidated mill standing next to this building. Caroline Bancroft has a photo from 1954 with that same mill in ruins. What remains is not the mill itself but the hydroelectric power generator, last used in 1916, for that now-vanished mill. Inside the vertical wooden shaft, which you can still see extending from the powerhouse, was a wooden water wheel that powered an air compressor for the mill.

The town of Crystal is 0.2 of a mile beyond the "mill." One look at the clear river water running through the valley and you might surmise how Crystal got its name. But you would be mistaken. It was not named for the water but rather for the silver-bearing quartz shot with crystallite that was found by prospectors in 1880.

Seven working silver mines kept Crystal going, and a road built over Schofield Pass to Gothic and Crested Butte in 1883 helped get supplies in and ore out. A later road went to Carbondale via the route you take into town. By 1886, about four hundred people lived in the town, which had two newspapers (including one using a wonderful pun, the *Crystal River Current*), two hotels, saloons, a billiard parlor, a barbershop, and the men-only Crystal Club.

The 1893 Silver Crash nearly emptied the town, and by 1915 only eight people lived there. A one-year mining venture brought the population up to seventy-five the next year, but after its failure, the town became deserted.

Crystal today contains about a dozen old cabins and the Crystal Club, made of stout logs except for the refinement of a lumber false front.

East of Crystal 0.3 of a mile, sitting in a ravine to your left, is the old schoolhouse. The road eventually ascends Schofield Pass, which I have not attempted in a motorized vehicle, but I did ride on a mountain bike, coming into Crystal from Gothic. On that occasion, the road was closed, and a large snowfield (in mid-July!) caused us to portage our bikes.

The hydroelectric power generator building for the Sheep Mountain Tunnel Mill (now a pile of rubble) is one of Colorado's most famous ghost town structures. *Philip Varney*

WHEN YOU GO

Crystal is 5.9 miles east of downtown Marble on Forest Road 314, the only road east from Marble.

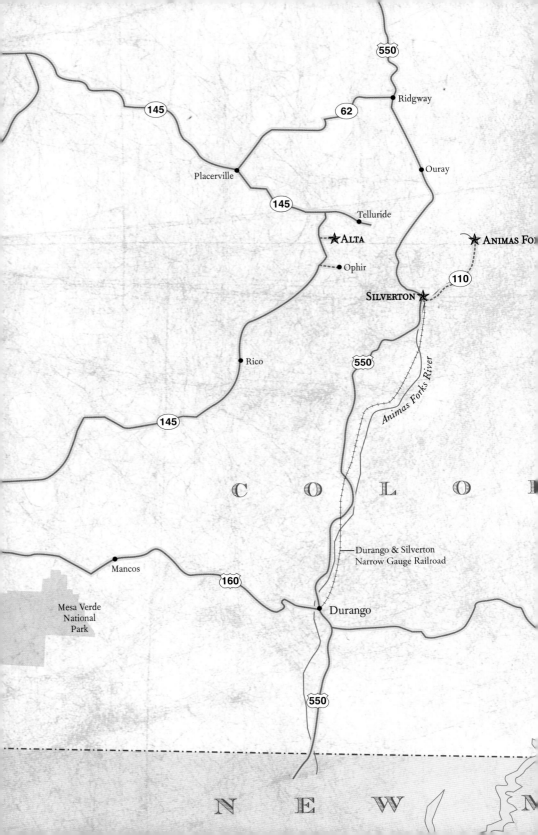

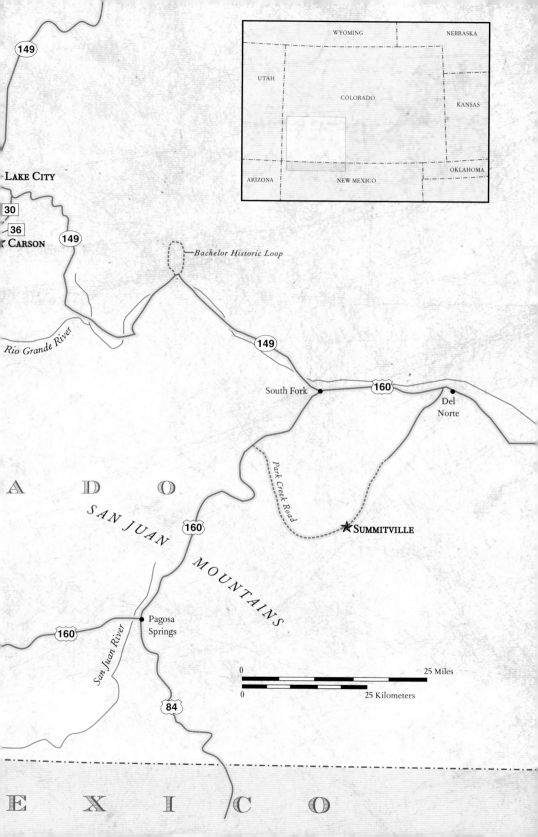

149

LAKE CITY

30

36

CARSON 149

Rio Grande River

Bachelor Historic Loop

149

South Fork ● 160 Del
Norte ●

WYOMING NEBRASKA

UTAH

COLORADO

KANSAS

ARIZONA NEW MEXICO OKLAHOMA

A D O

SAN JUAN

Park Creek Road

160

★SUMMITVILLE

M O U N T A I N S

160

Pagosa
Springs

San Juan River

84

0 25 Miles

0 25 Kilometers

E X I C O

LAKE CITY

Lake City rivals Georgetown as one of Colorado's most charming communities. Although smaller than Georgetown and not quite as splendid, it is also not nearly as crowded or tourist-oriented. Its downtown has some delightful buildings, while residential areas feature attractive homes and churches.

The region's most infamous incident occurred in late 1873 or early 1874, before Lake City existed. Alfred "Alferd" Packer was hired by Utah prospectors

Lake City's Silver Street has several excellent examples of wooden commercial buildings. Each features an attractive cornice atop its false front. *Philip Varney*

to guide them through the San Juan Mountains. Many gave up as winter approached, but five men continued with Packer. Two months later, when he arrived, alone, at Los Pinos Indian Agency, Packer claimed he had become separated from his companions and had nearly starved.

A search party found the men near Lake San Cristobal. All were dead, four from ax blows, the fifth from a bullet. All had been, literally, butchered. Remembering that the "nearly starved" Packer had seemed suspiciously well fed, the would-be rescuers reached a logical but grisly conclusion. By the time the search party returned, Packer had vanished.

Meanwhile, other prospectors were also combing the San Juans. Surveyor Enos Hotchkiss spotted the area's mineral deposits in 1874 while scouting a wagon route through the San Juans. He and his party abandoned the road project and spent the winter staking claims.

First Baptist Church's graceful off-center steeple and pretty stained-glass windows make it one of Lake City's most attractive places of worship.
Philip Varney

By the spring of 1875, a camp of four hundred citizens was firmly established where Hotchkiss's party had settled. Hotchkiss returned to roadbuilding long enough to create a toll road from Saguache with partner Otto Mears, who became famous as the "Pathfinder of the San Juans" for his ability to create a road where others could not. Improved roads meant cheaper transportation of ore, and the camp, called Lake City for Lake San Cristobal, boomed.

The arrival of the Denver & Rio Grande Railroad in the late 1880s added to Lake City's status. The town could boast of its five general stores, five saloons, three restaurants, three breweries, two drugstores, two bakeries, two blacksmith shops, two meat markets, a newspaper, and a public library.

Back to unfinished business. In 1883, nine years after he had been suspected of murder and cannibalism, Packer was apprehended in Wyoming and brought to Lake City for trial. When Packer had left his camp near Lake San

Cristobal, there was no Lake City; less than a decade later, he was being tried in its two-story courthouse. He was found guilty of murder and sentenced to death, but the sentence was later reduced to a prison term. After serving several years, Packer was paroled.

The Silver Crash of 1893 damaged Lake City, but enough gold was also being mined that the town held on into the twentieth century.

A natural place to start exploring Lake City stands at the south end of Lake City's business district, the Hinsdale County Museum. It is housed in the Finley Block, a single-story stone building constructed by stonemason Henry Finley, who fashioned the attractive storefront himself.

The museum has many unusual items and displays. For example, one exhibit features Susan B. Anthony's visit to Lake City in 1877; another shows a dollhouse made by Packer while he was in prison.

Downtown Lake City features several other historic buildings. At the corner of Silver and Third stands the 1877 Stone Bank Block, which served as a bank until 1914. It was then converted to other uses, including a forty-year stint as a hotel.

Around the corner is Armory Hall, originally the opera house, built in 1883. The restricted, posh Hinsdale Club for men used the building's second floor. The Hough Block, on the east side of Silver in the next block north, was built by John Hough between 1880 and 1882.

The 1877 Hinsdale County Courthouse is one block east of the highway between Third and Fourth Streets. The first-floor corridor displays documents on the Alferd Packer trial. The second-floor courtroom, except for a microphone and computer, transports you to 1877.

South of town 2.8 miles on Colorado Highway 149 is the Alferd Packer Massacre Site. Five metal crosses mark where Israel Swan, George Swan, Frank Miller, James Humphreys, and Wilson Bell were murdered.

The Lake City Cemetery is located 1 mile north of downtown along the highway. Another cemetery is 0.5 of a mile away. From the Lake City Cemetery, head north and then immediately turn left onto Balsam Drive, following the road to an attractive wrought-iron fence.

WHEN YOU GO

 ake City is 54 miles southwest of Gunnison and 52 miles northwest of Creede on Colorado Highway 149.

L ike many other true ghost towns, Carson sits in an unspeakably beautiful setting. Like a few others, it is unoccupied. This combination makes Carson one of my favorite mining camps anywhere.

Christopher J. Carson, prospecting along the Continental Divide, found gold and silver in 1881 and staked a claim for the Bonanza King. The small camp named for Carson struggled through the early 1880s because of transportation problems, but miners still managed to work 150 claims in which silver outproduced gold by a hundred ounces to one.

Transportation woes were eased when a road coming from Lake City was begun in 1883, led by an overseer named Wager, whose first name is unknown, for whom the gulch was named. Another road from Wagon Wheel Gap reached the south side of the divide in 1887.

The reliance on silver crippled Carson in 1893 when silver prices plummeted. But in 1896, promising gold deposits were found, bringing more than four hundred miners back, principally to the St. Jacobs and Bachelor Mines. At

The living quarters for the mine's foreman and the superintendent have a touch of class that the other five buildings at Carson do not: tongue-in-groove interior woodwork. Unfortunately, the residences, like the others in town, are marred by graffiti. *Philip Varney*

this time, buildings were constructed north of the pass at a "new" Carson. "Old" Carson was on the south side. By 1902, however, the *Gunnison Times* reported, "Carson with its many promising properties is practically abandoned."

Standing at the new Carson today are seven structures, one made of logs and the others of cut lumber. Each has a sturdy metal roof, thanks to the town's owner. (Carson is private property, but it is not posted against trespassing at this writing.) The largest building was a boarding house for Bachelor Mine employees and may also have served as a hospital. It is interesting architecturally because it was built as if it were three separate structures connected by hallways. The walls are covered with graffiti, one reason why sites like this become closed to the public.

Two nearby homes for the Bachelor Mine foreman and superintendent had tongue-and-groove interior woodwork, indicating that these buildings were not of slapdash construction. North of those homes is a buggy shed and stable.

The nearby Bachelor Mine is posted against trespassing, but you can see it nonetheless. Behind the Carson buildings is a faint trail that heads to the southeast. In perhaps thirty yards, you'll come out behind the mine, where, without trespassing, you can view the operation, including a boiler, cable winch, dumps, and rotting boards.

Very little remains at old Carson, south of the Continental Divide. When Muriel Sibell Wolle hiked there in 1948, she saw mine buildings, houses, an old hotel, and the post office.

WHEN YOU GO

From Lake City, head southeast on Colorado Highway 149 for 2.3 miles to County Road 30, the turnoff to Lake San Cristobal and Cinnamon Pass. Drive 9 miles to Wager Gulch Road (Road 36), which goes south. The next 3.6 miles to Carson require a four-wheel-drive vehicle, especially in wet conditions.

SUMMITVILLE

ummitville has hummed with activity well into the twenty-first century. However, it was not mining causing all the action; it was the removal of mining's detritus. Summitville was one of Colorado's several environmental Superfund sites, and the cleanup operation was immense. When I first visited the site in 1997, the renovation was in full swing, with huge trucks hauling contaminated waste from the site. When I returned in 2015, the cleanup seemed to be complete.

The ghost town of Summitville, fortunately, was not part of the decontamination area, and there remains much to see. Summitville is, however, a very vulnerable site, especially—at an elevation of 11,300 feet—to the elements, and it is a natural candidate for another kind of "superfund": preservation money from Colorado's gaming dollars.

In 1870, rancher James Esmund and a companion rode their horses into a high, park-like area in search of two runaway girls. They found the girls, and Esmund found something else: free gold in the

Several dozen buildings, most of them miners' cabins, stand at Summitville today. The main boom only lasted from 1870 until 1879, but gold was still being extracted from its mines into the 1970s. *Philip Varney*

rocks all around. He returned several times to remove high-grade ore, but he neglected to file claims.

In June 1870, a party of prospectors, including James and William Wightman, staked claims along the creek, now named for the brothers. Winter drove them out, but the next spring brought hundreds of argonauts. In 1872, hundreds more arrived, so when James Esmund returned once again, he discovered people swarming over the area, including on his find, by then known as the Little Annie. He nevertheless staked claims for the Esmund (later the Aztec) and Major Mines.

Summitville received its post office in 1876. By 1883, the town was Colorado's biggest gold producer, occupying several hundred miners and mill workers

Summitville's main pump house is, unfortunately, sagging toward the horizontal. The building is well worth resurrecting because of the unusual "chimney," which was a passageway to enter the pump house when snow covered the normal entrance. *Philip Varney*

for hugely successful mines, such as the Little Annie and the Bonanza. By 1889, however, the boom was over and only a few diehards remained.

A short-lived rebirth came in the late 1890s with the reopening of the Bonanza, but the mine's production fizzled by 1900. Miners tried again for two years beginning in 1911, for five years starting in 1926, and for about fifteen years commencing in the 1930s.

Another attempt was beginning after World War II, when Muriel Sibell Wolle visited Summitville. She was expecting a deserted ghost town but found instead a lively company town of tarpaper-covered shacks and a large community hall flying an American flag.

Further attempts were made in the 1970s, but not even the discovery of a boulder containing $350,000 in gold lying near a road could revitalize the town.

When you enter Summitville from the south, the first building will be on your right, along Wightman Creek. It is the sagging main pump house, architecturally interesting because it has a "chimney" passage so that it could be entered from above when winter snow covered the normal entrance. Above the pump house stands a two-story wood-frame structure that looks like a dormitory.

The only site you can explore without violating "no trespassing" signs is also the best of the townsite, but you'll need to hike up to it. North of the road, opposite the pump house and up on a hill to the east, stand almost twenty buildings: cabins, pump houses, and outhouses. About a half dozen are partially or completely collapsed, but most are under roof.

Beyond these buildings 0.3 of a mile, on the south side of the road, is a cluster of about a dozen residences and outbuildings on a small hill. At this writing, the wood-frame structures are under roof, partially covered with tarpaper, and posted against trespassing. From there, the road winds down for 27 miles to Del Norte. For that road, I'd recommend a high-clearance vehicle.

WHEN YOU GO

You can reach Summitville from either South Fork or Del Norte. The easier route by far is from South Fork (21 miles southeast of Creede) because the ascent to Summitville follows a haul road wide enough and level enough for huge trucks. From South Fork, head 7.1 miles southwest on US Highway 160. Turn left onto Park Creek Road and follow it for 14.6 miles, where a left turn onto Forest Road 330 takes you in 2.2 miles to Summitville. In good weather, a passenger car should have no difficulty reaching the townsite.

SILVERTON

A mong the first prospectors to reach the San Juan Mountains was a party led by Captain Charles Baker in 1860, lured by the captain's glowing accounts of a previous trip. Actual results were so meager that his disgruntled followers considered lynching him.

The area's isolation hindered exploration, but continued prospecting efforts in the 1870s brought pressure upon the federal government to "adjust" a treaty with the Utes, essentially forcing them to give up the San Juans in an 1873 agreement known as the Brunot Treaty.

Two years later, a small community named Baker's Park was established in a lovely valley surrounded by silver-bearing mountains. The town was carefully platted and featured wide main streets to facilitate wagon traffic. The post office was granted to Silverton, likely a shortened version of "Silvertown." An apocryphal story, however, claims the town got its name when a miner cried out that, although they had no gold, they had "silver by the ton."

Transportation of even the richest ore created considerable obstacles for miners, because ore had to be packed out by mules, transferred to wagons at the first road, and freighted to the nearest railhead, which originally was Pueblo. The arrival of the Denver & Rio Grande from Durango in 1882 alleviated that difficulty, cutting transportation costs by 80 percent. Silverton's isolation was over—as long as the rails were clear. Snowslides in 1884, for example, forced snowbound citizens to scrape down to their last bits of food as they endured for seventy-three days before a train could get through. The rail link to Durango was the community's lifeline.

In addition to food, the railroad could bring in everything that turns a camp

Most of the buildings on Silverton's Greene Street date from the 1880s and 1890s. Notice the handsome cornices and creative trim colors. *Philip Varney*

into a town. Silverton's Greene Street became an elegant thoroughfare, highlighted by the three-story brick Grand (later Grand Imperial) Hotel. Other commercial buildings vied for attention with attractive cornices and elaborate façades. Silverton has never suffered a major fire, so the fine buildings remain intact today.

One block east stood Blair Street, so notorious for its saloons and brothels that residents at either end called their sections "Empire Street" to avoid being tainted by association.

The Silver Crash of 1893 dealt a blow to Silverton, but by 1897 half of the town's ore production was for gold, followed by silver, lead, and copper. Output reached its zenith between 1900 and 1912 and continued until World War II. The new gold arrived after World War II when the Denver & Rio Grande's spectacular railroad began to attract tourists. Now called the Durango & Silverton Narrow Gauge Railroad, the train brings about two hundred thousand people to Silverton annually.

Silverton's stores offer a free visitors' guide that includes a walking tour. An appropriate place to begin is the San Juan County Museum, located at the north end of town. The museum is housed in the 1902 county jail, and much original equipment remains.

On your way downtown, visit the 1906 San Juan County Courthouse next door to the museum. Built in a cruciform configuration, its elaborate halls dramatically lead to a single central spot: a simple drinking fountain.

South of the courthouse on Greene is the 1902 Wyman Hotel, now a bed and breakfast. Across the street is the handsome 1908 town hall, gutted by a 1992 fire but beautifully restored by 1995. When you venture inside to see its graceful staircases, you will be amazed that skeptics considered the building beyond saving after the fire.

For the next four blocks heading south from the town hall, virtually every building on the west side of Greene dates back to the nineteenth century, as do many on the east side. Even the newer buildings look authentic. Your visitors' guide will give you information on individual buildings.

One block west of Greene is Reese Street, where you will find many attractive residences. In that same area are the school, Carnegie Library, and three churches. To reach Silverton's Hillside Cemetery, go north from town to a junction of roads. Take the north road and turn right at the first opportunity. The cemetery looks down upon the picturesque town and has a sweeping view of the mountains surrounding the valley.

WHEN YOU GO

Silverton is 49 miles north of Durango and 25 miles south of Ouray on US Highway 550.

Silverton's Hillside Cemetery, north of town, has hundreds of varied tombstones. Sultan Mountain is prominent in the background. *Philip Varney*

North of Silverton stand the remains of three mining towns: Howardsville, Eureka, and Animas Forks. The first two, at 3.9 miles and 7.6 miles northeast of Silverton, respectively, have rather scant remains. Howardsville has the tram terminus of the Little Nation Mine and a couple of cabins. Eureka features a restored water tank, which later was modified to become a firehouse and jail, and the immense foundations of the two mills of the Sunnyside Mine.

The William Duncan House, built in 1879, has been stabilized thanks to the attention of the San Juan County Historical Society. *Philip Varney*

If you are a bit disappointed with the remains at Howardsville and Eureka, you will be well rewarded by continuing north from Eureka 4.2 miles to see the considerable remnants of Animas Forks.

Animas Forks was founded in 1873 when prospectors built log cabins near their claims. Because three rivers met nearby, the camp was called Three Forks, or Forks of the Animas. The US Postal Service simplified the name to Animas Forks when a post office was granted in 1875.

At almost 11,200 feet, the town suffered from severe winters. Most of the miners retreated in the fall and returned the following spring. The hearty few who stayed were subjected to avalanches and isolation. In 1884, the year Silverton endured ten weeks without relief supplies, Animas Forks was snowbound for twenty-three days. Provisions had to come from Silverton, which had none to spare. Animas Forks emptied in 1891 as mining declined. A brief resurgence occurred in 1904 with the construction of the Gold Prince Mill, which was connected to its mine by a 2.4-mile tramway. The mill caused Otto Mears to extend his Silverton Northern Railway from Eureka to Animas Forks, further raising expectations for the town. But the mill closed in 1910, and Animas Forks lost its post office in 1915. In 1917, the mill was largely dismantled for use at Eureka's Sunnyside Mill.

At this writing, ten buildings stand completely or partially under roof around the townsite. As you cross the Animas Forks River entering town, the foundations of the Gold Prince Mill will be on your right.

One of Colorado's more photographed ghost town buildings is the 1879 William Duncan home, featuring a dramatic bay window. Historical signs at the site describe several other structures, among them the unusual jail. The jail is one of four in the area built using the same construction method: boards laid flat and stacked log-cabin style, so the structure has a stockade's strength. Similar structures stand in Silverton, Red Mountain, and Telluride.

WHEN YOU GO

nimas Forks is 12 miles northeast of downtown Silverton on Colorado Highway 110. It is 8.1 miles north of the turnoff at Howardsville to the Old Hundred Mine. I recommend a high-clearance vehicle to reach the townsite.

ALTA

Alta (Spanish for "high") was a company town for the Gold King Mine, discovered in 1878. Alta had a general store, an assay office, a school, miners' homes, and company offices. The town also became the upper terminus for a tram that extended almost 2 miles and dropped more than 1,800 feet to Ophir Loop, where a loading bin was located near the Rio Grande Southern depot. (Ophir Loop is located 1.8 miles south of the turnoff to Alta on Colorado Highway 145.)

The Alta-area mines produced into the 1940s under the ownership of the Silver Mountain Mining Company, but a fire in one of the shafts in 1945 effectively ended production.

When I first saw Alta in 1987, it was abandoned and deteriorating. Since then, efforts have begun to preserve and protect the buildings. The Alta I first saw, if left to the elements and vandals, would be in a sorry state today.

The weathered miners' dormitory at Alta once had an outside stairway to the second floor. Only its tilting roof remains. *Philip Varney*

When you enter Alta, you will be at the bottom of the townsite, where water tumbles off old waste dumps. Nearby are two crumbling wooden structures and, as you turn toward the upper site, five more miners' shacks.

You will come to a good place to park next to wooden fences that protect a roofless log building that has served as a mine office

Framed by the middle window of the Alta company store and mine office is one of southwestern Colorado's most recognizable landscapes: Lizard Head Peak. *Philip Varney*

and company store. Across the way, protected by the same fencing, is an impressive two-story boarding house built in 1939. To the west is an astonishing view of Lizard Head Peak, Wilson Peak, and Sunshine Mountain.

Also behind the fence, beyond the office and store, are four residences that housed mining officials. One of those houses has new siding on it and looks quite habitable, a change from my earlier visits. One home, probably the mining superintendent's, has an attractive bay window that likely has a spectacular view.

From the waste dump, you'll see lots of mining debris: buckets, pipe, slabs of concrete, and a geared wheel. Northeast of the boarding house are six wooden foundations and a log cabin. The schoolhouse once stood in this area, according to the 1955 topographic map.

WHEN YOU GO

From Telluride, head west to Colorado Highway 145. Turn south and drive 5.2 miles to the turnoff marked for Alta Lakes. The townsite comes into view in 3.5 miles. (The lakes are 1 mile beyond the Alta townsite.) Although I saw passenger vehicles on the road to Alta, I recommend a higher-clearance vehicle.

GLOSSARY
of Mining Terms

ADIT: A nearly horizontal entrance to a hard-rock mine.

ARGONAUT: A man who came to California during the gold rush (after the Argonauts of Greek mythology, who sailed on the ship *Argo* in search of riches).

ARRASTRA: An apparatus used to grind ore by means of a heavy stone that is dragged around in a circle, normally by mules or oxen.

ASSAY: To determine the value of a sample of ore, in ounces per ton, by testing using a chemical evaluation.

BONANZA: To miners, a body of rich ore.

CHARCOAL KILN (OR OVEN): A structure into which wood is placed and subjected to intense heat through a controlled, slow burning. Charcoal is a longer-lasting, more efficient wood fuel often used to power mills and smelters. If the kiln is used to convert coal to coke, it's called a coke oven.

CHLORIDE: Usually refers to ores containing chloride of silver.

CLAIM: A tract of land with defined boundaries that includes mineral rights extending downward from the surface.

CLAIM-JUMPING (OR JUMPING A CLAIM): Illegally taking over someone else's claim.

DIGGINGS (OR DIGGINS): Evidence of mining efforts, such as placer, hydraulic, or dredge workings.

DREDGE: An apparatus, usually on a flat-bottomed boat, that scoops material out of a river to extract gold-bearing sand or gravel; used in "dredging" or "dredge mining."

DUST: Minute gold particles found in placer deposits.

FLOTATION: A method of mineral separation in a mill in which water, in combination with chemicals, "floats" finely crushed minerals of value to separate them from the detritus, which sinks. Process used in a flotation mill.

FLUME: An inclined, man-made channel, usually of wood, used to convey water or mine waste, often for long distances.

GALLOWS FRAME: See "head frame" below.

GIANT: The nozzle on the end of a pipe through which water is forced in hydraulic mining. Also called a monitor.

GRUBSTAKE: An advance of money, food, and/or supplies to a prospector in return for a share of any discoveries.

HARD-ROCK MINING: The process in which a "primary deposit" (see below) is mined by removing ore-bearing rock by tunneling into the earth. Also known as quartz mining, since gold is frequently found in quartz deposits.

HEAD FRAME: The vertical apparatus over a mineshaft that has cables to be lowered down the shaft for raising either ore or a cage; sometimes called a "gallows frame."

HIGH-GRADE ORE: Ore rich in precious metals.

HIGH-GRADING: The theft of rich ore, usually by a miner working for someone else who owns the mine.

HOPPER: A structure with funnels from which the contents, loaded from above, can be emptied for purposes of transportation.

HORN SILVER: Silver chloride, a native ore of silver. Also known as cerargyrite.

HYDRAULIC MINING: A method of mining using powerful jets of water to wash away a bank of gold-bearing earth. Also known by miners as "hydraulicking."

INGOT: A cast bar or block of a metal.

LODE: A continuous mineral-bearing deposit or vein (see also "Mother Lode" below).

MILL: A building in which rock is crushed to extract minerals by one of several methods. If this is done by stamps (heavy hammers or pestles), it is a stamp mill. If by iron balls, it is a ball mill. The mill is usually constructed on the side of a hill to utilize its slope—hence, a "gravity-fed mill."

MINING DISTRICT: An area of land described (usually for legal purposes) and designated as containing valuable minerals in paying amounts.

MONITOR: See "giant" above.

MOTHER LODE: The principal lode passing through a district or section of the country; from the same term in Spanish, "La Veta Madre." In California, it refers specifically to the 100-mile-long concentration of gold on the western slopes of the Sierra Nevada.

MUCKER: A person or machine that clears material such as rock in a mine.

NUGGET: A lump of native gold or other mineral. The largest found in California's Mother Lode weighed 195 pounds.

ORE: A mineral of sufficient concentration, quantity, and value to be mined at a profit.

ORE SORTER: A structure, usually near a mine, in which higher-grade ore is sorted from lower-grade ore or waste before being sent to the mill or smelter.

PAN: The action of looking for placer gold by washing earth, gravel, or sand, usually in a streambed, by using a shallow, concave dish called a "pan."

PLACER: A waterborne deposit of sand or gravel containing heavier materials, such as gold, that have been eroded from their original bedrock and concentrated as small particles that can be washed, or "panned," out (see also "secondary deposit" below).

POCKET: In primary deposits, a small but rich concentration of gold embedded in quartz. In secondary deposits, a hole or indentation in a streambed in which gold dust or nuggets have been trapped.

POWDERHOUSE: A structure placed safely away from a mine that stored such volatile materials as gunpowder or dynamite. The building's walls are usually very stout, but its roof is intentionally of flimsier construction, so if the contents should explode, the main force of the blast would be into the air.

PRIMARY DEPOSIT: A deposit of gold or other mineral found in its original location. Ore is extracted by hard-rock mining, or hydraulic mining.

PROSPECT: Mineral workings of unproven value.

PROSPECTOR: Someone who searches for prospects.

QUARTZ MINING: See "hard-rock mining" above.

ROCKER: A portable "sluice box" (see below) used by prospectors.

SALTING: To place valuable minerals in a place in which they do not actually occur. Done to deceive. Therefore, a salted claim is one that is intended to lure the unsuspecting investor into a scam.

SECONDARY DEPOSIT: A deposit of gold or other mineral that has moved from its original location by water. Secondary deposits of ore are extracted by placer mining or dredging.

SHAFT: A vertical or nearly vertical opening into the earth for hard-rock mining.

SLAG: The waste product of a smelter; hence, "slag dumps."

SLUICE BOX: A wooden trough in which placer deposits are sluiced, or washed, to retrieve gold from the deposits.

SMELTER: A building or complex in which material is melted in order to separate impurities from pure metal.

SQUARE SET: A set of timbers that are cut so that they form a ninety-degree angle and so that they can be combined with other "sets" to create a framework that safely buttresses a mine. First used in Nevada's Comstock Lode.

STRIKE: The discovery of a primary or secondary deposit of gold or other mineral in sufficient concentration and/or quantity to be mined profitably.

TAILINGS: Waste or refuse left after milling is complete; sometimes used more generally, although incorrectly, to indicate waste dumps. Because of improved technology, older tailings have often been reworked to extract minerals that were left behind from an older, cruder milling process.

TRAMWAY: An apparatus for moving materials such as ore, rock, or even supplies in buckets suspended from pulleys that run on a cable.

TUNNEL: A horizontal or nearly horizontal underground passage open at one end at least.

VEIN: A zone or belt of valuable mineral within less valuable neighboring rock.

WASTE DUMP: Waste rock, not of sufficient value to warrant milling, that comes out of the mine; usually found immediately outside the mine entrance.

WORKINGS: A general term indicating any mining development; when that development is exhausted, it is "worked out."

INDEX

☞ ABOUT the AUTHORS and PHOTOGRAPHERS ☜

PHILIP VARNEY is the author of nine ghost town guidebooks, including *Ghost Towns of the Pacific Northwest*, *Ghost Towns of California*, *Ghost Towns of the Mountain West*, *Arizona Ghost Towns and Mining Camps*, and *New Mexico's Best Ghost Towns*. Varney visited his first ghost town—Central City, Colorado—at the age of eleven and has been an enthusiast ever since. He has toured and photographed more than six hundred ghost towns throughout the American West. *True West* magazine has honored Varney as one of the two "Best Living Photographers of the West." Varney lives in Tucson, Arizona.

JIM HINCKLEY's explorations began with a bicycle and a long bypassed segment of Route 66 in the rugged Black Mountains of western Arizona. They continued with time spent as a cowboy and wrangler for ranches in Arizona and southern New Mexico, a miner in Arizona, and as a travel writer and photographer for numerous publications. With fourteen published books that reflect his passion and zeal, Hinckley is also a popular speaker. He currently resides in Kingman, Arizona, with his wife of thirty-four years.

KERRICK JAMES has photographed the American West and Pacific Rim for over twenty-five years as a travel journalist, with more than two hundred magazine and book covers and hundreds of features illustrated. His credits include *National Geographic Adventure*, *Arizona Highways*, *Sunset*, *Popular Photography*, *Conde Nast Traveller UK*, *Alaska Airlines Beyond*, *VIA*, *Delta Sky*, *EnCompass*, *Outdoor Photographer*, and many more.